# day trips® from
# dallas/fort worth

# help us keep this guide up to date

We would love to hear from you concerning your experiences with this guide and how you feel it could be improved and kept up to date. Please send your comments and suggestions to:

editorial@GlobePequot.com

Thanks for your input, and happy travels!

day trips® series

# day trips® from dallas/fort worth

## first edition

**getaway ideas for the local traveler**

## sandra ramani

travel

Guilford, Connecticut

To buy books in quantity for corporate use or incentives, call **(800) 962-0973** or e-mail **premiums@GlobePequot.com.**

Editor: Kevin Sirois
Project Editor: Lynn Zelem
Layout: Mary Ballachino
Text Design: Linda R. Loiewski
Maps: Ryan Mitchell © Morris Book Publishing, LLC.
Spot photography throughout © David Woo courtesy of the Modern Art Museum of Fort Worth

Library of Congress Cataloging-in-Publication Data is available on file.
ISBN 978-0-7627-5707-7

Printed in the United States of America
10 9 8 7 6 5 4 3 2 1

# about the author

Based in New York City, writer-editor Sandra Ramani specializes in covering travel, spa, beauty, and lifestyle topics. Her work has appeared in such publications as the *New York Daily News,* The *New York Times*.com, *Travel + Leisure, Conde Nast Traveler, The Dallas Morning News, Elegant Bride, New York Magazine, 002 Houston,* and *Bridal Guide*, among others. She is currently a contributing editor for the lifestyle and wellness magazine, *Organic Spa,* as well as for luxury travel site Globorati.com, and has also served as an editor for NYMag.com, *Citysearch New York, Zagat,* and *Fodor's Gold Guides*. For an article she wrote on visiting Jane Austen's England, Sandra was the recipient of the 2006 VisitBritain Travel Journalism Award for Best Newspaper Feature.

A graduate of Vassar College, Sandra grew up in Dallas, Texas—where she still spends a few months a year—and has lived in England, Italy, France, and India. For more on her work, visit www.sandraramani.com.

# acknowledgments

This book couldn't have happened without the help of my mother, Avayam Ramani, and brother, Arun Ramani, who pretty much defined love and support throughout the process. Thank you for being so flexible with your time and space (and cars!), and for being such curious and enthusiastic day trip cohorts. Along with them, the book is dedicated to the memory of my father, Sankar V. Ramani (who would have loved the Historic Aviation Museum in Tyler).

Many thanks to my editor at Globe Pequot, Amy Lyons, for being such a pleasure to work with; my agent, Julie Hill, for bringing us together; and Divina Infusino for putting my name out there in the first place. For all her support and insight, a Texas-sized thanks to Traci Mayer and the Dallas/Fort Worth Area Tourism Council. I also appreciate the friends and family that have shown their support, both professionally and personally, along the way.

Researching this guide was an interesting, educational and thoroughly fun experience thanks to all the people who welcomed me so warmly to their towns. For their time, expertise, enthusiasm, and hospitality, my heartfelt thanks, in no particular order, to: Jean Mollard and Susan Cottle-Leonard in Palestine; Beth Shumate and Kim and Tim Loyd in McKinney; Steve Dieterichs and Todd Jones in Corsicana; Gina Rokas in Ennis; Kim Philips and Dana Lodge in Denton; Kym Koch Thompson at WinStar; Leigh Lyons in Fort Worth; Milton Babb, Janeen Cunningham, and Friendly in Greenville; Becky Semple, Judy Daniel, and David Ford in Paris; Debbie Schwanbeck in Athens; Frieda Hanley in Decatur; Bonnie Hamilton in Bowie; Wanda Wood in Nocona; Susan Travis, Chris and Lisa Garrett, and Les Ellsworth in Tyler; Karen Wright and Sandy Parker in Dublin; Billy Huckaby and Storie Bonner Sharp in Glen Rose; Lori Jarvis in Waco; Debbie Charbonneax in Salado; Jay Melugin in Pilot Point; Ninfa Holly in Mineral Wells; Peggy Hutton in Weatherford; Freeda Hose in Palo Pinto; Jerry Allen and Patricia Shepard in Granbury; Jacquelyn Kuykendall in Waxahachie; and all the dedicated, knowledgeable volunteers who staff many of these attractions. I feel like I've made some friends during these journeys, and I hope you day-trippers will, too.

# contents

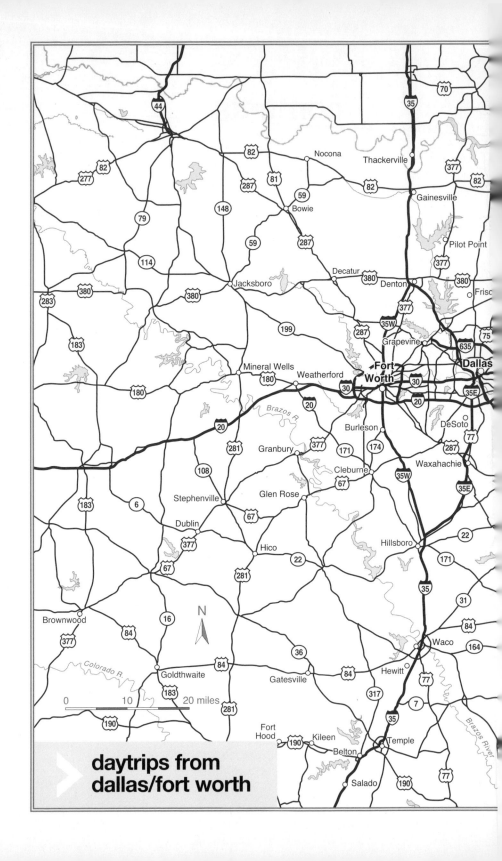

**daytrips from dallas/fort worth**

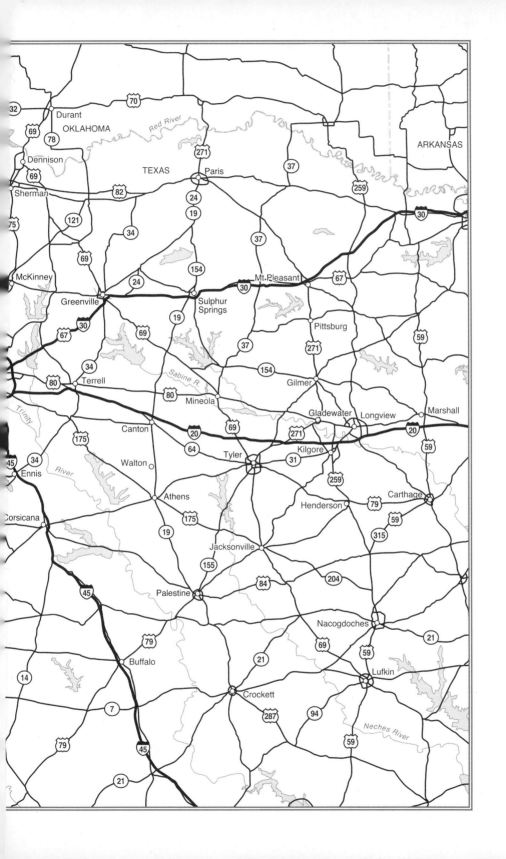

# introduction

Another state may officially boast the title of "Big Sky Country," but for my money, nothing beats the endless, deep blue heavens above Texas. The views above seem particularly majestic in the north central part of the state, where the Prairies and Lakes region's softly rolling grasslands and long stretches of wide, open spaces allow for plenty of unblemished skylines, over which the skies—with nothing to detract from them—seem that much grander. The varied weather of this area makes for some pretty breathtaking colors, too: bright, piercing blues, moody violets, stormy grays and fiery, jaw-dropping sunsets. When it's sunny, the grasslands almost seem electric green, and even when overcast, the sunshine manages to sneak through just enough to dramatically backlight the towering, round bales of hay that dot the farms, making the countryside look like a sort of outdoor sculpture garden.

Of course, you've got to get out of the city to see all this. Luckily, within miles of leaving the Dallas/Fort Worth area, the buildings get lower, and the views more expansive. The Metroplex sits in the upper part of the Prairies and Lakes region, which runs through the center of the state from the Red River border with Oklahoma to just southeast of Austin. With its loamy soil and fertile blacklands, this has historically been the area for cattle and horse ranching, and the seat of the cotton and oil booms. Drive through today and you'll still see working ranches and farms, and plenty of sunbathing cows and hay-chomping horses. Rivers, creeks, lakes, and ponds big and small decorate the plains; even along the highway, some of the tree-shaded swimming holes seem so pristine that, if not for the modern telephone lines overhead, you could almost imagine the "Little House on the Prairie" gang tumbling down to take a dip. But with its position near the top of this region, DFW is also close to some other Texas topographies. Drive west to Mineral Wells or Nocona and you're entering the Panhandle Plains, a more rugged area of flatlands and canyons that evoke the Old West. Head east to Tyler, Gladewater, Athens, or Palestine and you're in the Piney Woods, a lush, scenic region shaded by dogwood, maple, sassafras and, naturally, pine trees. Going south to Hico and Dublin brings you to the edge of Hill Country, where the wildflowers bloom brighter and the dips in the road get deeper.

Take a couple day trips and you'll soon find that it's not just the nature of North Texas that's inspiring. Whether in a town of under 1,500 people, like Nocona, or closer to 115,000, like Waco, you'll meet locals generous with their smiles and their stories. They're also doing some pretty interesting things: In Weatherford, you can visit a free museum of South and Central American artifacts started by a retired professor, while in Paris, the excellent museum of local history was built by a group of volunteers whose average age was seventy-two. In Dublin, unleash your creative side with the help of a craft queen (before downing some fresh Dr. Pepper, of course), or have a giraffe eat right out of your palm at a reserve for endangered animals in Glen Rose. In many of the towns, it's locals who are buying and restoring the empty historic buildings, ensuring that their heritage is preserved for future generations and creating some cool spaces along the way. And oh, there's the food: classic Texas barbecue and chicken-fried steak, mile-high scratch-made pies, and some of the best Tex-Mex around. It's worth the drive to Weatherford for the sandwiches and cinnamon rolls, Gainesville for the fried pie and sopapilla cheesecake, Nocona and Denton for their tomatillo enchiladas, Hico for the chocolate, and Athens for the "cakeballs." (See those chapters for details.) Every town has some type of trade day flea market and, depending on the season, farmers' market, too, which offer more opportunities to pick up goodies. Check the Festivals and Celebrations section for the top local events—a prime way to see the heart of a community—but most of all, enjoy slowing down and chatting with the people you meet, and seeing where the conversation takes you. Their suggestions and stories could fill several books.

And when you're out there hitting the road, take a moment to take in the great expanse of sky before you, or check the side mirror for a spectacular look at where you've been. It's just a small reminder of what's out there—because in North Texas, the sky really is the limit.

# using this travel guide

# hours of operation, prices, credit cards

In the interest of accuracy and because they are subject to change, hours of operation and attraction prices are given in general terms. Always remember to call ahead. You can assume all establishments listed accept major credit cards unless otherwise noted. If you have questions, contact the establishments for specifics. Note that in many of the smaller towns, shops, restaurants, and attractions are often closed on Mondays, and have shorter hours on Sundays. Some local attractions are also staffed by volunteers, so do call to confirm that they are open.

# pricing key

## accommodations

The price code reflects the average cost of a double-occupancy room during the peak price period (not including tax or extras). Always ask if any special discounts are available or, if applicable, check the Web site for any current deals.

| | |
|---|---|
| $ | less than $100 |
| $$ | $101 to $200 |
| $$$ | $201 and up |

## restaurants

The price code reflects the average price of dinner entrees for two (excluding cocktails, wine, appetizers, desserts, tax, and tip). You can usually expect to pay less for lunch and/or breakfast, when applicable.

| | |
|---|---|
| $ | less than $20 for entrees for two ($10 or less per entree) |
| $$ | $30 to $40 for entrees for two ($11 to $20 per entree) |
| $$$ | $40 and up for entrees for two ($20 or more per entree) |

# driving tips

On most numbered highways, the maximum speed limit for cars and light trucks (pickups, vans, etc.) in Texas is 70 miles per hour in the daytime, 65 mph at night, unless otherwise indicated. Note that the speed limits often drop substantially when the highway passes through a rural community, so be on the lookout for postings (or end up caught in a speed trap). When on a highway of two or more lanes, the left lane is for passing, the right for slower moving traffic; passing is illegal when there is a posted sign or a continuous yellow stripe on the driver's side of the center line.

Also be on the lookout for the dreaded orange barrels; those mean road construction and possible delays. It's especially wise to stay within posted speed restrictions in these areas, as fines may be more than doubled for offenders. Signs often designate alternate routes. Although these detours may require more actual driving, they save aggravation and, in some cases, travel time.

Law enforcement is also quick to help those in distress. If you're lost or having car trouble, call the Texas State Highway Patrol at (800) 525-5555 and they'll dispatch someone to provide assistance. The Highway Patrol also offers daily trip planning assistance, emergency road condition info, and general travel tips at (800) 452-9292.

For information on current road conditions and seasonal reports on the best spots to view scenic wildflowers or fall foliage, contact the Texas Department of Transportation at (800) 452-9292; a live counselor is there daily from 8 a.m. to 6 p.m., after which an automated system takes over. You may also visit their Web site at www.txdot.gov.

# highway designations

Just as within Dallas I-635 is also known as LBJ Freeway, and US 75 is called Central Expressway, you will find that most towns featured have a second name for the major highway within their city limits. (For example, in Paris, US 82 BUS is called Lamar Ave. east of the town square and Bonham St. west of the square.) These have been noted in each chapter wherever possible, but the best bet is to grab a local map from the convention and visitors bureau (CVB) or visitor center office, which should have these name variations noted.

**Interstates** are prefaced by "I" (for example, I-35) and are generally multilane divided highways.

**U.S. highways** are two- and three-lane undivided roads and prefaced by "US" (for instance, US 82).

**State highways** are paved and divided and prefaced by "TX" (for example, TX 6).

**Farm-to-Market roads** can be paved or even gravel and are prefaced by "FM" (e.g., FM 51).

**Country roads** can be paved or even gravel and are prefaced by "CR" (e.g., CR 178).

# travel tips

**Driving in Town.** Many of the towns featured are centered around a courthouse square or a Main Street. The streets surrounding these focal points are often one way, so be sure to note the signage. Often, streets will be designated as North, South, East or West based on their position to this central point; for example, in Waxahachie, College St. become N. College St. above the County Courthouse, and S. College below it.

**Parking.** Most towns offer free parking around their town square and on the side streets; check the chapters for tips on other free parking areas, when applicable. In some cities, town square parking is limited to two hours, so be sure to note the signs.

**Seasonal Issues.** While the weather is typically mild in North Texas, the area is more prone to thunderstorms and tornados than most other parts of the state; the latter generally might occur April–June. Check the latest weather forecasts for details. For prime flora-spotting, head out in April (for bluebonnets), early summer for crape myrtles, and October–November for fall foliage.

# where to get more information

*Day Trips* attempts to cover a variety of bases and interests, but those looking for additional material can contact the following agencies by phone, mail, or the Web. Regarding the latter, when checking out the various destinations, be aware that online reviews may be contradictory and conflicting. Everyone's experience can be different, and the Web allows for a forum for these diverse opinions. So call the place directly and be conscious of ratings such as AAA and the Better Business Bureau. Most all of the areas have chain hotels and restaurants, which are generally not included in the listings in each chapter. Within each chapter we provide contact information for chambers of commerce and/or convention and visitor bureaus. Here are some additional general resources:

**Dallas/Fort Worth Area Tourism Council.** (DFWATC) 701 S. Main St., Grapevine, TX 76051; (817) 329-2438; www.visitdallas-fortworth.com.

**Texas Lakes Heritage Trails.** (512) 463-6092; www.texaslakestrail.com.

**Red River Valley Tourism Association.** www.redrivervalley.info.

**TravelTex.** P.O. Box 141009 Austin, TX 78714-1009; (800) 888-8839; www.traveltex.com.

**Texas Association of Convention and Visitors Bureaus.** 311 South Station St. Port Aransas, TX 78373; (361) 749-0467; www.tacvb.org.

**Texas Hotel and Lodging Association.** 1701 West Ave., Austin, TX 78701; (800) 856-4328; www.texasloging.com.

**Texas Bed and Breakfast Association.** P.O. Box 301596, Austin, TX 78703; (800) 428-0368; www.texasbb.org.

**Texas Park and Wildlife Department.** 4200 Smith School Rd., Austin, TX 78744; (800) 792-1112; www.tpwd.state.tx.us.

**Texas State Historical Association.** 1155 Union Circle #311580, Denton, TX 76203; (940) 369-5200; www.tshaonline.org.

**Texas Historical Commission.** P.O. Box 12276 Austin, TX 78711-2276; (512) 463-6100; www.thc.state.tx.us.

**Texas Department of Agriculture/Go Texan Program.** (877) 99-GOTEX; www.gotexan.org.

# north

# day trip 01

north

**life on the square:**
mckinney

# mckinney

A straight shot off of North Central Expressway (US 75), this day trip is close enough to Dallas that you're not spending all day in the car, but full of enough unique attractions that it feels like a true getaway. While McKinney itself has boomed in recent years, almost doubling its population since 2000 and now stretching close to Frisco and Allen (being voted one of the "Best Places to Live" by *Money* magazine in 2008 probably didn't hurt), this trip focuses on the charming downtown, where the city's history meets its thriving present. McKinney boasts one of the livelier town squares in North Texas, with a roster of over one hundred boutiques, restaurants, bars, and independently owned stores. In this district, it's easy to imagine what life might have been like in a bustling small town—a feeling the city keeps alive through a full calendar of festivals and events, from Oktoberfest to ice cream "Crank-Offs."

Named for Collin McKinney, one of the signers of the Texas Declaration of Independence and an early North Texas settler, McKinney was first established in 1848 and quickly became a bustling county seat and commercial center. Thanks to the foresight and careful planning of city officials, the town has managed to preserve much of its historic downtown district and nineteenth-century buildings, many of which are still in use today—though they now house cafes and stores instead of cotton and fabric industry offices. As Dallas has expanded northward, McKinney's population has also grown, and today the city's prosperity is palpable; unlike some other towns in the region, particularly those a bit further away

2

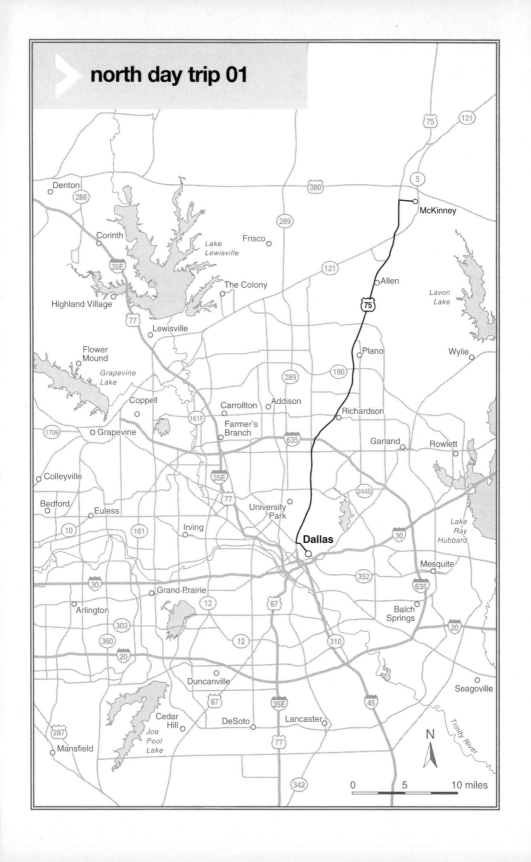

# north day trip 01

from the Metroplex, McKinney's historic downtown is happily free of empty storefronts and FOR LEASE signs.

Once you've experienced today's town square, take a short walk to the Chestnut Square Historic Village and the Heard-Craig House, both of which offer insight into the city's cotton-belt past. If you want to extend the day trip into night, the McKinney Performing Center for the Arts and McKinney Repertory Theater put on a full schedule of events, with the former attracting nationally known acts. And once the show's over, you're still only 30 miles away from Dallas.

# getting there

To reach the historic center, take N. Central Expressway (US 75) to exit 40A/Virginia-Louisiana Sts. Head east for approximately 1 mile (the street will become Louisiana St.), until you see the old Collin County Courthouse in the center of McKinney Square. Parking can be tough to find right off the square, but lot and street parking are available on the side streets. Note that Louisiana St. is one-way, so when heading back home, you'll take Virginia St. to US 75.

# where to go

**Chestnut Square Historic Village.** 315 S. Chestnut St., at Anthony St.; (972) 562-8790; www.chestnutsquare.org. Collin County history comes alive at this collection of nine historic homes and buildings—dating from the 1850s to 1920s—that have been moved to sit around a quaint square just a couple of blocks from downtown. Visit an original one-room schoolhouse, a turn-of-the-twentieth century Baptist church, a general store from 1918, and six homes, ranging from 1870s Victorians to a 1920s Arts and Crafts bungalow. (The Faires House, built in 1854, is the oldest still-standing home in Collin County, and survived being in the line of fire at the only Civil War battle fought in the area.)

Guided tours are given three times a week, but the complex is also open for various special events throughout the year, including concerts, Thanksgiving and Christmas home tours, a yearly Ghost Walk, and free monthly themed Living History days, during which reenactors demonstrate the days of the Civil War or Wild West. Between April and October, the village is also home to a Saturday farmers' market (open from 8 a.m. to noon), at which you'll find organic produce, grass-fed meats, honey, and native plants and flowers. Be sure to stop in the visitors center, which houses one of the largest collections of vintage ice cream freezers in the country (there are over 300). Guided tours of the buildings are given Tue, Thurs, and Sat, at 11 a.m.; admission $5 for adults, free for kids. The visitors center is open Tue through Fri, 9 a.m. to 3 p.m.

**Crape Myrtle Trails.** (972) 516-4235; www.crapemyrtletrails.org/trails. McKinney's public roads are lined with over 2,000 crape myrtles—those beautiful, bright flowers that thrive in the hot Texas sun. Found in five main colors (pink, white, lavender, purple, and red), the flowers are typically in bloom from May until September. Call or visit the Web site of The Crape Myrtle Trails of McKinney for driving tours and suggestions on where to spot the best blooms.

**Heard-Craig House.** 205 W. Hunt St., McKinney; (972) 569-6909; www.heardcraig.org. A couple of blocks off the main square, this beautiful 7,000-square-foot home was built by the prominent Heard family in 1900, who at the time were at the center of McKinney's cultural, social, and business circles. The Heard's daughter, Katie, wanted the home to benefit the women of McKinney, so since 1971, the gracious structure has served as a "club house" for cultural, educational, or literary groups. Now restored to reflect its heyday, with original furnishings, art works, and family heirlooms, the house is open for tours Tue and Thurs at 2 p.m., and Sat at 1 p.m., 2 p.m., and 3 p.m.; cost is $5 for adults, $3 for children. The on-site Center for the Arts also sponsors regular events like art talks and concerts in the garden.

**Heard Natural Science Museum and Wildlife Sanctuary.** 1 Nature Place, McKinney; (972) 562-5566; www.heardmuseum.org. One mile east of TX 5 on FM 1378/Country Club Road, this sanctuary houses more than 4 miles of hiking trails, indoor and outdoor exhibits, a two-acre native plant garden, and preserved environments for native birds and small exotic animals. You can also try your hand at a zip line course, tour wetlands and—for three to five months of the year—see dozens of life-sized robotic dinosaurs. Open Mon through Sat 9 a.m. to 5 p.m., Sun 1 to 5 p.m.; closed Thanksgiving, Christmas, and New Year's Day. Admission is $8 for adults, $5 for kids ages 3 to 12 and seniors.

**McKinney Convention & Visitors Bureau.** 1575 Heritage Dr., Suite 100, McKinney; (888) 649-8499 or (214) 544-1407; www.VisitMcKinney.com. Just a block south of US 380 and 2 blocks east of US 75 (take exit 41/University, and head east on US 380 to Heritage Drive), this office can set you up with maps, restaurant lists, and brochures on historic homes driving tours and walking tours of downtown (including the annual Legends of McKinney Ghost Walk). Though the bureau is only open on weekdays, feel free to call ahead or visit their Web site for tips and suggestions. Open Mon through Fri, 8 a.m. to 5 p.m.

**McKinney Performing Arts Center.** 111 N. Tennessee St., McKinney; (972) 547-2650 for the office, (214) 544-4630 for tickets; www.mckinneyperformingartscenter.org. Built in 1875, remodeled in 1927, and recently restored inside and out, the former Collin County Courthouse now serves as a multipurpose arts facility, with artist studios, galleries, and a 480-seat theater (complete with Wurlitzer pipe organ). Visitors can also spot the courtroom's original judge's bench, witness stand, and jury box, which have been left intact. The center books a regular schedule of events, from kids' shows and holiday plays to nationally known comedians and musicians. If you just want to get a glimpse inside, office hours are Mon through Fri., 9 a.m. to 6 p.m. and by appointment. Tip: Offering public restrooms, an ATM, and air conditioning, the center is a great place to take a break if you've been wandering around the square.

**North Texas History Center.** 300 E. Virginia St., McKinney; (972) 542-9457; www .northtexashistorycenter.org. This former 1911 post office is now home to exhibits on Collin County history. From January through May, the center focuses on the Civil War and its effect on the regions, while June through December, the exhibits celebrate the area's pioneers. Open Mon through Sat, 11 a.m. to 4 p.m., Sun, by appointment. Admission is $4 for adults, $2 for kids, and $8 for families.

**Third Monday Trade Days.** 4550 W. University St., McKinney; (972) 562-5466; www.tmtd .com. One of the oldest and largest monthly trade/flea markets in North Texas, this massive event features everything from train and pony rides and State Fair–type food stalls to rows and rows of for sale items Browse clothing, furniture, collectibles, antiques, sporting goods, and more. The market takes place on the Fri, Sat, and Sun before the third Monday of each month (see the Web site for exact dates), from about 8 a.m. to 5 p.m. Admission is free, parking is $3.

## where to shop

Stroll the streets around the central **McKinney Square** around Louisiana, Tennessee, Virginia, and Kentucky Streets, which are home to dozens of unique shops; some standouts include:

**The Book Gallery.** 207 N. Tennessee, McKinney; (972) 562-0533. If you're a book lover, budget a few hours to browse through this independent store packed to the rafters with rare and gently used tomes. Hours vary, so call ahead to avoid disappointment.

**Loco Cowpoke.** 206 E. Louisiana St., #102; (972) 548-0630; www.lococowpoke. It's all about Texas-style condiments at this tasty store, where you'll find everything from dips, queso, and BBQ sauces to preserves, mustards, and pickled items. The main focus is on salsas—dozens of flavors and heat-levels are on hand—but there are also unique sweet things like cactus sangria jelly and Dr. Pepper cake mix to help temper the fire. Almost everything is available to sample. Sun through Thurs, noon to 5 p.m.; Fri, noon to 8 p.m.; Sat 10 a.m. to 8 p.m.

**Main Street Magic and Fun Company.** 211 N. Tennessee St., McKinney; (972) 542-5010; www.mainstreetmagicandfun.com. Professional magicians man this family-friendly store, which sells all things magic-related. Browse puzzles, props, magic and card tricks, DVDs, gifts, and more. Once you've made a choice, the staff will even help explain how to perform the trick; classes are also available. Open Tue through Sat, noon to 7 p.m.; Sun, 1 to 5 p.m.; closed Mon.

**MOM & POPcorn.** 215 E. Louisiana St., McKinney; (972) 542-7605; www.momandpop corn.com. Owners Kim and Tim Loyd left the corporate world behind for this much more colorful and fun Candyland. No matter what your indulgence of choice, chances are you'll find it at their lively store, which stocks over forty flavors of saltwater taffy and shelves of retro and present-day candy, separated into categories like "Concession" (think Everlasting Gobstoppers, Jujubes, and Good & Plenty), Lollipops & Suckers, and Bulk (remember Mary Jane's?). There are also vintage lunch boxes and other accessories, but the real stars are the forty-five-plus flavors of popcorn that are made daily on-site using pure ingredients (and lots of real butter). Both sweet and savory flavors are available; favorites include spicy hot cheese, caramel espresso, dill pickle, tomato basil (tastes just like soup!), Texas Bumpy-road (chocolate-covered caramel-pecan popcorn with marshmallows and white chocolate), and McKinney Style (a sweet-and-sour mix of caramel and jalapeno-cheddar). Open Mon through Sat, 10 a.m. to 6 p.m.; Sun, noon to 4 p.m.

**Uptown.** 102 E. Louisiana St., McKinney; (972) 562-0303. Shoppers drive from miles to visit this upscale home decor store, which offers an eclectic mix of bath, bed, and kitchen items, plus furniture for the whole house. Owner Linda Day decorated all forty-six guest rooms of the nearby Grand Hotel, so is known in the area for her distinctive taste. Uptown also stocks some imported and specialty food items, and recently opened a gelato store in a separate location. Open Mon through Sat, 10 a.m. to 6 p.m.; Sun, noon to 5 p.m.

## where to eat

**The Pantry.** 214 E. Louisiana St., McKinney; (927) 542-2411; www.thepantryrestaurant .com. For over twenty-five years, this local favorite has been serving up delicious lunches, Sunday brunch, and homemade desserts out of what was once the Hope Hardware store (you can still see the old fabric rulers embedded in the floor). Munch on salads, sandwiches, fresh quiches, and daily specials like casseroles and meatloaf, but save room for the famous pies (available in flavors like chocolate chip, banana split, and pumpkin crunch). Known as "Pie Day," the days before Thanksgiving and Christmas are the busiest here, when seemingly all of McKinney stops in to pick up their holiday dessert orders. Open Mon through Fri, 11 a.m. to 2:30 p.m., Sat, 11 a.m. to 5 p.m., Sun, 9 a.m. to 2:30 p.m. $.

**Rick's Chophouse.** 107 N. Kentucky St. McKinney; (214) 726-9251; www.rickschop house.com. Located in The Grand Hotel (see more info on that below), Rick's main dining rooms and bar/lounge pay homage to the city—and building's—history. Guests feast on Texas-flavored standards like crab cakes, shrimp and grits, porterhouse steak, and buttermilk fried chicken, while surrounded by gas lanterns, chop-block tabletops, mahogany walls, a restored tin-pressed ceiling, and an original 1865 limestone wall. The bar hosts live music Thurs through Sat nights. $$$.

**Sauce on the Square.** 112 E. Louisiana St., McKinney; (214) 726-0251; www.sauceon thesquare.com. This recent addition to the square has become an instant favorite, thanks to its wood-stone-fired pizzas, authentic Italian pastas and appetizers, and well-curated wine list, boasting fifty bottles all under $50. Local, farm-raised ingredients, house-made cheeses, and imported Italian flour help make the dishes traditional and tasty. Open Mon through Sat for lunch and dinner. $$.

**Spoons Cafe.** 100 E. Louisiana St., McKinney; (972) 548-6900; www.spoonscafe.com. Popular with families, office mates, and groups of friends, this lively, casual spot with an open-style kitchen serves fresh salads, sandwiches, wraps, soups, and hot comfort food (baked spaghetti, chicken casseroles), as well as a full all-day breakfast menu. Mon through Wed, 7:30 a.m. to 3 p.m., Thurs through Fri, 7:30 a.m. to 9 p.m., Sat, 8 a.m. to 9 p.m., Sun, 8 a.m. to 3 p.m. $.

## where to stay

**The Grand Hotel and Ballroom.** 114 W. Louisiana St., McKinney; (214) 726-9250; www .grandhotelmckinney.com. After an extensive renovation in 2007, this forty-six-room hotel— set in a landmark 1880s building that once held an opera house and a mercantile—has emerged as a sumptuous boutique property with a killer location right on the main square. Each room is individually designed with one-of-a-kind furnishings, but all boast pillow-top mattresses, Frette linens, and granite bathrooms. Be sure to check out the restored ball-room, where composer John Philip Sousa reportedly once played. $$.

# day trip 02

north

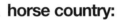

## horse country:
### denton, pilot point

**A 40-mile drive** north on I-35 brings you to one of the most significant horse breeding and training areas in the United States. Quarter horses, thoroughbreds, Andalusians, Arabians, Clydesdales—they can all be spotted grazing and playing along the winding roads of Denton County, where some of the top trainers, breeders, and riders in the world are hard at work all year-round. The area has proved popular with tourists, as well—particularly international ones, who come looking for the "cowboy" life you don't find so much in the Dallas area anymore.

Collectively, Texas is the nation's premier horse state, with over one million four-legged friends in residence, and Denton County alone is home to over 350 working farms and ranches—many of which have produced multimillion-dollar stock. While horses have always played an important part in Texas's commercial and social history, the current breeding and training boom in this area began in the 1970s, as ranch owners were attracted by the mild weather and the unique strip of horse-friendly sandy loam soil that stretches from here up to the Oklahoma border. (The soft, cushiony soil provides excellent support for the horses' hooves.) These days, the area is a designated national equine trading center, and turns out top-tier horses in all breeds and for all disciplines, from jumping and dressage to reining and cutting. The ranches are all private, but the Denton convention and visitors bureau offers behind-the-scenes tours four times a year, and self-guided driving tours can be taken at anytime (for more on that, and the best times to spot the new foal, see the Denton section below).

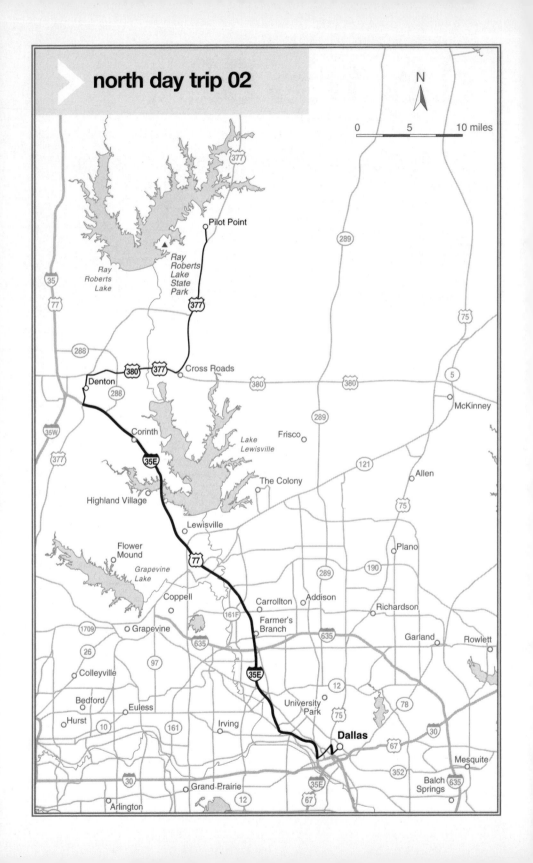

N

0     5     10 miles

377

Pilot Point

Ray Roberts Lake

Ray Roberts Lake State Park

35

77

288

377

380     377     Cross Roads

Denton

288

289

380     380

75

5

McKinney

35W

Corinth

35E

377

Highland Village

Lake Lewisville

Frisco

121

Allen

75

The Colony

Lewisville

Flower Mound

Grapevine Lake

77

Plano

190

289

Coppell

Carrollton     Addison

161F

Farmer's Branch

Richardson

1709

Grapevine

635

635

Garland

Rowlett

26

97

Colleyville

Bedford

Euless

10

Hurst

161

Irving

35E

University Park

75

12

78

Dallas

67

Mesquite

Balch Springs

635

30

Grand Prairie

12

35E

67

352

30

Arlington

Interestingly, the drive through scenic horse country is book-ended by two diverse towns: Denton, a larger city known for its thriving music scene, beautiful downtown, and cool, slightly edgy vibe; and Pilot Point, a tiny piece of the old West, where the fiddlers in the square and patrons propping up the Lowbrow bar are as authentic as you're bound to find. As a result, a day trip up this way combines a bit of Texas, old and new—the natural resources and traditions that helped build the state, along with a taste of the cuisine, art, and music that's coming up today.

# denton

Founded in 1857 as the county seat for the area, Denton's early days were—like that of most of the region—centered on horses. Famous cattleman John Chisum operated his first ranch in the area, and the Butterfield Overland Mail stage coach route, which led from St. Louis to San Francisco, made a stop on the courthouse square. The town's population nearly doubled with the arrival of two railroad lines a few decades later, and cotton and wheat farming along the blackland and grassland prairies, respectively, became the primary industries. In 1897, Denton's prosperity became visible for miles around with the dedication of the beautiful Courthouse-on-the-Square, a cream-colored, fairy tale castle-like limestone structure—complete with a clock tower and numerous domes—that still watches majestically over the downtown. It's one of the more than 140 restored historic buildings that have helped make Denton an award-winning Texas Main Street City.

With the arrival of what's now called the University of North Texas in 1890, and the opening of the present-day Texas Woman's University in 1901, Denton established itself as a center of higher learning—an image it still enjoys today. The city's residential population of about 111,000 is increased by another 50,000 during the school year, and UNT remains one of the area's biggest employers. Having two distinguished universities has also helped the city cultivate the creative, lively atmosphere of a smaller college town; funky cafes and dive bars abound, there are plenty of used book and clothing stores, and UNT's reputation as a premier music school has made Denton one of the best places for live music and up-and-coming bands in the country (even "*The New York Times*" says so). Most places are relaxed and casual, and the crowd is usually pretty eclectic.

At the same time, Denton County's history with horses continues, though now the focus is on big-money breeding and training. In addition to hundreds of ranches and farms, the area outside of town is also home to all manner of equine-related businesses, from mega-tack stores to veterinarian clinics, saddle shops, and feed shops. (Even the local FedEx trucks are kept busy with horsey matters, as sperm from the area's top stud stallions is regularly shipped to breeders all over the world.) There are also plenty of riding trails for those with their own horses, and several places out of town that offer horseback riding; contact the convention and visitors bureau for suggestions.

## getting there

To reach downtown Denton, take I-35E north to the exit for US 377/Ft. Worth Dr. Turn right onto Ft. Worth Drive, which will become Carroll Street in town, and take that to Hickory Street. Turn right for the downtown square.

## where to go

**Courthouse-on-the-Square Museum.** 110 W. Hickory, on the first floor of the courthouse in the middle of the town square, Denton; (940) 349-2850; www.dentoncounty.com/chos. Browse through a series of connected rooms filled with select items detailing Denton County history, including some furniture, books, and toys, as well as a lovely collection of Native American pottery and arrowheads. Most interesting of all are all the old photographs of generations of locals, along with brief bios about their lives and families. More than casefulls of memorabilia, these people spotlights offer real insight into the city's history. Free; Mon through Fri, 10 a.m. to 4:30 p.m., Sat, 11 a.m. to 3 p.m.

**Denton Convention & Visitors Bureau.** 414 Parkway, Denton; (940) 382-7895; www.discoverdenton.com. Brochures, maps, and the excellent North Texas Horse Country Driving Tour booklet are available from this welcome center. The office is only open Mon through Fri, from 8:30 a.m. to 5:30 p.m., so call ahead to have materials sent to you, or visit their Web site for more details.

**Denton Firefighters Museum.** 332 E. Hickory St., Denton; (940) 349-8840. Check out over 150 years of firefighting memorabilia and equipment, from a 1800s hose cart and breathing apparatus to fire logs from the 1920s to 1940s, an assortment of extinguishers and fired grenades, and uniforms spanning several decades. The collection is displayed in the lobby of Denton's Fire Station No.1. Free; Mon through Fri, 8 a.m. to 5 p.m.

**Historical Park of Denton County.** 317 W. Mulberry St., Denton; (940) 349-2865; www.dentoncounty.com/bsh and www.dentoncounty.com/dcaam. Driving into town from I-35, this complex is hard to miss, as the two historic houses stick out like a sore thumb in the middle of all the drab, modern office buildings. On the left is the Bayless-Selby House Museum, a two-floor Victorian Queen Anne mansion showcasing the history of Denton County in the late nineteenth and early twentieth centuries. Wander through the music room, kitchen, dining area, and two bedrooms, each filled with furnishings, decorations, and daily life-items from those times. There's also a brick-path-lined garden planted with herbs, antique roses, and vegetables, and shaded by pecan, oak, and magnolia trees.

Next door, find a 1904 house originally located in the town's historic African-American Quakertown Park neighborhood, and now containing the Denton County African American Museum. Inside, photographs, quilts, letters, and other memorabilia bring to life the traditions and history of the area's early African-American residents. Both attractions are free; open Tue through Sat, 10 a.m. to noon, and 1 to 3 p.m.

In June through September, the parking lot of the Historical Park is the site of the Denton Country Farmers' Market. On Tue, Thurs, and Sat, from 7 a.m. until sellout, check out seasonal fruits and veggies from regional farmers.

**Horse Country Driving Tour.** (940) 382-7895; www.discoverdenton.com. Four times a year, the Denton CVB organizes a Horse Country bus tour that features many of the top ranches in the area, where experts will offer a behind-the-scenes look at how the breeding and training operates, along with an equine presentation. The tour costs $35 and includes lunch; call the CVB for more info or to reserve a spot. Visitors are also encouraged to take self-guided driving tours through the area, and a detailed brochure with maps is available from the CVB. Because these are all working ranches, drivers are requested to stay on the main roads and off the private properties, unless a particular ranch has a sign up saying they accept drop-in guests. But even just driving along roads like FM 455 and US 377 will afford you plenty of looks at the prize-winning horses, since most of the pastures and paddocks border the main roads. For the best photo ops, do your drive by between February and June, when the majority of the year's baby foals will be outside with their mothers.

**Texas Women's University Attractions.** At Administration Dr. and Bell Ave., Denton; (940) 898-3644; www.twd.edu. Founded in 1901 as the Girls Industrial College (the name changed in 1957), Texas Women's University has a history of providing women with a well-rounded education as well as specific professional skills; it has a top-notch nursing school, and was the first college in the United States to have a building dedicated to library science (in 1956). Though men have been admitted since 1994, the university honors its heritage with several unique attractions that spotlight the achievement of women.

Perhaps most popular with visitors is the Texas First Ladies Historic Costume Collection, located in the administration building. Presented to the University by the Texas Society of the Daughters of the American Revolution in 1940, the collection boasts forty-two gowns from the 1800s until today that belonged to the wives of Texas governors and Texan presidents. There's Willie Hobby's deco-inspired number from the 1920s, Mamie Eisenhower's gold brocade from the 1950s, and the pink embroidered and fringed sheath of Miriam Ferguson, who took over the governorship from her impeached husband in 1925. Informative plaques opposite each dress take it beyond the fashion, offering details on each lady and her accomplishments. Only eighteen of the forty-two gowns are on display at any given time, with the exhibit rotating several times a year.

A short walk from the dresses is Hubbard Hall, site of the Texas Women's Hall of Fame; this is a simple display of all the commemorative plaques presented to the inductees, but it's interesting to read the bios and see the photos of the 114 women who have been honored. Next door is the library, where on the second floor lives the Cook Book Collection—over 15,000 cookbooks and 3,500 pamphlets and recipe books from as early as 1624, which offer a fascinating look at the evolution of the American home life, eating habits, and cultural trends. Also at the library is the WASP Collection, a growing archive of

## horse maneuvers

*Along with thoroughbreds, North Texas is known for raising some of the top cutting and reining horses in the world. Both names refer to types of equestrian events practiced in Western riding competitions, typically by quarter horses. In a cutting event, the rider and horse are tasked with separating a single cow away from a herd and keeping it isolated for a certain period of time. After separating (or "cutting") the steer or heifer away from its pack, the rider will loosen the reigns—or "put his hands down" in cutting terminology—and let the horse take over the job of isolating the cow; horses are judged for their style and skill. In reigning, the rider will take the horse through a pattern of spins, circles, and stops, alternating between a slow cantor and faster gallop. The horse should be easily guided and show no resistance to the moves—which include the signature "sliding stop," in which a galloping horse comes to an abrupt stop by planting his hind feet in the ground, but walking forward with his front legs, creating a graceful slide. The sliding stop is featured on the reigning competition trophies—many of which have been won by Denton's own Tom McCutcheon.*

papers, photographs, biographies, oral histories, and other memorabilia documenting the pioneering Women Air Force Pilots of World War II.

Head along the main path a bit further to reach the famous Little Chapel-in-the-Woods, among the campus's most visited sites. Designated as one of Texas's top twenty outstanding architectural achievements, the chapel was designed by noted architect O'Neal Ford in 1938, and built with the help of more than 300 TWU students and faculty. The stunning stained glass windows—each depicting women performing important "human acts"—were also designed by the students.

All the above TWU attractions are free; open Mon through Fri, 8 a.m. to 5 p.m., and on weekends by appointment.

## where to shop

Some notable stores are featured below, but for a complete list of shops and restaurants around the Courthouse-on-the-Square, as well as a list of events taking place in downtown, visit www.dentonmainstreet.org.

**2nd Street on the Square.** 116 N. Locust St., Denton; (940) 387-6280. Owners Jennifer Boncyk and Leah Wood describe their boutique as "where fashion, art, and music collide," and true to that description, the place carries a little bit of all three things: artwork and music by local artists, plus clothing, jewelry, and accessories from all over. There are new and vintage items, as well as pieces that have been recycled in-house or by other designers, like bracelets made of old vinyl records or patchwork-adorned travel bags. Mon through Thu, 10 a.m. to 6 p.m., Fri through Sat, 10 a.m. to 7 p.m., Sun, 1 to 5 p.m.

**The Candy Store.** 110B W. Oak St., Denton; (940) 382-1001. Since 1996, the Bertelsen's have been peddling all manner of confections and caffeine to an addicted crowd. The coffee and coffee beans come fresh roasted from a local purveyor, while the candies are handmade by four families that have been chocolatiers for four generations or longer. There are old-fashioned candy sticks, barks, and snowballs, dozens of flavors of truffles and even chocolate-covered fruits, sunflower seeds, graham crackers, and potato chips. A sugar-free section ensures no one feels left out. Mon through Fri, 8:30 a.m. to 6 p.m., Sat, 10 a.m. to 6 p.m., Sun, noon to 5 p.m.

**Downtown Mini Mall I & II.** 108 and 118 N. Locust St., Denton; (940) 387-0024 and (940) 387-2218. Together, these massive indoor flea markets take up most of the east side of the courthouse square. Over 110 booths stock everything from board games, army gear, and hats to collectibles and antiques. The selection is hit-or-miss, but the staff tells tales of "some really rare finds." Mon through Sat, 10 a.m. to 6 p.m.

**Recycled Books, Records & CDs.** 200 N. Locust St., Denton; (940) 566-5688; www .recycledbooks.com. Set inside the old purple Opera House, this legendary 17,000-square-foot store has been enticing book lovers from far and wide since the 1970s. The three levels are packed with every type of used book imaginable, all well-organized by category, plus a large selection of vintage vinyl, old cassettes, and new music by local bands. Recycled is also known for their selection of rare and collectible books, which has attracted professional dealers from as far away as New York. If you're a reader, budget a few hours in the itinerary for this place. Daily, 9 a.m. to 9 p.m.

## where to eat

**Beth Marie's Old Fashioned Ice Cream & Soda Fountain.** 117 W. Hickory St., Denton; (940) 384-1818; www.bethmaries.com. The lunch counter here serves comfort food like PB&J, Frito Pie, loaded baked potatoes, and sandwiches, but it's hard to focus beyond the lengthy list of homemade ice creams, which are all sold by the ounce to encourage mixing flavors. Some of the flavors change seasonally, but signatures include banana cream pie, cupcake, Courthouse pecan, strawberry cheesecake, and the more decadent Turtle Torture (butternut ice cream with caramel cups and chocolate-covered pecans) and Texas Doctor (praline-pecan in Dr. Pepper ice cream). Mon through Wed, 11 a.m. to 10 p.m., Thurs, 11 a.m. to 10:30 p.m., Fri through Sat, 11 a.m. to 11:15 p.m., Sun, noon to 10 p.m.; lunch served daily until 4 p.m. $.

**Denton County Independent Hamburger Co.** 113 W. Hickory St., Denton; (940) 383-1022. Denton's go-to burger joint has been serving patties topped with chili, hickory sauce, or jalapeños—as well as classic old-fashioneds and cheeseburgers—since 1977. Also find steak sandwiches, hot dogs, and, of course, chicken-fried steak. Mon through Sat, 11 a.m. to 3 p.m. $.

**El Guapo's.** 419 S. Elm St, Denton; (940) 566-5575; www.elguapos.com. The winking face of owner Mike Zampino smiles out from the menus and T-shirts at this perennial Tex-Mex favorite, located in a large, colorfully painted strip of buildings a few blocks from the square. The vibe is relaxed and friendly, while the menu satisfies with both classics (oversized burritos, chili rellenos, combo plates, tomatillo enchiladas) and the creative ("loca cola" marinated brisket, jalapeño-stuffed shrimp, Mexican Philly wraps, giant shrimp-and-jack cheese quesadillas). Everything is fresh and homemade, from the guacamole, salsa, and tortilla soup to the tortillas, which you can watch being made on-site. Free lunches and desserts are given away every weekday through "Lotto Lunch" drawings, which take place during peak lunch hours. Sun through Thurs, 11 a.m. to 10 p.m., Fri through Sat, 11 a.m. to 11 p.m. $–$$.

**Hannah's Off the Square.** 111 W. Mulberry, Denton; (940) 566-1110; www.hannahsoffthesquare.com. A former blacksmith's workshop is now home to Denton's largest wine selection and a creative menu of gourmet comfort food. Hannah's serves lunch, brunch, dinner, and a bar tapas menu, with an emphasis throughout on using locally sourced and seasonal ingredients. Settle into grilled shrimp with grit cakes and tomato-bacon gravy or roasted sea bass with blueberry-red pepper sauce for dinner, sandwiches paired with homemade kettle chips for lunch, or pork pot stickers and Kobe beef sliders over drinks. Open daily; call for hours and reservations. $$–$$$.

**Prairie House Restaurant.** 1001 US 380, Cross Roads; (940) 440-9760; www.phtexas.com. Located in Horse Country, this is the type of place that works perfectly with a day out on the ranch: ribs, wings, homemade buffalo meatballs, BBQ, burgers, steaks, catfish, and more, all with tasty sides. Sun through Thurs, 11 a.m. to 10 p.m., Fri through Sat, 11 a.m. to 11 p.m. $–$$.

**Ravelin Bakery.** 416 S. Elm St., Denton; (940) 382-8561. Whether you like your baked goods straightforward—eleven kinds of muffins, legendary cinnamon Danish, cake-like chocolate chip cookies—or a bit more adventurous (black pepper-prosciutto bread, savory stuffed croissants, "Russian Tea" cookies), this is the place for you. The selection is vast, and it's all made on-site using natural ingredients and European-style recipes—meaning things are a little less sweet, and there's not so much deep frying. Tue through Sat., 6:30 a.m. to 5:30 p.m., Sun, 8 a.m. to 5:30 p.m. $.

## where to stay

**Meritt Hotel at the Meritt Bois D'Arc Buffalo Ranch.** 2946 Ganzer Rd. West, Denton; (940) 482-3409; www.buffalovalleyeventcenter.com. Sleep where the buffalo roam at this spot just outside of town, where the nineteen hotel rooms all come with high-speed Internet, microwaves, and fridges, and access to a common lounge overlooking the courtyard, gardens, and waterfall. The vast property also includes event spaces, RV hook-up sites, and a ranch offering a long list of animal- and Western-related activities. The husband-and-wife owners make everyone feel at home, and have been known to dole out a hug or two before bedtime. $.

**Wildwood Inn.** 2602 Lillian Miller Parkway, Denton; (940) 243-4919 or (866) 840-0713; www.denton-wildwoodinn.com. A few exits south of downtown, on the way from (or back to) Dallas, this romantic, European-style inn set on four wooded acres combines the intimacy of a B&B with the amenities and service level of a larger hotel. The fourteen individually decorated rooms boast luxe details like feather beds, see-through fireplaces, and whirlpool tubs, while the property features a pool and a four-star restaurant (breakfast is served daily for inn guests, but reservations are required for the multicourse Thursday and Friday dinners). $$.

## notorious in north texas

*Pretty much any town you go to in this part of North Texas claims some connection to Bonnie and Clyde, the notorious robbers and outlaws that roamed the central United States during the Great Depression—and who were born and raised in the Dallas area. The couple robbed banks in Grapevine and Pilot Point, and hid out in hotels in Fort Worth and Decatur; in Corsicana's Pioneer Park, there's even a small museum dedicated to them, filled with items donated by Clyde's uncle. In 1967, the movie* Bonnie & Clyde, *starring Warren Beatty and Faye Dunaway, filmed all over the area, from Waxahachie to Pilot Point, where the bank on the town square doubles for one of the banks taken by the duo. The premiere of the Academy Award– winning film took place at Denton's Campus Theater, a 1949 movie house that now serves as the city's performing arts theater.*

# pilot point

From Denton, a drive through Horse Country along FM 428, FM 455, and US 377 will bring you to Pilot Point, the oldest town in Denton County. Set on the edge of the Cross Timbers region of the state, the location first attracted settlers in the 1840s with its expanse of blackland prairies to the east and sandy-soiled woodlands to the west. At the highest point in the area stood a small hill coved with oak trees and one towering cottonwood; the latter served as a navigational landmark for travelers, giving the town its original name of Pilot's Point. The town square now sits where that hill once was.

The town was officially plotted in 1853, and over the next couple of decades became a stop on the Butterfield Overland Mail stage route, home to lots of German immigrants and the site of a respected seminary school. The first brick building in the county was built along the square in 1872, using locally made brick, and the first telegraph line came through in 1877, connecting the town to the rest of the region before the arrival of the railroad three years later. (One fun side note: Pilot Point's first telegrapher was Ed Reaves, who went on to become the chief telegrapher at the White House.)

Over the years, the town thrived thanks to farming, ranching, and cotton mills; at one time, it even boasted the largest cotton gin in the United States. These days, the city of about 5,100 is at the center of the booming North Texas horse breeding and training industries, with many of the major ranches set just outside of town. At the same time, Pilot Point has made a name for itself as a top spot for custom cabinetry and furniture making. As the Dallas area has grown northward, many of the grand new homes and sprawling subdivisions feature interiors by Pilot Point craftsmen, and many Metroplex residents drive up here to custom order their own pieces at one of the over fifteen local cabinet shops.

Thanks to these thriving industries, the town is enjoying a bit of an upswing. While the historic buildings around the town square are mostly empty, plans are underway to restore and revive some of the spots, including the old hotel. One of the unique things about Pilot Point is that despite economic ups and downs over the decades, it has managed to maintain a lot of its history—the first town bank, which opened in 1884, is still serving customers, for example, and the local Masonic Lodge, chartered in 1862, is one of the oldest in Texas. So even as the town is growing, this is still a place where there's gospel on the square on Saturday nights, and where even a drop-in visitor is bound to hear a colorful story or two.

## getting there

To reach the town square, take US 377 north to Pilot Point. The highway will fork just outside of town; stay left to take it into downtown, where it will become Washington St./State Loop 387.

# where to go

**Greenbelt Corridor & Lake Ray Roberts State Park.** (940) 637-2294 or (940) 686-0261; www.tpwd.state.tx.us. Spread out around the 30,000-acre Ray Roberts reservoir, this state park offers bird-watching, water sports areas, fishing, camping, swimming, hiking and biking trails, and wetlands (and for the less outdoorsy, Wi-Fi hotspots). The park is made up of two main units—the Isle du Bois section in Pilot Point and the Johnson Branch in Valley View—as well as six satellite parks. The Sanger Unit is home to the Lake Ray Roberts Marina, where you can rent boats and slips, buy fishing licenses and bait, and pick up groceries for a picnic (940-458-7343; www.rayrobertsmarina.com). See below for info on the Jordan Unit, which offers overnight accommodations and horseback riding. The Pilot Point park entry is located along PW 4137, off of FM 455.

The park is also connected to the Greenbelt Corridor, a 20-mile multiuse trailway connecting Ray Roberts Dam with the beginning of Lake Lewisville. Bikers, hikers, equestrians, and kayakers favor the corridor, which takes you along the wooded Elm Fork branch of the Trinity River. Trailhead access points are located at FM 455, FM 428, and Hwy. 380. For info on canoe and kayak rentals, call Greenbelt Canoe Rentals at (817) 228-9496.

**Historic Square Walking Tour.** Between Main and Liberty Streets and Jefferson and Washington Streets, Pilot Point; www.pilotpoint.us. Pick up or download a map for this short stroll around the square. What's fun about this walk is that, in addition to details about architecture and building dates, the brochure gives some colorful anecdotes about the town's past—like that the west side of the square used to be geared toward men (because it was considered "unladylike" to cross the busy main street), and that the man who ran the shoe store was often the butt of teenage pranks (legend has it an outhouse ended up on his roof one Halloween night). Be sure to pop into the old bank building on the northwest corner (used as a location in the movie *Bonnie and Clyde*) to see the art collection and controversial mural of Eve.

**Pilot Point Chamber of Commerce.** 300 S. Washington St., Pilot Point; (940) 686-5385; www.pilotpoint.us. This visitors center doles out maps and local info. While it's only open on the weekdays, a lot of the information—including downloadable walking tour brochures—can be found on the city's Web site, as well as at various businesses around the square. Mon through Fri, 8:30 a.m. to 4:30 p.m.

# where to eat

**Jay's Café & Museum.** 110 W. Main St., Pilot Point; (940) 686-0158; www.jayscafe museum.com. Stop in for a bite and you'll discover so much more: This popular eatery on the town square serves a diverse menu of Texas comfort food in a space packed with over 500 items on the history of Pilot Point, plus over 10,000 other pieces of antiques and memorabilia. Take it all in while noshing on huevos rancheros with jalapeño bacon, loaded three-egg omelets, homemade chips and salsa, Greek salads, chicken- and chili-fried steak, over a dozen types of sandwiches, and tortilla soup made with seventeen ingredients. No credit cards accepted. Open Tue through Sat, 8 a.m. to 2 p.m. $.

**Lowbrow's Beer & Wine Garden.** 200 S. Washington St., Pilot Point; (940) 686-3801; www.lowbrows.us. There are no neon beer signs or fancy cocktail menus at this relaxed local hangout—instead, the stylishly restored historic building (home to Dad Robins' restaurant in the late-1800s) features wooden tables, a 1930s shuffleboard set, and a cool curved back bar usually surrounded by a cast of characters telling stories and shooting the breeze. There's also a back garden, domino matches every Thursday, and live music most Thursdays through Saturdays, all overseen by Bob, the legendary owner with a real flair for deadpan wit. (Just check out the Web site for a taste.) Open "whenever the light is on" (generally noon to 12 a.m.). $.

## where to stay

**Lantana Lodge.** 2200 FM 1192, Pilot Point; (940) 686-0261; www.lantanaresortmarina .com. Tucked into Lake Ray Roberts State Park, and surrounded by cedar and oak trees, this lodge and restaurant is an ideal spot to get away from it all. The rooms are well appointed and casual, with a rustic Western decor, while the lovely Bronze Buffalo Grill (a popular place for special occasions) serves cooked-to-order lunch, dinner, and weekend breakfast overlooking the lake. (The restaurant is closed Mon and Tues.) The resort also offers seven horse stalls for customers who want to ride up on the Greenbelt trails, park their horse, and enjoy lunch. If you don't have your own steed, the Black Mustang Ranch nearby provides horseback riding and guides (817-915-8455; www.blackmustangranch.com). $.

# day trip 03

north

**Located about 67 miles** north of Dallas, Gainesville is a little over an hour away when cruising along I-35, and only minutes from the Red River border between Texas and Oklahoma. A varied history kept the town booming for much of the late-nineteenth and twentieth centuries, and these days tourism—and a picturesque downtown—keep the crowds coming. Along with the unique shops and restaurants along the square, and a notable zoo, one of the main draws is the city's wealth of historic Victorian homes, many of which can be viewed on a drive through the historic neighborhood south of downtown.

This day trips pairs this slice of old Texas—where back during the cattle trail days, cowboys used to do their shopping, carousing, and gambling—with a bit of contemporary entertainment. Just under 12 miles from the fried pies and antiques of Gainesville is the Win-Star World Casino, the fifth-largest casino in the world (as of this writing). Multiple gaming areas, concerts by top national acts, and a hotel and spa (just opened in 2009) give North Texan day-trippers the chance to get a little Vegas along with their Victorians.

# gainesville

Established in 1850 on a forty-acre tract of land on the Red River frontier, the town was originally called Liberty—a name that didn't stick, as there already was a Liberty, Texas. Colonel William Fitzhugh from nearby Fort Fitzhugh suggested naming the town after one of his military bosses, General Edmund Pendleton Gaines, a United States General who had sympathized with the Texas Revolution. And thus Gainesville was born. By 1858, the

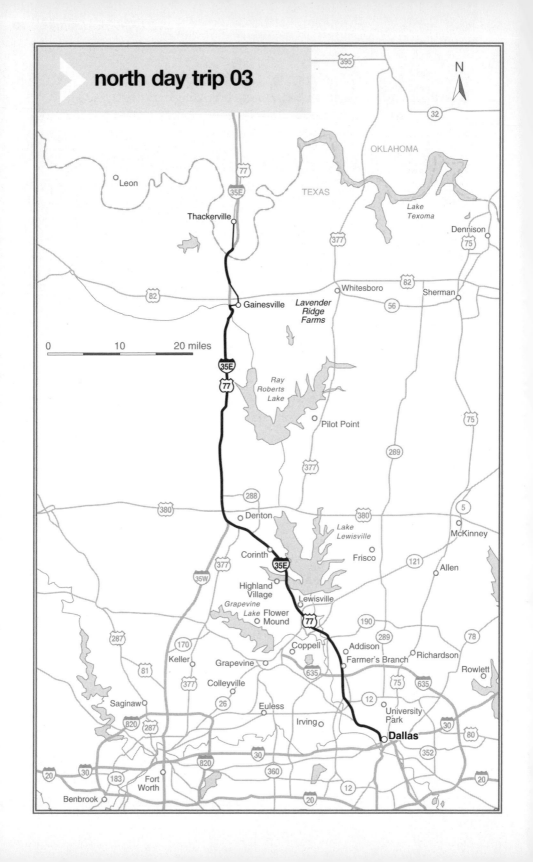

town had become a stop on the Butterfield Overland Mail stage coach route, and was soon designated the seat of Cooke County—though a steady number of Native American attacks kept it from growing too fast.

Gainesville first earned notoriety as the scene of the tragic Great Hanging during the Civil War, in which a number of suspected Union sympathizers were killed; a small marker at the corner of I-35 and California Street honors the fallen of that event. But after the war, the town boomed along with the cattle industry, serving as a supply and entertainment center for cowboys leading stock across the grasslands and north to Oklahoma (Gainesville is only 7 miles from the Oklahoma border). Located in between the Chisholm Trail and the Shawnee Trail, Gainesville became a hotbed of stores, saloons, casinos, and houses of ill repute, all catering to the cowboy. The town continued to grow for the remainder of the century and into the 1900s, as the railroad, cotton farming, and retail businesses helped bring in the bucks. (It was even the first place in Texas to sell barbed wire.) In the 1930s, the town weathered the Depression thanks to both nearby oil fields and the all-volunteer Gainesville Community Circus, which gained national prominence and drew crowds of thousands. During World War II, Camp Howze, an army infantry training camp, brought more jobs to the area.

Today, the city's population lingers at just under 17,000, and tourism is one of its main draws. In 1999, Amtrak added a stop here along its route from Oklahoma City to Forth Worth; the train stops at the Santa Fe Depot twice a day (once before noon, and again around 6:30 p.m.), and has brought in a whole new group of day-trippers. The city now offers free trolley service Fri and Sat, 11 a.m. to 9 p.m. and Sun, 11 a.m. to 6 p.m. The trolley links the Santa Fe Train Depot, the downtown square, Frank Buck Zoo, many local hotels, and the Gainesville Factory Shops on an hourly loop, making it a convenient way to see the town. Park at the square and hop on; for more information, contact the Gainesville Chamber of Commerce at (940) 665-2831 Mon through Fri, or visit www.gogainesville.net.

## getting there

Gainseville proper sits at the intersection of I-35 and US 82, but to reach the historic downtown, take I-35E north from Dallas and exit 496B for California Street. The courthouse square is less than half a mile east along California Street.

## where to go

**Frank Buck Zoo.** 1000 W. California St., at I-35, Gainesville; (940) 668-4539 and (940) 727-9097; www.frankbuckzoo.com. In the 1930s, A. Morton Smith debuted his Gainesville Community Circus at the Cooke Country Fair, and the show went on to delight both local and national audiences for close to three more decades. In 1954, after a fire wiped out much of the circus equipment, the animals stayed together in what became the zoo. (They moved to their current home on the banks of Elm Creek in 1962.) The facility was named in honor of Gainesville native Frank Buck, an early-twentieth-century modern zoo pioneer who traveled the globe dozens of times collecting animals for various zoos around the world—a skill that earned him the nickname "Bring 'em Back Alive" Buck.

These days, all manner of wildlife call the zoo home, from big fellas like giraffe, camels, kangaroo, black bears, and zebra to African crested porcupines, two-toed sloth, and leopard tortoise. VIP packages are available that offer a behind-the-scenes look at the zoo and the chance to see some feedings up close. Admission is $6 for adults, $5 for seniors, and $4 for kids 12 and under. Open daily, year-round, except for Thanksgiving and Christmas Day; hours vary depending on the season, so call ahead.

**Morton Museum.** 210 S. Dixon St, Gainesville; (940) 668-8900; www.mortonmuseum .org. Located 2 blocks south of the courthouse, this building was constructed in 1884 to house the town's city hall, fire station, and jail—all under one roof. Back then, the bell in the second-floor tower rang every night at 9 p.m. to signal curfew for the settlers. After new city buildings were built in the 1920s, this one served as a warehouse for many years before falling into disarray, but was then saved from demolition in the 1960s (though the second floor and bell tower were already gone) and turned into a museum. Inside, find part of a 1870s log cabin, and a series of rotating exhibits; the themes change—popular ones include Civil War, Outlaws, Baseball, and the Circus—but the focus is always on Cooke County, its history, and its role in larger world events. The museum also maintains an extensive archive of documents and photographs that's available to researchers. Admission free; open Tue through Fri, 10 a.m. to 5 p.m., Sat, 10:30 a.m. to 4 p.m.

In addition to operating the museum, the historical society also offers guided walking tours of the downtown and the Victorian homes district, as well as several other themes; these are available by appointment, so call for more info. Visitors interested in a self-guided tour may also rent or buy audio CDs detailing the historic buildings. The chamber of commerce is another good resource for tips on which streets offer the best house-spotting.

**Santa Fe Depot and Museum.** 605 E. California St, Gainesville; (940) 668-8900. Built in 1902 to handle Gainesville's increasing rail traffic (the town was a stop on the Gulf, Colorado, and Santa Fe line), this beautiful red brick building was renovated in 2002. The ground floor is where passengers arriving on Amtrak's twice-daily Heartland Flyer train (running between Fort Worth and Oklahoma City) disembark. Upstairs, there's a museum, opened in 2002, highlighting different parts of local history. There's a room on transportation, including info on the old Harvey Restaurant that used to serve travelers, plus rooms on the Gainesville Community Circus and various local industries, and a re-created bedroom of one of the Harvey House waitresses. A small theater shows a 1930s short film made about the circus. Free. Wed through Sun, 11 a.m. to 2 p.m.

## where to shop

**Gainesville Factory Shops.** North I-35, at Exit 501, Gainesville; (888) 545-7220; www .gainesvillefactoryshops.com. If you're in the market for outlet-priced clothing and accessories, make this easy stop along I-35 between Gainesville and Thackerville. The complex include factory outlets for twenty-two brands, including The Gap, Reebok, Van Heusen, Kitchen Collection, Oshkosh B'Gosh, Perfumania, RSI Toys, Sunglass Hut, and Rocky Mountain Chocolate Factory. The outlet is serviced by Gainesville's free weekend trolley and the public TAPS bus, which runs from both the depot and downtown; call (800) 256-0911 for details.

**Historic Downtown Square.** Along California, Commerce, Main, and Dixon Streets, Gainesville; www.shophistoricgainesville.com. Close to two dozen shops line the edges of the town square, with not a chain store among them. Park on one of the side streets and wander. Note that most of the places are open Mon through Fri, 10 a.m. to 5 p.m. and Sat, 10 a.m. to 3 p.m., but call ahead to make sure.

Some notable spots to check out include:

**Barron's** (101 E. California St.; 940-665-4223). The place for unique, handcrafted jewelry.

**Bella Matiz** (103 W. California St.; 940-668-8418). "Pampering" and "natural" are the key words here, where you'll find a range of boutique skin and body care brands, flax-based clothing, comfy robes and slippers, botanical-based candles, and a smattering of folk art.

**Kelly Lane Jewelry** (205 S. Commerce St.; 940-665-2138). Beautiful, hand-twisted jewelry using semi-precious stones and silver- and gold-filled wire.

**Lindsay House/Powell Fine Art** (318 E. California St.; 940-665-7171). Along with jewelry, antiques, gourmet foods, and other gift items, find a large collection of original and limited-edition artwork and decorative objects, much of it by local artists.

**Otts Furniture** (115 S. Commerce St.; 940-665-6861). Catering to Gainesville's home decor and furniture needs since 1960, with four generations of the Otts family working on-site.

**Paige Davidson Studio & Cahoots Handbags** (205 S. Commerce St.; 940-665-2138). Two stores for the price of one: The one-time Byrd Drygoods Store, still with its original wood floors and mural, now showcases stylish accessories by Cahoots Handbags, handmade with vintage textiles, and paintings and drawings by respected artist Paige Davidson.

# where to eat

**Edelweiss Tea Haus.** 105 S. Commerce St., Gainesville; (940) 665-6540. Tortilla wraps, homemade soups, German fare, and daily made-in-house desserts bring lunchers to this square-side cafe. Daily home-style specials, like chicken spaghetti, come with soup or salad and a roll. Mon through Sat, 11 a.m. to 3 p.m. $.

**Fried Pie Co. & Restaurant.** 202 W. Main St., Gainesville; (940) 665-7641. A regional icon since 1981, this homey eatery made its name with—you guessed it—dozens of kinds of homemade fried pie, including classics like apricot and coconut and newer additions like pecan and blueberry. The doughy goodies are all displayed in a center case, making them convenient for take-out. The rest of the two-room space is made up of seating for the restaurant, which serves a lengthy—and super-affordable—breakfast and lunch menu, featuring everything from omelets and grits to chili-cheese hot dogs and close to twenty kinds of sandwiches. Mon through Fri, 6:30 a.m. to 4:30 p.m., Sat, 6:30 a.m. to 3 p.m. $.

**Main Street Pub.** 216 W. Main St., Gainesville; (940) 668-4040. Settle in to pub-style comfort food like nachos, pastas, and wraps, plus best-sellers like the rainbow trout and hand-breaded fried steak. With dark wood accents and a relaxed atmosphere, the vibe is as comforting as the eats. $–$$.

**Sarah's on the Square.** 115 California St., Gainesville; (940) 612-4782. Fresh, gourmet eats, an upscale-casual vibe, and sense of humor define this standout, which does a brisk trade for lunch and dinner—and boasts a few regulars who drive over 100 miles to eat here once a week. "Monster" quesadillas, sandwiches on homemade breads, chicken spaghetti, and burgers are local favorites, along with homemade soups "so delicious, you'll wish you were sick." (The Tomato Gin Bisque in particular is worth coming in for.) Save room for the famous desserts: sopapilla cheesecake bars, Reese's peanut butter pie, and "mile high" coconut creams. This building used to house a brothel in the 1850s–1860s, and the restaurant is named for the madame of that establishment (for more on that, see "Where to Stay"). The crew behind Sarah's also owns Sweet Thangs soda shop, Amelia's Antique Mall, Miss Olivia's B&B, and The Shady Lady B&B—all named after women. Tues through Wed, 11 a.m. to 4 p.m., Thurs, 11 a.m. to 9 p.m., Fri and Sat, 11 a.m. to 10 p.m. $.

**Sweet Thangs.** 103 S. Commerce St., Gainesville; (940) 612-4386. Everyone's a kid at this colorful retro candy and soda shop, which opened in late-summer 2009. Enjoy lunch staples like hot dogs and sandwiches—made using the same recipes from the soda shop that was here fifty years ago—but save room for all the sweets: homemade peanut patties, pecan pralines, Kaluha cake, and "funky" cupcakes, plus chocolates from Hico. Many of the treats are named for local connections, like Leopard Brownies (for the Gainesville High School Leopards football team) and the Black & White Shake (for the Lindsay Knights team colors). Root beer floats and Blue Bell shakes are made at the fountain, and in keeping with the old-fashioned theme, the owners often sell coffee for a nickel. Tues through Sat, 10 a.m. to 7 p.m., Sun, 1 to 5 p.m. $.

## where to stay

**The Shady Lady.** 115 California St., Gainesville. (940) 665-5239. Set above the Sarah's on the Square restaurant (and owned by the same people), this four-room B&B opened in 2008 in what was—in the 1850s and 1860s—the town brothel. That colorful past is acknowledged in the decor of the Madame Suite, which is done-up in velvets, animal prints, and rich colors like plum and garnet (there's also a Jacuzzi), and in the Chisholm Trail room, where the six-foot copper tub is matched by a sink that was created from the old brothel washstand. The other suites boast Victorian Garden and Santa Fe Depot themes, and all include breakfast. $–$$.

## worth more time

If time permits before leaving the Gainesville area, stop by **Lavender Ridge Farms** (2381 CR 178; 940-665-6938; www.lavenderridgefarms.com) to pick your own herbs, veggies, and sweet-smelling lavender. Originally a melon and strawberry farm in the 1920s and 1930s, the idyllic spot reopened in 2006 as a place for cut flowers and fresh herbs. Today, there are about two acres of lavender on-site, as well as a pesticide-free vegetable and strawberry garden and a greenhouse. Visitors are welcome to come by at cutting season to pick their own blooms, plants, or edibles (or eat strawberries right off the vine); the rest of the year, the gift shop stocks perennials, herbs, and lavender-based bath and body products. The cafe is open Fri through Sat, 11 a.m. to 3 p.m. for lunch, and for dinner by reservation. Call for details on the various cutting seasons for the lavender and the fruits/ veggies. The farm is located about 8 miles from Gainesville, and one hour from Dallas. From Gainesville, take Hwy. 82 east for about 8 miles, then turn south on FM 678 and travel for about 1 mile. Turn right on CR 178 and follow that road for 1.5 miles until you see the farm entrance on the right.

# thackerville, ok

Despite recent efforts to get the laws changed, casino-style gambling is still illegal in Texas. For years, North Texan card players and slots enthusiasts had to head out to Louisiana to drop (or win) a few bucks, but now that privilege can be had a lot closer to home. Southern Oklahoma's Chickasaw Nation operates close to fifty casinos and related businesses, including WinStar—the biggest casino in Oklahoma, the fifth largest in the world, and a slice of Vegas in our neck of the woods.

## getting there

Continue north on I-35 about 12 miles from Gainesville, pass the Oklahoma border, and take exit 1—the first exit past the Red River. Follow the signs for WinStar Casino; the road will curve around for a few minutes and you will see the entrance to the golf course and other WinStar properties on your right, but keep driving until you spot the façade of the casino section, which is designed to represent the different cities featured in the casino, like Rome and Paris (you can't miss it).

## where to go

**WinStar World Casino.** Exit 1, I-35, Thackerville, OK; (800) 622-6317; www.winstarworld casino.com. Operated by the Chickasaw Nation, the WinStar World Casino and complex underwent a massive expansion in 2009, beginning with the opening of new gaming sections that nearly doubled the size of the casino to 519,000 square feet. (For more on the complex's other facilities, see below.) There are eight gaming plazas in total, all connected under one roof, and each boasts the name of an international city—like Paris, Vienna, Cairo, and Madrid—with a decor of marble fountains and hand-painted murals to match. Most sections house mainly slot machines, of every style and monetary amount, plus roulette wheels and other electronic games; the Beijing section, watched over by eight crystal dragons, is the main place for table games. The casino is open twenty-four hours a day.

As in most casinos, the lighting here is kept low (so you never really know what time it is) and smoking is allowed inside. For when you need a break, there are several eateries tucked between the different halls. Find Italian fare at Zar's and Matador, tender steaks at Stone Ranch, burgers and pub grub at Red River Grill and Chips 'N Ales. Kahn's Fire Mongolian, a particular standout, offers made-to-order rice bowls using a wide selection of fresh ingredients. Country artist Toby Keith is set to open a branch of his restaurant, I Love This Bar & Grill, on-site in 2010.

At the center of the casino building sits the Global Event Center, a 2,500-seat theater that hosts blackjack and poker tournaments and nationally recognized entertainment acts. B. B. King, Willie Nelson, Tony Bennett, Patti Labelle, Journey, Kelly Clarkson, Miranda Lambert—they've all played here; check the Web site for an upcoming schedule.

## where to stay

**WinStar World Casino Hotel.** Adjacent to the WinStar World Casino; (866) 946-7787; www.winstarworldcasino.com/amenities/winstarworldhotel. Officially opened over Labor Day weekend, 2009, this twelve-story, 395-room hotel finally offers patrons (and artists performing in the theater) somewhere to stay in the casino complex. Rooms are spacious and well appointed, with flat-screen TVs, free high-speed Internet, plush bedding, and iPod docking stations; corner, Player and Governor suites take things further with wet bars and glass showers. Downstairs there's a pool and whirlpool, a fitness center, the Aces bar/lounge, and an outpost of Dallas-based Spa Habitat, a green-minded spa that uses only natural, healing ingredients in their pampering services. Dinner can be taken at The Grill, a steak, seafood, and wine place that's a step up from most of the other places in the gaming rooms.

WinStar also operates an 18-hole, D.A. Weibring-designed golf course, spread out over 225 acres adjacent to the casino center. The hotel can coordinate tee times and transport, so just ask when you get there. (www.winstargolfcourse.com) $–$$.

# northeast

# day trip 01

## northeast

**where cotton was king:**
greenville

# greenville

Head east on I-30 into the Blackland Prairies for an easy forty-five-minute drive to Greenville, the seat of Hunt County and the town that cotton built. Today, the place is in the midst of a revitalization, with new businesses moving into the semi-abandoned downtown and progressive city programs—like an eco-friendly "smart garden," a "My Downtown Is Back" campaign, and a push to encourage walking and biking—taking hold. There are regular concerts featuring new and established Texas songwriters, and a popular winery with live music that's drawing patrons from as far away as Austin. Some of the major companies based in the area make military surveillance equipment and robotic technology—which has helped the local high school establish an award-winning robotics team.

At the same time, there are still plenty of reminders of the town's past. Greenville was declared the county seat in 1846, and named for Thomas J. Green, a general in the Texas Army. (The first choice for a name had been "Pinckneyville," in honor of James Pinckney Henderson, the first Governor of Texas, but thankfully that idea fell by the wayside.) The town was established along a stretch of blackland prairie covered in tall grass, where the rich soil tended to stick to boots and buggy wheels. But what might have irritated settlers ended up being their cash cow: The soil proved ideal for growing the high-grade cotton coveted by English weaving mills, and soon the town was booming. Six railway lines blew in, the world's largest inland cotton compress was built here, and the population grew to

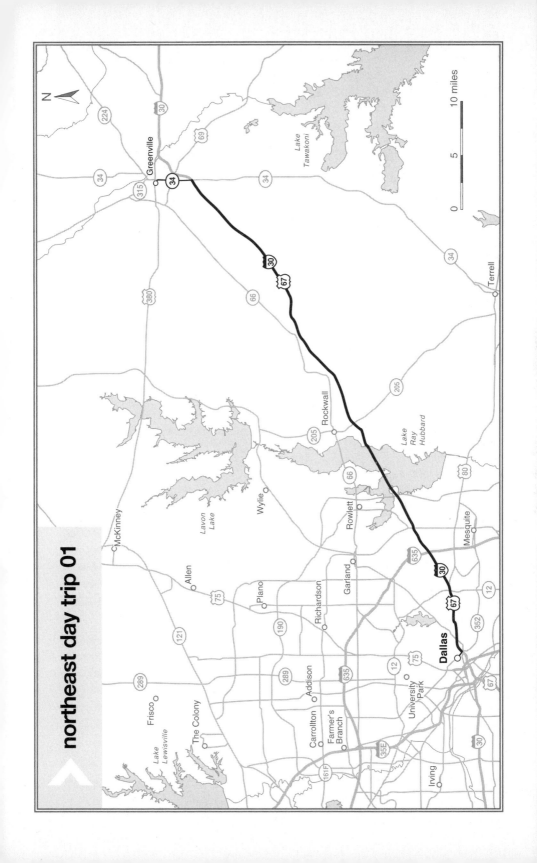

northeast day trip 01

N

Greenville

Lake
Tawakoni

Terrell

Rockwall

Lake
Ray
Hubbard

Mesquite

Wylie

Lavon
Lake

Rowlett

Garland

McKinney

Allen

Plano

Richardson

Frisco

The Colony

Lake
Lewisville

Addison

Carrollton

Farmer's
Branch

University
Park

Dallas

Irving

0    5    10 miles

8,500 by 1900. It must have been a magical scene at harvest season then, when prospective buyers would pull out white tufts of cotton from the bales to examine the quality, causing little "snowflakes" to waft through town.

Greenville diversified as the cotton industry began to wane, and during World War II was home to Majors Field Army Air Corp base; postwar, the Texas Engineering and Manufacturing Company leased part of the base, and over the years—and though various mergers and incarnations—has remained one of the area's largest employers. (On a sports-themed side note: It was after the war, in 1949, when Joe DiMaggio and the New York Yankees came to town to play an exhibition match against the Greenville Majors—and famously lost.) With a current population of around 26,000, Greenville remains an interesting mix—close enough to Dallas to attract businesses and visitors, but happily on the edge of scenic, relaxed-pace East Texas.

## getting there

To reach Greenville, take I-30 east about 60 miles. If visiting the Audie Murphy/American Cotton Museum or Mary of Puddin' Hill first, follow those directions below. For the historic downtown, take exit 96 for TX 302/US 67/Lee Street, which will lead into town. (Those are all the same street—TX 302 and US 67 are called Lee Street within the city limits.)

## where to go

**Audie Murphy & American Cotton Museum.** 600 Interstate 30 East, at exit 94B, on the north service road, Greenville; (903) 450-4502; www.cottonmuseum.com. Greatly expanded in early 2010, this museum covers a lot more than its name lets on. One of the primary focal points is Audie Murphy, a local boy, World War II hero, Hollywood movie star, cowboy singer, and all-around interesting guy. Born in Greenville to very humble beginnings, Murphy went on to receive every medal of valor that the United States gives, some more than once, as well as the Medal of Honor—a feat that got him into the pages of *Life* magazine, and attracted movie producers. This led to a career in Hollywood, where he eventually starred in forty-four films, including one based on his autobiography, *To Hell and Back*.

Visitors to the museum may first watch a fifteen-minute video detailing Murphy's story, then browse through sections on his childhood, his military career, and his acting and singing days; included are photos, memorabilia, and costumes. Past the Murphy exhibits, find a few areas on local history—including an original cotton compress—as well as several rooms on military history, with a focus on local connections. The largest section covers World War II, but there are items on the Civil War, World War I, Vietnam, and Korea, as well. There's a recreated trench, so guests can feel how cramped quarters were on the field, as well as a diorama depicting various important battles.

Also interesting are a few exhibits telling the stories of other notable locals, including Monty Stratton, the 1930s major league baseball pitcher whose biopic, *The Stratton Story,* starred Jimmy Stewart. The museum also hosts several events throughout the year, such as the popular adults-only "Easter after Dark" egg hunt, movie nights, and the annual Audie Murphy Day. Visit their Web site for details. Adults, $5, students (K–college), $1. Tues through Sat, 10 a.m. to 5 p.m.

**Greenville Chamber Convention & Visitors Bureau.** 2713 Stonewall St., Greenville; (903) 455-1510; www.greenvillechamber.org. Stop in for maps, brochures, and assistance. The office is open Mon through Fri, 8 a.m. to 5 p.m., but several local merchants also stock pamphlets and info sheets when the center is closed. The Friends of Main Street Web site (www.greenville-texas.com) provides downloadable maps for walking tours, shopping, and more; see below for more info.

**Greenville Historic Downtown.** Between Wright, Crockett, Henry, and Gordon Streets, Greenville; www.greenville-texas.com. Stroll through the old downtown for a look at its significant buildings, and to get a feel for what Greenville was like when cotton was king. Many of the structures have historical markers explaining their story, but for even more insight (and interesting local tidbits), follow the Historic Downtown Walking Tour map put out by the Greenville Main Street program. You can download the map from their site (www .greenville-texas.com) or visit them at 3216 Washington St.

While walking around town, stop by the **Heritage Garden of Hunt County** (2217 Washington St., 903-455-9885). Once a plain old parking lot, the site has been transformed by an all-volunteer team into a small, sweet garden showcasing a number of trees, shrubs, plants, and flowers that thrive in North Texas; signs throughout indicate what's what. There are also a few benches and tables for those who want a quiet place to picnic.

## worth more time:

**Northeast Texas Children's Museum.** 2501 Hwy. 50, Commerce; (903) 886-6055; www .netxcm.com. Travelers with kiddies may want to check out this fun attraction, located about 15 miles away in the city of Commerce. There are various interactive theme rooms for the little people to play in, including ones depicting a frontier living room, a grocery store, and the "jungle"; it's all geared toward creative learning. There are also some art exhibits, as well as the railroad history collection and model trains that used to be in the Greenville Railroad Museum. Adults, $2, kids 2 to 16, $5. Tues through Sat, 10 a.m. to 5 p.m., Sun, 1 to 5 p.m.

## where to shop

**Greenville Historic Downtown.** Between Wright, Crockett, Henry, and Gordon Streets, Greenville; www.greenville-texas.com. The slowly regenerating downtown is home to dozens of retail businesses, from antique stores to quilting suppliers and clothing boutiques. A complete list and detailed maps are available on the Friends of Main Street Web site, or at their office at 3216 Washington St. It's best, though, just to park the car and wander the few blocks around and adjoining the courthouse square. Along with the Uptown Forum (detailed below), some standouts include **My Sister's Closet** (2601 Johnson St.; 903-454-2056) for vintage clothing and "juntiques," benefitting victims of domestic violence; **The Coin Shop** (2813 Lee St.; 903-454-9198), to browse an interesting array of gold and silver coins from around the world; and **Redneck Jems** (2418 Lee St.; 903-456-1617), for gifts, jewelry, and home goods with a Texas twist.

## a local mystery

*One of Hunt County's most intriguing tales has all the makings of a Hollywood movie: wealth, romance, and the mysterious deaths of several prominent citizens. Though cotton and the railroads helped Greenville grow, the town's first million- aire was cattle and horse baron Thomas Oswin King, born in 1848. After making his fortune out on the ranch, King went on to open a bank near the town square (which today is home to the Blue Armadillo Winery) and also helped finance water and electric companies and a luxury hotel for the area. In addition to being a shrewd businessman, King also had a deep interest in the arts, and in 1891, he built the King Opera House, which became the town's cultural center for over forty-five years. Back then, regional theaters like this would typically host shows that were part of a traveling vaudeville circuit, but King—never one to do things on a small scale—instead took Greenville to the big time: He would personally travel to New York City to view shows on Broadway, then offer the shows he liked big bucks to perform at his Opera House. Not only was this bypassing the established syndicates, but it also succeeded in bringing top shows of the day— like John Philip Sousa's band, the Marx Brothers' comedy act, and Helen Keller's lectures—to Greenville, making it the entertainment capital of the region.*

*King's mansion in town was located on Washington Street—right across from the cottage of one Miss Kate Austin, rumored to be his mistress. On June 16, 1897, King and one of his bank employees, J. F. Norseworthy, took a buggy out to King's 800-acre ranch, located about 6 miles out of town. With them were Miss Austin and another woman, Miss Ida Schenck of Sherman, who may have been Norseworthy's paramour. Sometime that evening, the foursome took a dip in a pond on the property—and only one, Norseworthy, came out. Though ruled a drowning at the time, the mystery surrounding the death of Greenville's most notable citizen has never been fully solved, and the rumors continue to swirl: Was his mistress pregnant, and King trying to get rid of her? Was Norseworthy stealing from the bank, and trying to cover it up? To this day, locals still don't know for sure.*

**Uptown Forum.** 2610 Lee St., Greenville; (903) 454-3311. In the 1970s, long before the current move to repopulate downtown, some forward-thinking folks turned the 1910 former Perkins Department Store building into a specialty mall housing a collection of different boutiques. Though the roster of stores is always changing, one mainstay since the beginning has been Calico Cat (www.calicocatgreenville.com), where owner Janeen Cunningham supplies the women of the region with an eclectic array of clothing, jewelry, and accessories, including pieces by Brighton. There's also a yoga studio, artists' workshops, a hair salon, and a cafe (see "Where to Eat" below).

## where to eat

**Blue Armadillo.** 2702 Lee St, Greenville; (903) 455-WINE; www.bluearmadillowinery.com. A former old bank—complete with 1888 floors and an early-1900s ceiling—is now home to Greenville's own (much cooler) version of *Cheers*. Owner Friendly (no last name, thanks) was already known to many as a popular regional radio DJ before he teamed up with winemaker Joe Anselmo to open this relaxed hangout. There's no food menu, but patrons are encouraged to bring their own grub from other restaurants and settle down with a glass of Texas Turkey chardonnay or merlot, or perhaps a Texas Moon Riesling. ("We will not serve food," Friendly says, "but sometimes we give it away.") The warm, upscale-rustic space—much of it handcrafted, including the bar—gets packed most nights with a regular local crowd, while the weekend no-cover live music shows are drawing patrons from Texarkana to Austin. Though technically the place closes between 9 p.m. and 10 p.m. on the weekends, on rocking music nights, Friendly will take it to what he calls "Armadillo time": the doors get shut at the official time, but as long as people are buying wine and tipping the musicians, things will keep going until whenever. All types of music are featured, from blues and traditional to experimental; check the Web site for a calendar. Wed through Thurs, 4 to 9 p.m., Fri, 4 to 10 p.m., Sat, 1 to 10 p.m. (Hours sometimes vary in the winter, so call ahead.) $.

**C. B.'s Sandwich Shop.** 3304 Wesley St. Greenville; (903) 455-7661. Sure, there are sandwiches here—ham and cheese, egg, BLT—but anyone who grew up in Greenville knows this as the place for burgers for the last sixty-plus years. Pop in for a small (now $1.95, but many in town remember when they were a nickel), large or double meat, all served with fixins on a warm bun. The small dining area has old schoolhouse desks and not much else, but a lot of character all the same. Mon through Fri, 9 a.m. to 6 p.m., Sat, 9 a.m. to 3 p.m. $.

**Mary of Puddin' Hill.** 201 Interstate 30 East, exit 95, Greenville; (903) 445-2651 and (800) 545-8889; www.puddinhill.com. More than a restaurant and a famous mail-order gourmet shop, this is a Greenville institution—and one of its main attractions. Its story begins in 1839, when James and Mary Horton moved to a 620-acre piece of land in this blackland prairie region. On the day they arrived, it had been raining, so as the couple walked around their new property, the thick black mud was sticking to their boots. "This is like walking in pudding," Mary said, to which her husband replied, "Well then, welcome to Puddin' Hill!" Cut to more than one hundred years later, in 1948, when Mary's great-granddaughter, Mary Horton Lauderdale, and her husband were students at U.T. Austin. To help supplement their student income, Mary and Sam began making Christmas fruitcakes out of their apartment using Mary's family recipes—passed down from that first Mary of Puddin' Hill. Five hundred pounds of cake later, they decided to head back to Greenville and make a business out of baking. Since then, the company has grown into a major gourmet purveyor, shipping homemade chocolates and cakes all over the world.

Set a short drive from downtown, the homey facility includes the Mary's "Luncheon Experience" café, with its sandwiches and po' boys, fresh salads, and much-loved homemade soups and desserts. Then there's the gift shop and chocolate store, stocking all the delectable signature sweets and cakes, from the Texas Snowballs (praline pecan pie filling covered in dark chocolate), Thingamajigs (pecans and caramel), and milk-chocolate covered Nutter Butters to jalapeño peanut brittle and the legendary fruit and nut cakes, made with pecans, apricot, walnuts, and more. Around the corner, past a mural of Lucy and Ethel's famous candy-making experience, you can watch the chocolates being handcrafted and sent down the conveyor belt; tours are available Mon through Fri, 9:30 a.m. to 4 p.m. for groups of ten or more. The store is open Mon through Sat, 9 a.m. to 5 p.m., and lunch is served Mon through Sat, 11 a.m. to 3 p.m. $ (or more, depending on how many cakes you buy).

**Sally's Especially For You Cafe.** 2610 Lee St., in the Uptown Forum, Greenville; (903) 454-1913. Tucked into the first floor of the Uptown Forum shopping center, Sally's is a cozy, quintessentially local spot for tasty lunches and friendly service. Choose from an array of sandwiches, including tuna, chicken, and egg salads, meatloaf, and homemade pimento, all served with carrots, chips, and homemade pickles. There are also seven types of salads, available alone or in combo plates, but the real draw is the one daily special, which includes a main dish, some type of salad or veggies, and a dessert for under $6. The featured items always rotate, but might include tater tot casseroles, barbecue "sundaes" (pulled pork, beans, and slaw), beef fajita salads, or French onion burgers, finished with s'mores pie, monster cookies, or sopapilla cheesecake. Mon through Fri, 11 a.m. to 2 p.m. $.

# day trip 02

northeast

>>> **a dairy day:**
sulphur springs

# sulphur springs

Eighty miles from Dallas along I-30 sits Sulphur Springs, the county seat of Hopkins County. Once considered the Dairy Capital of Texas, the county still boasts well over one hundred working dairy farms, collectively producing the second largest amount of milk in the state. In addition to learning about that industry at the Southwest Dairy Center and Museum, visitors to town will enjoy a glimpse into the area's history at a well-done heritage park, through a unique music box collection, and by wandering the regenerating downtown—at the center of which sits the distinctive, multiturreted courthouse made from red Texas granite.

While milk may be Sulphur Springs' most recent claim to fame, it was another liquid that led to its creation. For years, local Native Americans had set up camp in this area to be close to the over one hundred natural springs that bubbled up around the verdant woodland, under shade of oak and catalpa trees. In the mid-1800s, pioneers and workers hauling commodities from the southern ports began stopping here, too, and soon businesses began opening along the Jefferson Road. (One such shop was started by Eli Bibb, who sold whiskey, persimmon beer, and his wife's ginger cake to weary travelers.) The town was officially founded in the late-1840s and named Bright Star, though people referred to it as Sulphur Springs in honor of the mineral-rich water. In 1871, the name was changed to its present-day moniker, and the next year the railroad stop was created, bringing visitors and settlers from far and wide who were attracted by the health benefits of the natural springs.

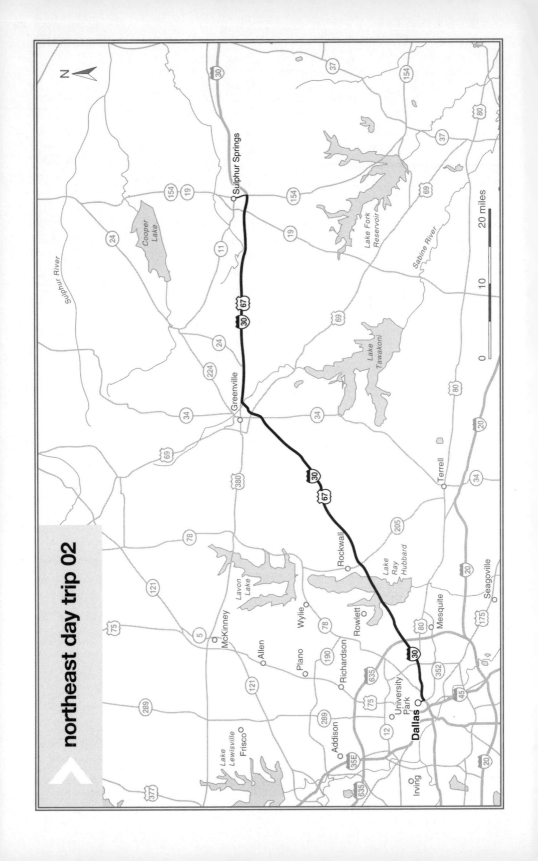

northeast day trip 02

Over the next few decades, the town continued to flourish. The unique sulphur water and freshwater springs proved beneficial to both humans and crops, making the area rich in corn and wheat as early as the 1860s. Toward the end of that century, cotton became king, and that cash crop sustained the community for the next several decades. In 1937, the Carnation Milk Company opened a plant in town, kicking off the region's dairy industry. Over the years, Hopkins County has been home to over 600 grade A dairies, and while the number is less today, it—along with beef production—continue to be a major source of employment. In recent years, horse breeding has started to flourish in the area, as well, and the town—which now has a population of 16,000—has diversified to other industries. And what about the original springs? While they've all been covered-over and dormant for decades, some recent construction work unearthed a couple of still-gurgling wells. There's now talk about perhaps opening up some of the springs again—bringing the town's history full circle.

## getting there

To reach downtown Sulphur Springs, take I-30 east, then TX 154 North, which leads into town. For more information, contact the Sulphur Springs Department of Tourism at (888) 300-6623 or (903) 885-5614, or visit them online at www.sulphurspringstx.org.

## where to go

**Coleman Park.** Various exits off Main St./US 67 BUS, Sulphur Springs; www.coleman park.com. Up to 3 miles of walking and jogging trails take you around Lake Coleman and through natural wetlands and native East Texas foliage at this city recreational hangout. There's also fishing at the lake, picnic areas, waterfalls, and several kids areas, including a children's water activity site and the Imagination Mountain playground. Free.

**Hopkins County Museum and Heritage Park.** 416 N. Jackson, Sulphur Springs; (903) 885-2387; www.hopkinscountymuseum.org. A short drive from downtown brings you to this capsule of county history. The complex includes the Hopkins Country Museum, set in a notable 1910 house with carved columns, double-bricked walls, pressed tin roof, and a Regency-style domed ceiling. Inside, find a collection of Caddo Indian relics, antiques, Civil War artifacts, period clothing, an original stockade, and more.

Wandering the rest of the grounds takes you on a trip through the small town of times past. There are eleven original buildings on site, including a working blacksmith shop, a country store, farm and log houses, a grist mill, a fire station, and a chapel. The park also hosts events throughout the year, like bluegrass concerts, Dutch oven cook-offs, and arts and crafts festivals. Adults, $2; kids under 12, $1; Tues through Sat, 10 a.m. to 2 p.m.

**Leo St. Clair Music Box Museum.** 611 N. Davis, inside the Sulphur Springs Public Library, Sulphur Springs; www.sslibrary.org. In the foyer of the local public library, find one of the most unique collections in the area: over 200 elaborate, antique music boxes collected by early twentieth–century local resident Leo St. Clair. In 1919, St. Clair was serving as storekeeper on the USS *George Washington* when he was charged with overseeing the forty-two pieces of luggage accompanying the king and queen of Belgium on their U.S. state visit. When one of the suitcases fell, St. Clair heard the melodious sound of a music box coming from within; he reported the incident to one of the queen's ladies in waiting, mentioning that the sound had reminded him of his grandmother's music box back in Texas. At the end of the journey, the lady-in-waiting presented St. Clair with the music box, which was shaped like a miniature gilt chair and played a tune from the opera *Faust*.

Inspired by the gift, St. Clair began collecting unusual music boxes, most of which are now housed in the over ten cases located here. Check out one shaped like a squirrel family eating dinner, Asian-inspired creations, and fancy, multilayer ones covered with intricate designs. Mon through Wed and Fri, 9 a.m. to 6 p.m., Thurs, 11 a.m. to 8 p.m. Free.

**Southwest Dairy Center and Museum.** 1200 Houston St., Sulphur Springs; (903) 439-MILK; www.southwestdairyfarmers.com. Once called the Dairy Capital of Texas, Hopkins County is still home to a number of working milk production facilities. Opened in 1989 and designed to look like a typical white-stone dairy farm, this 10,000-square-foot facility traces the history of the dairy industry in the southwest, explains the steps involved in the process and details the various forms of dairy and their benefits. There are life-sized replicas of a 1930s farmhouse kitchen, exhibits on the creamery process and the art of cooling milk (before there was ice or refrigerators), a cutaway cow showing how the bovine turns grass into milk, and a human skeleton demonstrating the importance of calcium. With advance reservations, visitors may also take part in interactive demos, such as one on how to separate cream from milk, or how to whip milk into ice cream. It's all designed for kids, but just as interesting for adults—plus there's a soda fountain serving lunch, milkshakes, sundaes, and cones that's fun for all ages. Mon through Fri, 9 a.m. to 4 p.m. Free.

# where to shop

**Town Square.** Along Jefferson, College, Church, and Main Streets, Sulphur Springs. www.sulphurspringstx.org. Browse the antique shops, gift stores, and boutiques around the historic courthouse. Though the selection isn't as wide as in some other towns, new businesses are starting to roll in, and the square and adjacent Main Street are quite lively during the days. Plus, you can still find unique pieces and good deals in the antique stores here, where the stock isn't as picked over. One notable spot is Town Square Antique Mall (102 College St.; 903-438-0286), which typically has an interesting selection of furniture and collectibles. Note that most stores are open Mon, noon to 5 p.m. and Tues through Sat, 10 a.m. to 5 p.m.

# where to eat

**LouViney Winery.** 206 Main St., Sulphur Springs; (903) 438-8320; www.louviney.com. What was once Sulphur Spring's first movie theater now houses a lively restaurant and winery, opened in 2008. Enjoy a selection of Texas wines, including a number of house label vintages; some are made for LouViney by other wineries, while the Blanc du Bois is from their own grapes. (There are also some winemaking facilities on site.) The menu includes blackened tilapia, steaks, pastas, flatbread sandwiches, and things to nibble, like cheese and humus plates; daily lunch specials are also available. Free live music takes place several nights a week (and there's always complimentary Wi-Fi). Tues through Thurs, 11 a.m. to 9 p.m., Fri through Sat, 11 a.m. to 10 p.m. $–$$.

**Pioneer Cafe.** 307 Main St.; Sulphur Springs; (903) 885-7733. Blue-and-white checked tablecloths and Texas memorabilia set the scene for down-home cooking at this spot, which opened in 2009 (it was formerly Judy's Kitchen.) Stop in for hearty breakfasts and lunch. Mon through Fri, 6 a.m. to 2 p.m. $.

**Plain & Fancy Sandwich Shoppe.** 120 Main St., Sulphur Springs; (903) 885-9225. The decor may be somewhat plain—wooden tables and chairs, lazily circling ceiling fans—but the food's better than fancy. Tuck into soups, salads, chili-topped Frito Pie, baked potatoes, and a roster of creative sandwiches, from chicken salad, pimento cheese, and veggie wraps to the sourdough pileup (chicken breast, bacon, cheese, and honey mustard dressing). Finish with tasty cookies, cheesecake, and other baked goods. Mon through Fri, 7:30 a.m. to 3 p.m., Sat, 10 a.m. to 3 p.m. $.

# day trip 03

## northeast

**jewel of the north:**
paris

# paris

Drive about 105 miles northeast of Dallas, almost to the borders of Oklahoma and Arkansas, and you'll spot a gun-metal colored Eiffel Tower topped by a bright red cowboy hat—just in case you thought for a second that you'd made a wrong turn and ended up in France. Named the "Best Small Town in Texas" by *The New Rating Guide to Life in America's Small Cities*, Paris, Texas, may not have the Mona Lisa, but it does have a few things in common with that similarly named city: On a day trip here, you'll find history, natural beauty, unique shopping, and mouth-watering food. The Red and Sulphur Rivers substitute for the Seine, but the newly revitalized historic downtown is so charming (and a touch quirky), and the people so friendly, it won't be long before you're saying, "Bonjour, y'all."

Broadcasting legend Paul Harvey once described Paris as a town "where yesterday fell in love with tomorrow," and these days the description couldn't be more apt, as the distinctive local history is partnered with an exciting revitalization movement. The presumed father of Paris was George Wright, who came to Red River Valley with his family in 1816, when he was seven years old. Wright eventually went on to own various pockets of land in the area, including once parcel that was located on a divide between the Red and Sulphur Rivers, on a ridge reaching over 600 feet; he used this area for his home and store. At the time, smart settlers were looking to live away from the river bed, to protect themselves from mosquitoes and disease and be in a drier climate, so when the newly formed Lamar

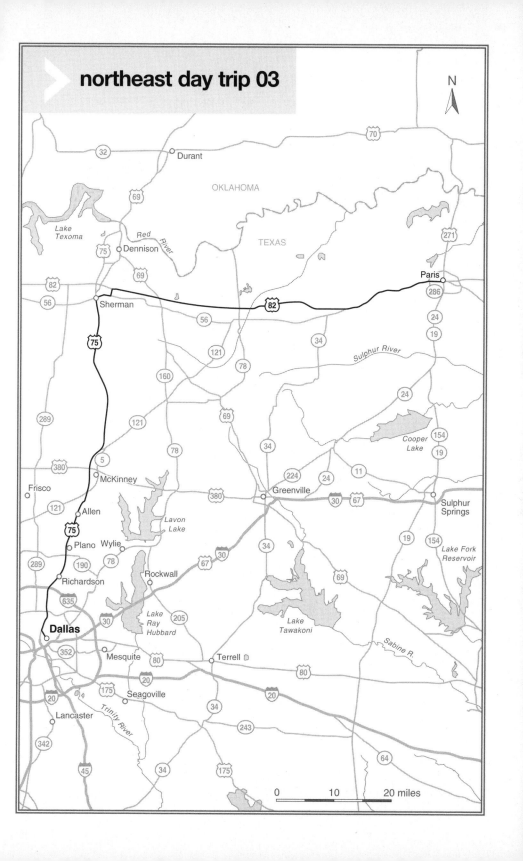

County was looking for an appropriate county seat, Wright donated fifty acres of his land to the commissioners. And so Paris was born, and officially designated the county seat in 1844. As far as historians can tell, there's no clear-cut story about how it got its name: The theories vary from that it was named by a Frenchman working in Wright's store to the idea that the name was inspired by the "Helen of Troy" story (which has a character called Paris). However it came about, the new town was soon attracting an influx of settlers.

One of the more interesting aspects of Paris's past comes courtesy of its location at the northeast border between the United States and what was then the Republic of Texas. Because of its position, the town tended to look north for its commerce and expansion, and was a touch more "northern" than "western" in its sensibilities. Because this Red River border also formed the boundary between Anglo Texas and the Choctaw and Chickasaw Nations—educated and independent (and relatively wealthy) Native American nations that were recognized by the United States—Paris became a major Native American trading hub, as well as home to the U.S. District Court for the Nations. For ten years beginning in 1889, the imposing Paris courthouse handled all Native American trials and lawsuits that didn't fall under tribal law.

Like many Texas towns, Paris thrived in the late 1800s thanks to cotton, commerce, and the railroad. Many new residents arrived from Europe, lending the town a cosmopolitan flair, and the town also attracted "free thinkers" and other unique characters, like William McDonald, a lawyer with a passion for astronomy (the University of Texas at Austin's McDonald Observatory was built with his endowment). The Gibraltar Hotel, built in 1915 and still standing, was considered the "finest hotel between Dallas and St.Louis," and hosted many dazzling balls and notable guests. All the wealth led to the construction of plenty of mansions and grand downtown buildings—many of which were, tragically, affected by the infamous 1916 fire. Sweeping from southwestern Paris up through the square and Pine Bluff Road, the fire wiped out countless landmarks, as well the courthouse, banks, post office, and dozens of newspaper and court archives. (The Gibraltar was one of the few left standing.) But in true Paris fashion, the town picked itself up and moved on—and the fact that so many buildings today bear the years 1916–1918 shows how quickly the town regenerated.

That same attitude has helped the town in the years since cotton and the railroad lost their pull. During World War II, Camp Maxey served as an important military facility, and in the years since, the town (population now about 26,000) has attracted major businesses and production facilities; Campbell's Soup is made here, along with Pace Picante Sauce and some goods by Sara Lee. (On a side note, the acclaimed 1984 movie, *Paris, Texas,* was not filmed here and had little to do with the actual town—though the association still draws a lot of European tourists to the area.) Head around the downtown now and you'll spy cute bakeries, an eco-themed shop, a winery. and a custom clothing designer along with the antique peddlers. Loft apartments have been built near the square, artists and musicians call the area home, and there's talk of turning the historic 1915 dry goods building into a swanky event space or hotel—making this an exciting time to be a Parisian, even just for a day.

# getting there

To reach Paris, take US 75 (Central Expressway) north to Sherman, then US 82 east into town; the trip should take about two hours. Note that US 82 is called Bonham Street west of the town square and Lamar Avenue to the east, and that Grand Avenue becomes Clarksville Street once it hits the square. Whatever the street name, the block that borders the square is called North, South, East, or West Plaza. Lamar and Clarksville are the two main thoroughfares, and when locals refer to "The Loop," they're talking about TX 286, which forms a ring around the city. Note that much of the parking right around the main square is limited to two hours.

# where to go

**Eiffel Tower.** At the corner of Jefferson Rd. and Collegiate Dr., next to the Love Civic Center, Paris; www.paristexas.com. You can't go up it, and you probably wouldn't want to propose here, but this whimsical local icon makes for a fun photo op. Stop by to take a snap of the 65-foot tall mini-Eiffel, compete with jaunty red cowboy hat.

**Evergreen Cemetery.** At South Church St. and Jefferson Rd., Paris. In operation since 1866, this vast cemetery is known for its many uniquely carved headstones and markers (about 18,000 people are interred here). Most famous is the towering Babcock Monument, the final resting place of 1880s resident William Babcock. To honor this volunteer fire chief and avid Shakespeare enthusiast (he would frequently stage plays on the square), Babcock's family hired a sculptor to create a 12-foot statue of Jesus to place on his tomb. When the original artist couldn't finish the sculpture, another was brought in—one who, as the story goes, didn't know how to depict bare feet. So since the 1800s, this statue has been known as "Jesus with Cowboy Boots," for the truly Texas footwear adorning the otherwise traditional Jesus. Call the Paris CVB for directions on how to find the monument, and for cemetery hours.

**Lamar Country Historical Museum.** 1009 W. Kaufman St., in Heritage Park, Paris; (903) 783-0064; www.lchparistx.com. Built by a dedicated team of ten volunteers—whose average age was seventy-two!—this very well-done, 7,000-square foot center houses lots of unique curios that help evoke the area's rich past. There are photos of the town before and after the great fire, a collection of vintage Paris postcards, exhibits on notable locals, a restored buggy, nineteenth-century artwork and collectibles, and memorabilia from long-gone local businesses. (There's also the famous "Smile" sign—see the sidebar for the story.) Further in, find a 1920s family parlor recreated with period furniture, the Sunday school room from the famous Buckner Children's Home orphanage, and a large back area containing farm equipment, a blacksmith shop, an iron lung, and the oldest still-standing cabin in Lamar County. A side room details the area's African-American heritage, next to which there's a section on military history. Every detail of the place is related to the area—from the columns in the central gallery (taken from a local Judge's home) to the beautiful photos of old residences that line the walls—so be sure to soak it all in. Friendly and knowledgeable volunteers are available to show visitors around. Tip: Be sure to check out the restrooms, located in the very back. Guides love to surprise guests by leading them to the door of what looks like a dilapidated old outhouse—but which opens up to a fancy, fully stocked powder room. Admission is free (donations accepted); open Fri through Sat, 10 a.m. to 4 p.m.

**Paris Chamber of Commerce.** 8 West Plaza, Paris; (903) 784-2501; www.paristexas .com. Stop in the square-side visitor center for brochures, maps, and suggestions. The CVB shares this space with The Plaza Art Gallery, which features works by about fifteen artists, many of them local. Mon through Fri, 8:30 a.m. to 5 p.m., Sat, 10 a.m. to 4 p.m.

**Sam Bell Maxey House.** 812 S. Church St., Paris; (903) 785-5716; www.visitsbmh.com. This 1868 High Italianate–style structure was the longtime home of noted Paris resident Sam Bell Maxey—a Confederate general and two-term U.S. Senator—and his family. Stop in for a look at the upstairs and downstairs rooms, all of which feature period furnishings and original family antiques. Tours are offered daily, 9 a.m. to 5 p.m. Adults, $3, children, $2.

**Trail de Paris.** From 12th St. SE to Loop 286, Paris (see the Web site for maps); www .traildeparis.org. What began as a project for the Lamar Leadership County Class of 2004 has evolved into nearly 4 miles of scenic, all-weather trails for hiking, biking, or walking. Park benches, labeled trees and plants, and a butterfly/hummingbird garden line the trail, and there's an observation deck from which to view the beautiful East Texas canopy.

## just smile

*On March 21, 1916, a fire that started on Paris' s southwest city limits quickly spread through town. By the time they were subdued, the flames had caused about $11 million in property damage and wiped out much of the main square— including the post office, federal building, city hall, courthouse, jail, and several churches—along with countless homes. Needless to say, the once-thriving town was devastated, but the next morning, as people came into town to survey the damage, they saw a small sign attached to a lamppost bearing a single word: SMILE. This became a rallying cry for the town, as the mayor encouraged folks to accentuate the positive, help each other out, and begin the reconstruction. By the very next year, most of the square-side buildings had been re-built, in a true tes- tament to the "smile" philosophy. Today, visitors can view the original motivational sign in the Lamar Country History Museum—a touching reminder of the positive Parisian attitude that still holds true today.*

# where to shop

**Downtown Antiques Shops.** Around the main square, Paris; www.paristexas.com. There are several quality antiques and collectible shops and minimalls around the main downtown square, so be sure to take a stroll around. The stock is generally pretty good, and the prices reasonable. While in the square, be sure to check out one of the town's own prized antiques: The ornate Culbertson Fountain, set at the intersection of the four streets, was a gift to the city in 1916 to commemorate the rebuilding after the big fire.

**Downtown Records.** 101 Grand Ave., Paris; (903) 739-2237; www.myspace.com/down townrecordsparis. After living out of state, most recently in Portland, Oregon, local boy David Ford came home and opened Outlaw, a place for new and used music, movies, and games. In 2009, the store moved to this location right on the main square, and changed its name to Downtown Records, but the stock is still the same: hundred of CDs, DVDs, video games, and LPs, plus a smattering of posters and offbeat tees. The place carries both new and used items, the latter culled from stuff the owner finds, or things customers bring in to sell. A few boxes near the door hold LPs that are yours for free with any purchase—and you never know what you may score. Mon through Sat, 11 a.m. to 8 p.m.

**Farmers' Market.** Market Square, 410 S.W. First St., Paris; www.paristexas.com. A seasonal farmers' market runs daily, from dawn to dusk, from mid-March to the end of September. Contact the chamber for details.

**Green Eco-Boutique.** 111 Lamar Ave., Paris; (903) 785-2397; www.shopgreenparis .com. Sharing space with the generations-old Daniel family framing shop (and operated by the younger members of the family), this spacious boutique has introduced the concepts of sustainability and fair trade to the Paris retail scene. Find unique handcrafted jewelry, accessories, and home decor pieces from all over the world, most made by traditional craftsmen and artisans who are compensated per fair trade policies. There are also some artwork, clothing, and gift items, all chosen for their eco-friendliness—and modern style. Mon through Sat, 10 a.m. to 6 p.m.

**Junk Divas & Smalltown Girls.** 102 Clarksville St., Paris; (903) 784-7766; www.small towngirlshg.com. Two stores share this space about a half a block from the main square. Downstairs, find modern clothing and sassy accessories at Smalltown Girls; upstairs, there are interesting antique, vintage, and flea-market-found furnishings that have been restored or reworked by a mother and her two daughters. The stock at both stores is a little funky and offbeat—in different ways. Smalltown Girls is open Mon through Fri, 10 a.m. to 6 p.m., Sat, 10 a.m. to 4 p.m.; Junk Divas is open Thurs through Fri, 10 a.m. to 6 p.m., Sat, 10 a.m. to 4 p.m.

**Paris Vineyards.** 2 Clarksville St., Paris; (903) 785-9463; www.parisvineyrds.com. Sample wines from all over Texas as well as house-brand vintages, made at the store's own vineyards about 7 miles from town. The selection includes the Cabernet "Tex Red," the white Blanc du Bois, and newer additions like a Tempranillo. The pleasant, loftlike space sells bottles and wine-related merch, and is outfitted with table and chairs for the serious samplers. Tues through Sat, 11 a.m. to 8 p.m.

**Smalltown Rags.** 3 S. Plaza; (903) 784-5333; www.smalltownrags.com. The custom T-shirts and designer clothing at this cool shop would be stylish in any town, big or small. Customers can have items created based on in-house designs or their own; all the basic colored tees, jeans, shoes, and other pieces are displayed in the front, so you just choose your base and then confab with the staffers, who will work their magic using spray and splatter paint, appliqués, and other techniques. In the back, find ready-to-wear clothing for men and women, most with a trendy, street edge. They ship finished pieces (and take orders online), so no worries if you're not in town to pick up your creations. Mon through Fri, 10 a.m. to 6 p.m., Sat, 10 a.m. to 3 p.m.

# where to eat

**A Piece of Cake.** 1205 Clarksville St., Paris; (903) 739-2940; www.apieceofcakeparis .com. "A balanced diet is a cookie in each hand," reads the tagline of this large-scale bakery, but they also serve soups and deli sandwiches to have before you hit the sweet stuff. Cookies, muffins, and brownies are available by the slice; cakes whole or to order. There's a large patio for outside dining, as well as a drive-through window for those in a hurry. Mon through Fri, 6:30 a.m. to 5:30 p.m. $.

**Crawford's Hole in the Wall.** 202 3rd St., Paris; (903) 737-9025; Locals and visitors alike swoon for this long-standing favorite, where the walls are covered with vintage signs, the vibe is low-key, and your ice tea glass will never be empty. Order at the front counter for homemade plate lunches, sweet potato fries, and excellent burgers and enchiladas—then try to find a seat among the ravenous crowd. Mon through Fri, 10 a.m. to 2 p.m. $.

**Fish Fry.** 3500 NE Loop 286, Paris; (903) 785-6144. Tuck in to best-sellers like the "steak-and-tails" plate, rib eyes, shrimp, and more at this dinner-only place, which many consider the best fish purveyor in town. Of course, the fried catfish gets most of the oohs and aahs— residents and visitors alike have been known to drive out of their way to get some when a craving hits. Mon through Sat, 5 to 10 p.m. $$–$$$.

**Jaxx Gourmet Burgers.** 10 Clarksville St., Paris; (903) 739-2955. An airy, brick-walled space is the home to one of the town's favorite burgers. Though this location is relatively new, the owner has been serving the community for years, cooking up fresh patties served on focaccia buns and with multiple ingredients; over twenty-five choices are available, from the classic bacon-and-cheese topping to others with sauerkraut, feta, or habanero hot sauce. Chili, chicken-fried steak sandwiches, and a lengthy list of salads, sides, and starters give non–beef eaters something to chew on. Sun through Wed, 11 a.m. to 2 p.m., Thurs through Sat, 11 a.m. to 8 p.m. $.

**Mom Mom's Cafe.** 102 Lamar Ave. Paris; (903) 784-4515; www.mommomscafe.com. The focus is on heart-healthy items at this casual diner-style eatery, so the BLT wrap uses turkey bacon, the sandwiches feature lean ham and fat-free mayo, and the "Wacky Pasta Salad" is topped with a fresh apple vinaigrette. Specials might include spinach lasagna or chicken enchiladas, the sides range from slices of carrots, celery, and beets to baked sweet potato fries, and desserts like the apple taco and peach cobbler are made with less sugar. Think of it as Mom's food—only healthier. The calories, carbs, and nutritional values are listed for every item, for those who want to know. Mon through Fri, 10 a.m. to 2 p.m. $.

**Paris Bakery.** 120 N. Main St, Paris; (903) 784-1331. Fresh daily breads, scrumptious pastries, and a creative lunch menu based on seasonal ingredients make this charming cafe a place you just might move to Paris for. A mixed local crowd of everyone from old-timers to the hipster set stream in for scratch-made bagels, juicy blueberry muffins, and chocolate croissants in the morning, and soup, tangy salads, and a choice of four sandwiches for lunch. The special changes daily, but might include bacon, braised greens, and white bean puree on pumpkin-cranberry sourdough bread, or oven-fried green tomatoes with Monterey jack on cheddar-scallion bread. The ingredients are as local as possible: eggs and honey from farms surrounding Paris, and coffee freshly roasted by the town's own "That Guy" brand. Tues through Fri, 7 a.m. to 3 p.m., Sat, 8 a.m. to 2 p.m. $.

**Scholl Bros. Bar-B-Que.** 1528 Lamar Ave. Paris; (903) 739-8080. Named one of the 50 best BBQ joints in the state by *Texas Monthly* magazine, Scholl Bros. dishes out down-home classics like smoked turkey and brisket, chopped beef sandwiches, huge stuffed potatoes, pecan cobbler, and banana pudding. Though some say the quality is not quite what is used to be, this is still a popular local hangout and a favorite with BBQ connoisseurs. Mon through Fri, 11 a.m. to 8 p.m., Fri through Sat, 11 a.m. to 9 p.m. $–$$.

# where to stay

As of this writing, Paris doesn't yet have any B&Bs or independent inns, but there are several chain hotels in the area, including recent additions like the Holiday Inn Express and Comfort Suites. Contact the visitors center for the latest info at (903) 784-2501; www.paristexas.com.

# east

# day trip 01

east

**market mania:**
canton

# canton

Whether you're in the market for antique furniture or vintage LPs, have a hankering for fried pie, or just like looking through other people's junk, Canton's legendary First Monday Trade Days are a must-see. Started over 150 years ago as a one-day farmers' market, the event has grown to become the world's largest trading extravaganza, attracting over 200,000 shoppers on the Thursday, Friday, Saturday, and Sunday before the first Monday of every month. (To put that in perspective, the town of Canton itself is home to just about 4,000 people.) As a result, the market is pretty much Canton's calling card and the focus of most of its tourist offerings, though locals do tout it as a relaxed, friendly place to live (most likely for the other twenty-six days of the month).

The generally accepted story of the market goes that in the 1850s, the Van Zandt County circuit judge would stop in Canton to hold court proceedings on the first Monday of the month, leading people from across the rural county to also come in on that day to conduct business, visit family, and stock up on supplies. Many brought things to trade or sell, ranging from extra crops to farm equipment and livestock, and soon Canton earned a reputation as a good place to buy a horse. When the need for horses declined with the advent of the tractor, the market became a source for pigs (proudly billed at the time as "cholera free") and top breed dogs. Animals were so signature to the market back then, with buyers coming from as far as Arkansas and Oklahoma, that it was called "Dog Day" or "Hoss (Horse) Day" by regulars.

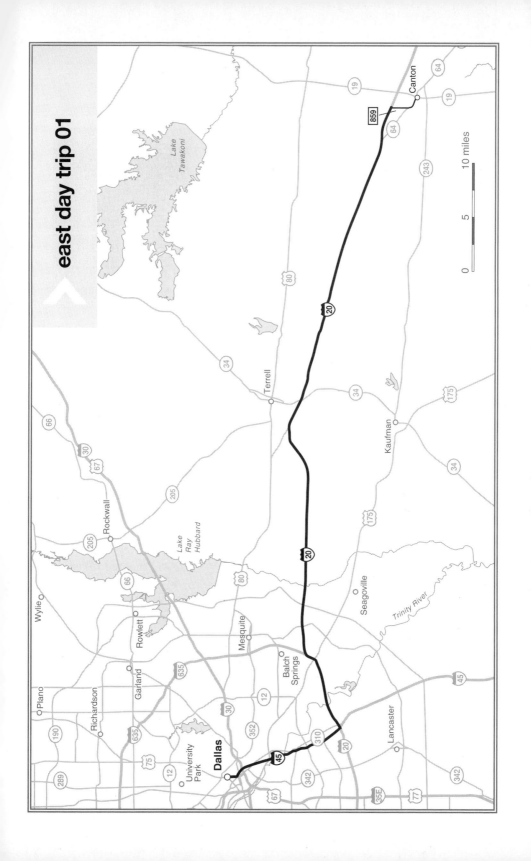

east day trip 01

Canton

Lake
Tawakoni

Lake
Ray
Hubbard

Trinity River

Dallas
University
Park

Plano

Richardson

Garland

Rowlett

Wylie

Rockwall

Terrell

Kaufman

Seagoville

Balch
Springs

Mesquite

Lancaster

0    5    10 miles

While other trade days around Texas shrunk or died out during the 1930s and 1940s, Canton's kept growing, moving past the downtown streets around the courthouse. Residents soon grew resentful of the influx of people stomping around their land—and the mess they were left to clean up. (So many stray dogs were released after the market days that the town eventually had to hire a dog catcher.) In the 1950s, a few savvy locals began renting out parts of their property to vendors (with some even making big money by charging for use of their bathrooms), but in 1965, the city took matters into its own hands and purchased six acres near the town square specifically for the trade days. Today, the indoor/outdoor complex stretches to over one hundred acres (owned and operated by various entities) and features pretty much anything that can be grown, eaten, made, used, or petted—and quite a few things that defy categorization.

There are several Web sites dedicated to First Monday, offering printable maps and tips on parking, planning, and navigating the vast complex; some also list vendors by category and give background info. Check out the city's official site at www.chambercantontx.com, as well as Canton Trade Days (www.cantontradedays.com) and First Monday Canton (www.firstmondaycanton.com.) Above all, remember to dress comfortably in layers and good walking shoes, bring sun protection, and stay hydrated. Scooter and wheelchair rental is available at several points through the park, as are ATMs (some stalls are cash only). Note that Thursdays are usually less crowded, and the busiest months for the market are October and November.

## getting there

To get to Canton, take N. Central Expressway (US 75) and I-45 south to I-20 East, toward Mesquite and Terrell. Take exit 526 and travel south on CR 859 (First Monday Lane), or exit 527, heading south on TX 19 (N. Trade Days Blvd.); both lead to the Original Trade Grounds. The venues for First Monday Trade Days stretch from between CR 859 to TX 19, between I-20 and TX 64. The Historic Main Entrance, with its commemorative statue, is located at the corner of Groves Street and Capitol Street. Car and RV parking is available off all the major streets; most car lots cost $4, while the VIP parking at the grove's St. Main Gate is $10. The lot behind the Original Grounds, off CR 859 (exit 526 from I-20) is often quieter and easier to navigate (there are even trolleys to ferry you from the lot to the market entrance), and it leads you to the "back entrance" of the complex, directly to the outdoor section. Entrance to First Monday Trade Days is free; the hours are dawn to dusk.

## where to go & shop

There are over 8,000 vendors on any given trade day, with the stock constantly fluctuating. Stalls are not separated by themes or types of goods, so it's all about wandering and exploring.

The outdoor Flea Market section, located on the CR 859 side of the Original Grounds, is a yard sale on steroids, where the only prevailing aesthetic is "random." Row after row of stalls hawk old records and magazines, kitchenware, homemade jewelry, rabbit skin hats, medical equipment, Grandma's hair dryer—if it's been made in the last one hundred years, it's probably here. These vendors don't have to meet any merchandise requirements and can rent lots for just $50 a weekend, so the crowd tends to be mainly individuals (as opposed to established stores), and the selection more eclectic; there's also an "Unreserved" section for last-minute sellers suddenly inspired to get rid of their 8-track tapes. The vibe here is that of a giant garage sale, and while there are definitely deals and quirky things to be found, this area requires a lot of patience and good bargaining skills.

In the covered Civic Center, also in the Original Grounds section, vendors have to meet more exacting standards: only antiques and collectables are allowed—no reproductions or new goods—and 80 percent of the collectibles must be at least twenty years old. Here you'll find furniture, linens, china, estate jewelry, and more. Further on, in the nearby Trade Center, Pavilion, Arbor, and Eastgate buildings, it's back to unrestricted items, but the layout is a bit more orderly than outside (and there's blissful air conditioning). Browse arts and crafts, antique coin and guns, dolls, jewelry made from old watches, and tons of other unique items.

Across TX 19 from the Original Grounds are two more indoor/outdoor sections—The Old Mill and The Mountain—which offer more of the anything-goes variety. On the southeast corner of TX 19 and TX 64, however, are the Curry Animal Grounds, a menagerie of living creatures. Nicknamed "Dog Alley" and "Guy Town" (there are also tools, farm equipment, and other manly things), this area sells everything from dogs, cats, horses, and cattle to exotic swans and kangaroos.

## where to eat

The food choices at the markets are just as eclectic as the things for sale, and some of the restaurants have been cooking up their specialties for years, to generations of fans. The Original Grounds section has a central Arbor Food Court where a network of stalls waft out enticing smells to a main seating area. A lot of the treats are state fair inspired—fresh kettle corn, sausage-on-a-stick, corn dogs, funnel cakes, homemade ice cream, hand-cut fries—but there are also more substantial eats like chicken-fried steak, smoky BBQ, juicy burgers, and fresh salads. Only non-alcoholic beverages are allowed on market grounds, but there's plenty of sweet tea and fresh-squeezed lemonade.

# day trip 02

east

>>> **coming up roses:**
tyler

# tyler

Further east along I-20 and southeast on US 69, into the shady pine and oak groves of East Texas, sits the "Rose Capital of America"—so officially named in honor of the city's long history with the thorny bush. With a present population of close to 100,000, Tyler has many other industries and major employers—including the East Texas Medical Center, a branch of the University of Texas, and the locally based Brookshire Grocery chain—but it's its success with the delicate flower that helped put the city on the map and that keeps visitors coming in droves.

Originally home to several Native American tribes, including the Caddo, or Tejas, Indians and later, the Cherokee and Kickapoo from the west, this area of East Texas was designated as Smith County in 1846. The settlers chose three hundred hilltop acres in the center of the region to house the country seat, and called the new town Tyler after President John Tyler, who had supported the annexation of Texas into the Union in 1845. Early life in Tyler centered around the brick buildings of the main square, many of which can still be seen today.

Though the town grew steadily over the next few decades, things really started to boom with the Civil War. About 15,000 Confederate troops were stationed in camps around Tyler in mid-1862, as they prepared to march to the front in Arkansas. The Confederate Medical Department established the largest pharmaceutical factory west of the Mississippi

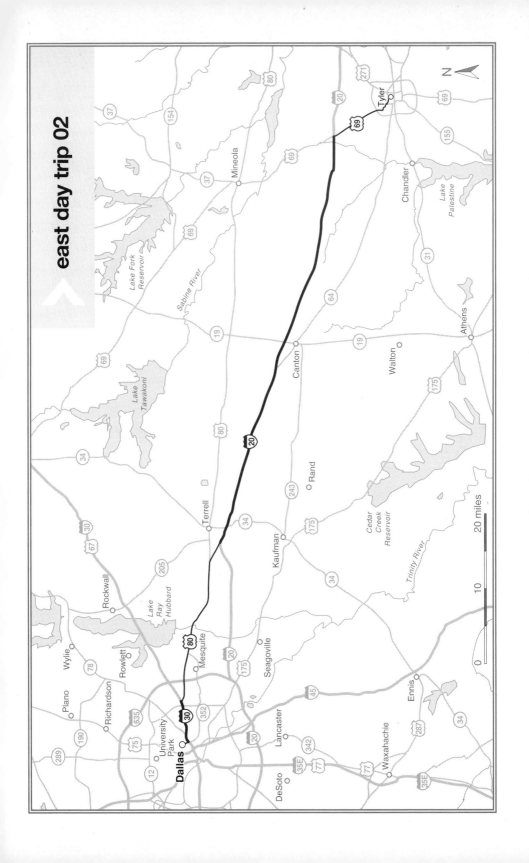

east day trip 02

River 3 miles southeast of here, while a depot 4 miles northeast manufactured wagons and shoes for the Transportation Department, and a local gun factory was expanded to produce rifles, small arms, and cannon cartridges. Most notably, Smith County also served as home to thousands of federal prisoners of war, many of whom were held northeast of town in what's now called Camp Ford; now open to the public, the site includes historic structures and POW databases. (See the "Worth More Time" section below for more information.) The area played a key role in World War II as well, with over 200,000 G.I.s processed at the camp, along with a substantial number of German prisoners of war.

In the years after the Civil War, agriculture became the main business of the county, thanks to the area's moderate climate, year-round rainfall, and sandy soil. With the arrival of the railroad, cotton and finished materials from local gins and mills were shipped to outside markets, along with fruits and vegetable from its farms. It was at this time that the rose-growing industry took off, too: After most of the area's peach crop was destroyed one year, many nurserymen tried their hands at cultivating roses. By the 1920s, millions of rose bushes covered the local fields, and for the rest of the century, close to half of all the rose bushes in the United States were located within 50 miles of Tyler. (Even today, over half of all the commercial rose bushes marketed annually in the United States are packaged and shipped from Smith County.) Inspired by the rose grower's floats included in small local parades, the town officially created the Texas Rose Festival in 1933—a legendary event that continues to draw hundreds of thousands of visitors to Tyler every October.

During the mid- and late-twentieth century, Tyler was spared from the decline experienced by many towns thanks to the discovery of oil in East Texas in 1930, and today, that industry, along with major medical and educational facilities, still helps keep the area thriving. While the city has expanded far beyond the old square (now mainly home to county- and courthouse-related offices) and is home to more than its fair share of chain restaurants and stores, visitors who explore its shaded downtown streets and unique historical sites can still get a feel for how things might have been. It's here, among the gabled Victorian mansions, hilly residential neighborhoods, and brick streets of downtown, that this growing city still feels small—and where a day-tripper can stop and smell the roses.

## getting there

To reach Tyler, take I-20 east through Canton, then US 69 right into town.

## where to go

**Brookshire's World of Wildlife Museum & Country Store.** 1600 W.S.W. Loop 323, at the corner of Old Jacksonville Hwy., Tyler, just south of Brookshire's distribution complex; (903) 534-2169; www.brookshiremuseum.com. Founded in Tyler in 1928, Brookshire's now boasts over 150 supermarkets in four states; drive around town for even a day and you'll see their big red signs beckoning from most major intersections. But along with groceries, the company is also responsible for one of the more unique local attractions: a museum featuring over 450 taxidermied animals displayed in exhibits evoking their natural habitats. The collection was begun by Wood T. and Louis Brookshire in 1975 in the lobby of the company's head office, with animals they had hunted on three African safaris (and later, in Alaska). Today, spot such diverse creatures as polar bears, seals, mountain lions, and zebras. The museum also contains a life-sized replica of a 1920s country grocery, complete with antique furnishings and old-fashioned candy, plus a restored 1952 fire truck and 1926 farm tractor. Free admission. Open Tues through Thurs, 9 a.m. to 5 p.m. (Mar 1 through Sept 30) and 10 a.m. to 4 p.m. (Oct 1 through Feb 28); closed Sun, Mon, and major holidays.

**Caldwell Zoo.** 2203 M. L. King Blvd., Tyler; (903) 593-0121; www.caldwellzoo.com. What began as a private children's playground—housing not much more than a couple of squirrels and a monkey—in the backyard of prominent Tyler resident D. K. Caldwell in 1937 has turned into a compact but well-stocked zoo featuring elephants, rhino, giraffes, jaguars, and tons of unusual birds. The park is divided by geographical region—lions and zebras in the East Africa section, bald eagles and buffalo in North America, monkeys and the world's largest rodent in South America—but it's very walkable and easy to navigate. There are also picnic areas and a cafe on site. Adults, $8.50; children 3 to 12, $5; seniors, $7.25. Open daily, 9 a.m. to 5 p.m. (Mar through Labor Day) and 9 a.m. to 4 p.m. (Labor Day through Feb), closed for some major holidays.

**Cotton Belt Depot.** 210 E. Oakwood St., Tyler; (903) 533-8057; www.cityoftyler.org. From 1905 to 1952, this tidy brick bungalow in downtown served as the passenger depot for trains in and out of Tyler. Today, find the extensive Bragg Collection, which features thousands of model train locomotives, rail cars, and other related pieces, plus memorabilia related to the history of the depot and nineteenth- and twentieth-century train travel. Visitors can also take a turn running the controls for a model train system. Open Mon through Fri, 9 a.m. to 4 p.m. Free (donations are accepted).

**The Goodman-LeGrand House.** 624 N. Broadway Ave., Tyler; (903) 531-1286; www .goodmanmuseum.com. Built in 1859 by a Civil War captain, this majestic house eventually passed into the hands of Dr. William J. Goodman, a Confederate Army surgeon whose descendents continued to live here until 1936. Today, the "Texas Colonial" structure (with a distinctive Greek Revival façade) showcases what life was like in the late-nineteenth and early twentieth centuries through original family furnishings, memorabilia, and photographs, including rare medical books, silver and china pieces, surgical tools, and a Colonial-era grandfather clock. Wander through the rooms and soak up the history. Tues through Sat, 10 a.m. to 4 p.m.; suggested donation $2.

**Historic Aviation Museum.** 150 Airport Dr., Tyler; (903) 526-1945 and (903) 526-1939; www.tylerhamm.org. A group of dedicated volunteers—many of them with military or aviation backgrounds—put together this excellent facility focusing on flying, set in an old terminal and hangar at the Tyler regional airport. Browse exhibits detailing aviation from 1900 to 2000, including sections on the various wars, training, commercial flight, space travel, local connections, and women in flying. There are uniforms, vintage advertisements, headgear, and a lunar sample from *Apollo 15,* but the real stars are the dozen or so historic aircrafts displayed outside, which include a rare North American FJ-4 fighter plane (one of only three left in the world) and the oddly shaped AD5 Skyraider. Tues through Sat, 10 a.m. to 5.p.m., Sun, 1 p.m. to 5 p.m. Adults $5, children ages 6 to 12, $2.

**Tiger Creek Wildlife Refuge.** 17552 FM 14, Tyler; (903) 858-1008; www.tigercreek.org. Forty "big cats," including tigers, leopards, and lions, have found a home among the pine trees of East Texas, thanks to this sanctuary dedicated to rescuing abused or neglected members of the species. Watch them frolic through the exercise yards, explore the caves, or tease each other under the waterfall. Guided tours are offered Mon through Sat, 10 a.m. to 5 p.m. (weather permitting); Adults, $10, kids 4 to 12, $8.

**Tyler Convention and Visitors Bureau.** 315 N. Broadway, Tyler; (903) 592-1661 or (800) 235-5712; www.tylertexas.com. Located on the first floor of the Blackstone Building in downtown, the visitors bureau offers brochures, maps, and help with planning itineraries. They are only open during the weekdays, so call ahead for phone advice if you're planning to visit on the weekend.

**Tyler Museum of Art.** 1300 S. Mahon Ave., Tyler; (903) 595-1001; www.tylermuseum .org. While the museum's permanent collection consists of over 600 works from all different periods, with more on the way thanks to donations and endowments, at the moment they only have two main galleries in which to highlight a select few; luckily, plans are underway for a new, larger facility to open in the next few years. For now, stop by to check out special exhibits featuring both borrowed and museum-owned pieces. Suggested donation $3.50 for adults; Tues through Sat, 10 a.m. to 5 p.m., Sun, 1 to 5 p.m., closed Mon and most major holidays.

**Tyler Rose Museum and Municipal Garden.** 420 Rose Park Dr., Tyler; (903) 597-3130; www.tylerrosemuseum.com. For over a century, roses have been a big part of Tyler's identity, influencing both its commercial growth and social scene. This 30,000-square-foot center pays homage to this relationship with a museum detailing the annual Rose Festival, with exhibits and videos on the parade, the participants, and all the rose queens; there are also dozens of the elaborate queens' gowns on dazzling display. A small area explains the history of the flower itself, touching upon cultivation and grafting, before guests are let loose in the vast gardens to admire the real things. Opened in 1952, the 14-acre municipal Rose Garden—the country's largest—has many sections, including the Heritage Rose and Sensory Garden, where the over thirty varieties are mainly from the nineteenth century (the oldest is from 1867). The center is also home to an All-America Rose Selection (AARS) trial

## the royal rose

*Full of pomp, pageantry, and all those beautiful flowers, the Texas Rose Festival is one of the state's major annual events. In 1933, while the rest of the country was in the throes of the Great Depression, Tyler continued to grow, thanks to the East Texas oil boom. To celebrate their success and honor the importance of the rose industry in their economy, the women of the Tyler Garden Club organized the first festival—drawing thousands to the town where "everything was coming up roses." Over the years, the event grew, attracting first ladies, presidential candidates, governors, and other notable guests; the festival has run every year since, except for the period around World War II.*

*Along with the main parade, the major events of the festival center around the Rose Queen and her court, which is made up of duchesses, ladies-in-waiting, attendants, train bearers, and more. Most of these participants are from families who have a history with the festival and the town: The Duchess of the Rose Growers typically comes from a rose-growing family; ladies-in-waiting are college sophomores with ties to the festival; and the out-of-town duchesses are sponsored by prominent Tyler residents. (Aside from the first rose queen, who was from Palestine, all queens have been from Tyler.) The public can meet and mingle with the royal court at events like the Vespers service (traditionally held at the queen's church), the Men's and Ladies Luncheons, the Coronation, and the famous Queen's Tea, held at the Tyler Municipal Rose Garden. For more on the festival, visit www.texasrosefestival.com.*

garden, one of only twenty-four in the United States, which evaluates new rose breeds over a two-year period. Because most of the working rose farms are not open to the public, this is where everyone—local and visitor—comes to see all the unusual varietals, and get a fragrant whiff of what made the town famous.

Note that after Labor Day, most of the garden's bushes are pruned in preparation for the Texas Rose Festival in October, so it's best to call in advance to check the state of the blooms if you are visiting in September. Mon through Fri, 9 a.m. to 4:30 p.m., Sat, 10 a.m. to 4:30 p.m., Sun, 1:30 to 4:30 p.m.; closed Mon from Nov until Feb. Adults $3.50, children $2.

## where to eat

**Fat Catz Louisiana Kitchen.** 3320 Troup Hwy., Ste 170, Tyler; (903) 593-1114; www.fat catzkitchen.com. East Texas is not too far from the Louisiana border, so it's only natural that the Tyler restaurant scene should boast a little Cajun flavor. The friendly joint serves crawfish étoufée, jambalaya, seafood fondue, alligator tail meat and down-home staples like dirty rice and fried pickles and okra, all made with hand-blended seasoning and house-made sauces. Sun through Thurs, 11 a.m. to 9 p.m., Fri through Sat, 11 a.m. to 10 p.m. $–$$.

**Jake's.** 11 E. Erwin St., on the downtown square, Tyler; (903) 526-0225; www.jakestyler .com. A historic brick building is now home to this hopping bar and restaurant, which boasts a clubby decor of dark woods and warm leathers, a long curved bar, two floors of dining, and a rooftop lounge. The menu's mainly meat and fish, with the blackened sea bass, Creole-spiced Red Snapper Pontchartrain, tenderloin burgers with smoked bacon, and Kobe steaks as particular standouts. Tues through Fri, 4 p.m. to midnight, Sat, 5 p.m. to 1 a.m. $$$–$$$$.

**Mercado's.** 2214 W. Southwest Loop 323, Tyler; (903) 534-1754; www.posados.com. If traveling with kids or a group, head to this lively, spacious Tex-Mex spot, one of the original outposts of a popular local chain. There are coin-operated games to distract the kiddies, an extensive menu of generously portioned combo platters, and free soft-serve ice cream for everyone on the way out. Sun through Thurs, 10:30 a.m. to 10 p.m., Fri through Sat, 10:30 a.m. to 11 p.m. $$.

**The Potpourri House.** 3320 Troup Hwy., Tyler; (903) 592-4171; www.potpourrihouse .com. In 1981, the Ellsworth family opened a tearoom and antiques store in a yellow Victorian house near downtown—a space they quickly outgrew. Since 1997, they've been serving folks out of this much larger strip mall space, a combination gift store and restaurant that regularly fills up with 300 to 400 diners for lunch and dinner. There are many claims to fame here, from the homemade soups and breads, extensive salad bar, chicken crepes, creative meat and fish entrees, and the legendary strawberry salad—spinach, strawberry slices, and almonds topped with their addictive strawberry-poppy seed dressing (also sold by the bottle). The buttermilk pie has received national praise, but the coconut cream cake, crème brûlée, and chocolate ganache are just as tasty. The scene here is a little quirky (and charmingly old school), the food great, and the place a long-standing Tyler tradition, especially on Thursday through Saturday nights, when couples hit the dance floor to live music from Bobby and Ken. This is somewhere where everyone's a regular—whether you've been here before or not. Mon through Sat, 11 a.m. to 9 p.m. $–$$.

**Rick's.** 104 Erwin St., Tyler; (903) 531-2415; www.rix.com. Since 1992, Tylerites have enjoyed a cigar or two at this square-side restaurant, known for its market-fresh seafood, top-grade steaks, and creative appetizers like barbecued smoked shark tacos, Cajun-battered potatoes with cheese and bacon, and smoked salmon "cheesecake." The spacious patio boasts three 46-inch TVs for watching the game, while inside there's live music on Thurs through Sat. Mon through Fri, 11 a.m. to midnight, Sat, 5 p.m. to 1 a.m. $$$–$$$$.

**Sonoma Grill.** 5875 Old Bullard Rd, Ste. 500, Tyler; (903) 534-9779; www.sonomagrilltyler .com. California meets Texas at this lunch and dinner spot. The menu's got hearty pastas, grilled chicken sandwiches, and burgers topped with your choice of smoked bacon, mushrooms, cheese, or fresh guacamole (the Sonoma Baja Burger already comes with grilled green chilies and pepper jack cheese). There are also substantial salads and a dozen meats and fish entrees prepared over a wood-burning grill. Daily, 11 a.m. to 9 p.m. $$–$$$.

**Villa Montez.** 3324 Spur 124, Tyler; (903) 592-9696; www.villamontez.com. A beautiful, 1930s oil baron's mansion set atop a hill is the setting for this gourmet Mexican restaurant, where two brothers from California are serving up unique Latin-flavored dishes to an appreciative crowd. Dig into favorites like Yucatan Sweet Pork Quesadillas, tequila-lime chicken fettuccine, seafood seviche, and "Chino Latino" rolls—spring-roll-like wrappers filled with roasted chicken, veggies, black beans, and cheese, served with jalapeño jelly. Seating is spread out through all the rooms of the mansion, including the wine cellar, as well as along an expansive patio overlooking the large grounds and gardens. Both the service and presentation are a cut above, but the vibe is casual—it all feels like you've wandered into some 1930s Hollywood star's Mexican hideaway, and have been invited to stay for dinner. Mon through Thurs, 11 a.m. to 9 p.m., Fri through Sat, 11 a.m. to 10 p.m., closed Sun. $$–$$$.

# where to stay

Tyler is home to outposts of all the major hotel and motel chains, most of which are located a short drive from downtown. For something more unique, personal, and authentically Tyler, check in to some notable B&Bs:

**Centaur Arabian Farms.** 10271 FM 2813, Flint; (903) 561-6929; www.centaurarabian farms.com. Spread out over ten acres just a few minutes' drive from central Tyler (the property is across the street from the city limits), this family-run facility features a thirteen-stall horse barn plus four charming guest suites. Owners Bill and Eva Sealy have decorated each room in a fun theme, like "Scout," "Captain," and "Nostalgia" ("When we got married and combined all our stuff, the themes just kind of happened," explains Eva), and each features satellite TV and wireless Internet; two have private baths, while the other two share. Every guest enjoys a bountiful home-cooked breakfast of eggs, biscuits, grits, meats, and specialty items like strawberries-and-cream pancakes. Relax around the pool, fireplace, or barbecue area, or book a horseback ride with one of the in-residence animals; rates vary depending on the horse's breed (there are Arabians, thoroughbreds, and quarter horses around), so call ahead for details. $$.

**Woldert-Spence Manor.** 611 W. Woldert St., Tyler; (903) 533-9057; www.tylertexasinn .com. The lingering scent of fresh-baked cookies and buttermilk biscuits welcome guests to Tyler's oldest B&B, set in a restored 1859 Victorian mansion in the leafy Azalea District near downtown. Proprietors Chris and Lisa Garrett—a young couple who traded in the tech world for inn keeping back in 2008—keep things relaxed and friendly at the manor, which includes six rooms in the main house and two carriage house suites; all rooms have private baths (some with claw-foot tubs), antique furnishings, cable TV, and free Wi-Fi, while some boast balconies, fireplaces, or stained glass windows. Rates include a hearty home-cooked breakfast that might include eggs, bacon, and fruit-infused coffee cake made using Lisa's grandmother's recipe. $–$$.

## worth more time

Less than a mile outside of town sits **Camp Ford,** home to the largest Confederate prisoner of war camp west of the Mississippi River during the Civil War. Established in 1863, and closed two years later, the camp housed over 5,300 prisoners at its peak. Nowadays, the site is a public historic park overseen by the Smith County Historical Society. Visitors can walk the trails (which are marked with informative signage), see a reconstruction of the lt. colonel's cabin, POW housing, and other historic structures, and enjoy a picnic area. The park is open daily from dawn to dusk; admission is free. Camp Ford is located on US 271, about 0.8 miles outside of Loop 323; www.smithcountyhistoricalsociety.org.

# day trip 03

east

**antique treasures:**
gladewater

# gladewater

A quick drive northeast from Tyler on US 271 leads to Gladewater, a town of about 6,300 that sits at the intersection of US 271 and US 80, straddling both Gregg and Upshur counties. Today, things are a little sleepy here—Longview is just 13 miles away, and meets most of the residents' commercial needs—but visitors interested in oil history and antiquing will hit pay dirt in this East Texas gem.

Gladewater was founded in 1873 by the Texas and Pacific Railway Company, which bought the land from two local residents, and was most likely named for nearby Glade Creek. When the railroad announced that the only rail (and mail) stop in the area would be in this new town, settlers from neighboring villages like St. Clair and Point Pleasant moved into Gladewater, forming its earliest community. Throughout the late-1800s and early-1900s, lumbering, cotton, and farming kept the town growing, but things changed forever on April 7, 1931, when someone struck oil a mile outside of town, at the bottom of the Sabine River. With the East Texas oil boom underway, Gladewater grew from a town of 500 to, at its peak, about 8,000. Over the next few decades, oil profits helped fund projects like a city airfield, the Rosedale Cemetery (for more on that interesting story, see below), and in 1954, Lake Gladewater, still a popular recreation site today. (On a musical side note, the town served as Elvis Presley's home base when he toured Texas during the early days of his career, and was also the town in which Johnny Cash wrote "Walk the Line.")

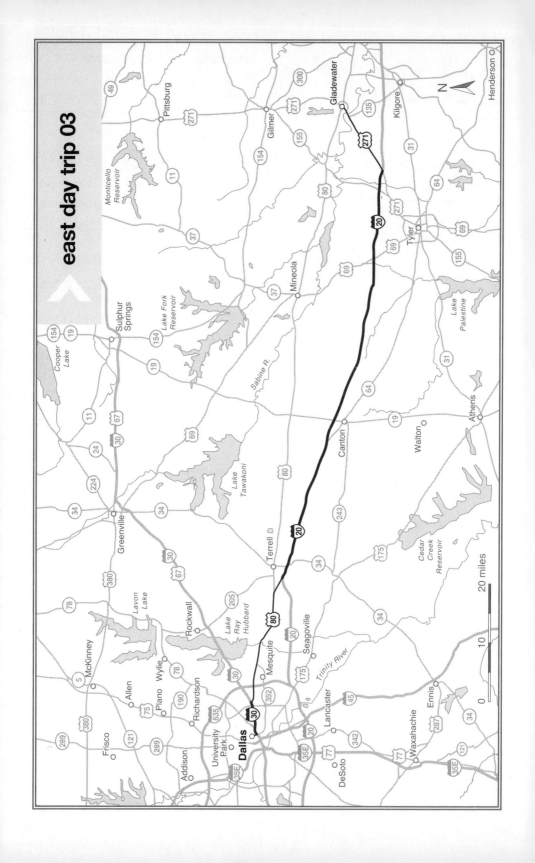

As the black gold rush began dying down toward the middle of the twentieth century, the town's economy diversified, and today it survives on lumber, agriculture, some manufacturing (of furniture, paper products, and boats), and a few oil industry-related businesses. In the 1990s, Gladewater became known for its wealth of antiques stores—close to 300 purveyors crowded the downtown in its heyday—and stories about its quality stock and rare finds still draw professional dealers and decorators from as far away as New York and California. While eBay and changing design trends have affected the antiquing business in recent years, it's still the town's biggest draw, and it's most recent claim to fame.

## getting there

To reach the downtown and antiques district, take US 271 directly into town. US 271 will become S. Tyler Street and then, in downtown, Main Street.

## where to go

**East Texas Museum at Gladewater.** 116 W. Pacific Ave., Gladewater; (903) 845-7608; www.gladewatermuseum.org. Housed in a 1939 art-deco-style building that once held the town library, this collection highlights the history of the area through photographs, memorabilia, antiques, and stories about past residents. Just opposite the museum, along Pacific Avenue, check out the replica of the Snavely #1, an important oil derrick that once produced 26,000 barrels a day. The museum is open Sat, 10 a.m. to 4 p.m. and by appointment.

**Gladewater Chamber of Commerce.** 215 N. Main St., Gladewater; (903) 845-5501; www.gladewaterchamber.com. Call or stop in for help planning your trip. The office is open Mon morning only 9 a.m. to noon, then Tues through Fri, 9 a.m. to noon and 1 to 5 p.m. If you arrive at a time when the chamber is closed, most of the stores in town have maps and brochures handy.

**Gladewater Saturday Night Opry.** 108 E. Commerce, Gladewater; (903) 845-3600; www.thegladewateropry.com. Enjoy a two-hour, family-friendly comedy and country music show every Saturday night at this lively community theater, which showcases both working and aspiring talent from all over Texas. Auditions are held every Saturday at 4:30 p.m. for those who want to try their luck.

**Rosedale Cemetery.** At the corner of US 80 (E. Broadway) and TX 485, Gladewater. With grounds shaded in pine, oak, holy, and cedar trees, and brightened by crepe myrtles when in season, this cemetery is both one of the oldest in the area (the first burial was in 1856) and one of the prettiest. Interestingly, at one time it was also labeled the "richest cemetery in the world," thanks to the discovery of oil on either side of its grounds. In 1932, the Gladewater Cemetery Association signed a contract allowing for the drilling of two wells—one on its east side, one on the west—for the terms of $13,000 up front, plus a one-eighth royalty on future profits. The quirky catch: All profits were to go to those buried in the cemetery—no living person could touch a cent. So as the profits rolled in, the dead of Rosedale were earning a monthly income—proof, the Cemetery Association felt, that you *could* "take it with you." Ultimately, funds were used to build a full-time caretaker's cottage, improve landscaping, and build a pergola on the north side to balance the arched brick entrance opposite. While the wells were plugged up in 1973 and no trace of them remains, the cemetery is still an interesting place to visit for its unique headstones spanning over 150 years. Pioneers, transient railroad and oil field workers, wealthy oil barons—all are resting here.

## where to shop

**Antique District.** Along Main Street and its side streets, in downtown Gladewater; www .gladewaterchamber.com. What started as a way to revitalize a deserted, post–oil-boom downtown in the 1980s helped turn Gladewater into the Antique Capital of East Texas. Culling from flea markets, estate sales, and private collections, hundreds of vendors showcase their wares in the numerous shops and mini-malls that line the main streets of town. In recent years, the popularity of antique hunter-friendly Internet sites like eBay, along with changing decor trends, have had an effect on the foot traffic, forcing some stores to cut their weekday hours or close for good. But come most weekends, the streets are still bustling, and Gladewater still boasts a reputation as a place to score some finds—a fact that attracts dealers and decorators from all over the country, who descend on the town on yearly buying trips. Most stores also now carry collectibles and some new items, to help draw in customers.

The best way to experience the district is to park along Main Street and just start wandering. Most of the multivendor stores don't specialize in anything in particular—"whatever we find" seems to be the prevailing aesthetic—but a few places carry more furniture than others, and some might have more locally sourced items. In general, most stores are open Tues through Sat, 10 a.m. to 5 p.m., with a fair number open on Sun, noon to 5 p.m. Most places are closed on Monday, but call ahead to confirm.

Shops to check out include:

**Gladewater Antique Mall** (100 E. Commerce; 903-845-4400). The town's original antique mall, opened in 1988, carries furniture, antiques, and memorabilia from dealers spanning several states.

**Gladewater Books** (109 E. Pacific; 903-845-4843). One of the few non-antique stores in the neighborhood, this temple of books (mainly used) and toys takes up the entire length of its building. As the sign outside proudly claims, READERS AND OTHER ODD FOLK: PLEASE COME IN, YOU ARE GOING TO LOVE IT HERE.

**Good Old Stuff** (114 S. Main; 903-845-8316). This spot specializes in furniture stripping, refinishing, and repair, should you need to have something you just bought taken care of.

**Now & Then Antique Mall** (109 W. Commerce; 903-845-5765). Along with collectibles, knives, and old LPs, find a smattering of new items like toys, plus a selection of Texas gourmet foods (jams, salsas, peach syrup), and candy.

**Red Rooster Antiques** (106 E. Commerce; 903-844-9240). Run by an interior decorator, this standout shop focuses on design-conscious furniture and home decor, including primitives, folk art, quilts, and furniture made from recycled or repurposed wood (most by local artisans).

**R&S Clocks and More** (111 S. Main St.; 903-844-2130). Clocks new and old, of every shape and size, make up just some of this large store's eclectic stock. There's also quality antique furniture, unique items like a Victrola record player, some artwork, and a huge collection of salt and pepper shakers.

**St. Clair Antique Emporium** (104 W. Pacific; 903-845-4079). Another of the larger multivendor malls, this one's got tons of collectibles, furniture, and Victoriana.

**Yesterday's Treasures** (105 W. Commerce; 903-845-7800). Comics, collectible Barbies, vintage vinyl, arrowheads, antique tin cans, and tons of glassware—all that and more is packed into this multiroom shop.

## where to eat

**Glory Bee Baking Company.** 111 N. Main St., Gladewater; (903) 845-2448. Featured in publications like *Southern Living* and *The Dallas Morning News,* this celebrated baker has served a steady breakfast, lunch, and afternoon treats crowd for over twenty years. (There's now a second location in Longview, too.) Find soups, salads, sandwiches, and more—and, if you've been good, Bodacious Brownies, flavored lattes, and elaborately

### a texas staple

*Whether they have a German or Czech heritage, or were built by the railroad, cotton, or cattle industries, every town in North Texas has one thing in common: chicken-fried steak. Head into any restaurant—even a Tex-Mex place—and you're sure to find this staple dish on the menu. Just what is it? In the classic version of the entree, a piece of tenderized cube steak is rolled in seasoned flour, pan fried, and typically topped with brown or peppered milk gravy. (The name most likely came from the fact that the dish resembles a piece of fried chicken—albeit minus the bone.) Over the years, variations of the meal have sprung up—chicken-fried chicken is now another popular option, as are fancy spicy gravies—but purists will still find the real thing in eateries all through the region.*

decorated cakes. There are also weekly dinner specials, like Gumbo Night, when chicken-and-sausage gumbo, homemade cornbread, and bread pudding are yours for well under $10. Mon through Wed, 6:30 a.m. to 6 p.m., Thurs through Fri, 6:30 a.m. to 8 p.m., Sat, 7:30 a.m. to 3 p.m. $.

**Guadalupe's.** 101 E. Pacific, Gladewater; (903) 845-2318. Gladewater's other Tex-Mex favorite sits in a big corner building right on Main Street. Favorites include the shrimp cocktail, chicken enchiladas with sour cream sauce, the homemade salsa, and the fajitas grande, which comes with sizzling beef, chicken, and shrimp, plus all the fixins. Tues through Sat, 11 a.m. to 9 p.m. $.

**Linda's Place Gourmet Bakery.** 104 S. Main St., Gladewater; (903) 845-7315. Another favorite with both visitors and merchants along Main Street, this cheery spot cooks up soups, sandwiches, salads, quiches, and daily specials, along with pound cake, baked (not fried) pies, and other treats. Tues through Sat, 11 a.m. to 5:30 p.m. $.

**The Pea Patch.** 201 E. Upshur Ave. (US 80), Gladewater; (903) 845-3920. Located just a few blocks north of downtown, this majestic old house on a hill is hard to miss. Built in 1875, the colonial-revival-style Bumpus House boasts gables, grand windows, a porch swing, and every other picturesque touch. By contrast, the inside, which has housed The Pea Patch restaurant for a few years, is like your basic country diner: plain tables and chairs, speedy service, and a menu that takes you from breakfast (omelets, hash browns, grits) to burgers, sandwiches, potato skins, chicken strips, and catfish fillet. Daily, 5:30 a.m. to 9 p.m. $.

**Tele's Mexican Restaurant.** 401 South Tyler St. (US 271), Gladewater; (903) 845-5999. Part of a family-owned minichain with locations in a few East Texas towns, this popular place serves satisfying Mexican fare made with family recipes, as well as a couple of regional specialties that go beyond the usual offerings. So along with nachos, grilled chicken, steak, fish, and combo platters, you'll find avocado enchiladas (tortillas stuffed with guacamole and topped with cilantro sauce), salsa homemade with lots of fresh lime, and famous fajitas. Sun through Thurs, 11 a.m. to 9 p.m., Fri through Sat, 11 a.m. to 9:30 p.m. $–$$.

# where to stay

**Honeycomb Suites.** 111 N. Main St., Gladewater; (800) 594-2253; www.honeycomb suites.com. The smell of fresh bread from the Glory Bee Bakery downstairs might wake you up at this B&B, but it's worth it—all guests enjoy a gourmet breakfast in the bakery dining room, included in the rate. (The two places have the same owner.) The seven suites here boast different decor themes—from the dramatic "Harlow" to the country cottage "Hide-away" and the clubby "Gentleman's Quarters"—but all feature private baths, queen beds, and cable TVs. All suites can be upgraded to the "Romance Package," available on the weekends, which includes a four-course dinner and carriage ride. $$–$$$.

# southeast

# day trip 01

southeast

## at the crossroads:
corsicana

# corsicana

It's about 55 miles along I-45 to Corsicana, a town that the railroads helped build and oil helped boom. A lot of ground was broken here: This is the home of the first commercial discovery of oil in Texas, as well as the first commercial refinery west of the Mississippi, and the birthplace of Mobile Oil (and around the same time, Wolf Brand Chili). Culturally, the town had one of the first brick schools for African-American students (built in 1881), and went on to boast such a respected African-American high school that students would take the train in from Dallas to attend it. A few noted musicians were born here, including country legend Lefty Frizell and blues great Blind Lemon Jefferson. These days, as the downtown slowly regenerates, Corsicana is making its name in other ways. A day trip here will bring you to some beautiful historic homes, fascinating museums—from a stellar Civil War center to a Pioneer Village and a unique homage to hunting—and food so good, *O Magazine* and The Food Network have approved.

In 1848, this spot was designated as the seat of the new Navarro County, named for Texas Revolution hero Jose Antonio Navarro. Navarro himself was given the honor of naming the new settlement, and he suggested Corsicana, after the Mediterranean island of Corsica, the birthplace of his parents. Within a couple of years, the town had grown to a little over 1,200 folks, though the Civil War stunted its expansion somewhat over the next decade. Once the railroad came to town in 1871, new settlers moved in, along with dozens

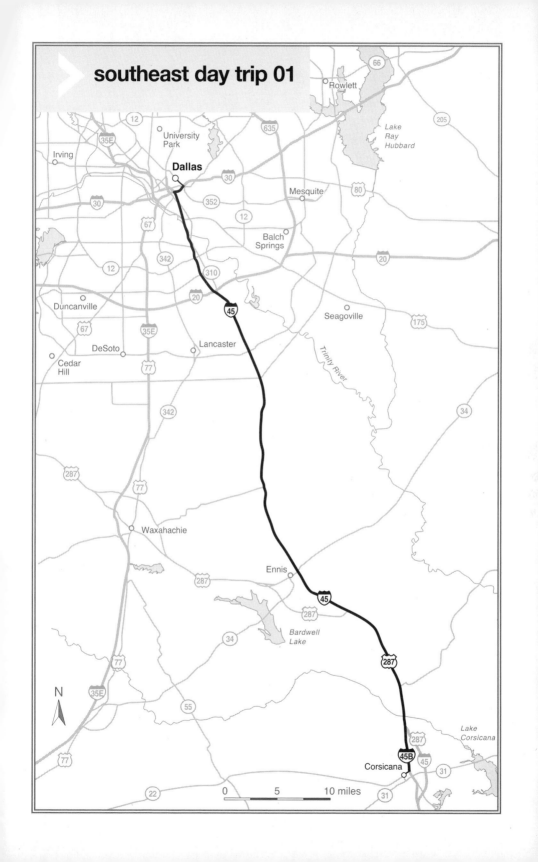

# southeast day trip 01

of new merchants; among the latter were the Sanger Brothers, whose mercantile business eventually evolved into the Sanger-Harris department stores of Dallas, which went on to become Foley's. Set at the crossroads of three rail lines, Corsicana became a trading and shipping center for the northern blacklands, and by 1885 housed over 5,000 souls.

With the influx of residents, the town needed a better water supply, so in 1894, the city's newly formed Water Company started drilling for a well. Instead, they struck oil. The first major discovery of oil west of the Mississippi kick-started Texas's oil boom (predating the gusher at Spindletop by six years), and Corsicana became home to its first refinery; by 1900, there were 600 producing wells in the area. Men that had previously been farmhands, businessmen, or water well drillers became the first generation of Texas roughnecks and oil men. Big-wig executives came in from the East, and a few of them founded the Magnolia Oil Company—which went on to become Mobile Oil. With all the money coming in, Corsicana was able to build a new courthouse (the 1905 neoclassical, Beaux-Art building, complete with stained glass panels, is now on the National Register of Historic Places), as well as neighborhoods full of majestic homes, both of which can still be seen today. As more oil fields were discovered in the 1920s, the town was spared from some of the harsher effects of the Great Depression, and when even more were drilled in the 1950s, it's said that Corsicana had at least twenty-one millionaires in town—and the highest per capita income in Texas.

These days, oil is still a major source of the economy here, though manufacturing, canning, and a few other industries are also in play. One of the biggest businesses is the Collin Street Bakery, whose famous fruitcakes are shipped around the world. You can still see a lot of the grand homes in the residential neighborhoods, but the old downtown—set up as blocks of streets instead of around a courthouse square—seems a little dusty at times, home to empty storefronts and slow foot traffic. Happily, though, a regeneration is underway, with the Arts District undergoing a restoration and new businesses and restaurants moving in to the area—making Corsicana, once again, a city at the crossroads.

## getting there

To reach the visitors center and downtown, take I-45 south to exit 231, and turn west onto Martin Luther King Jr. Boulevard/TX 31. This becomes W. 7th Avenue/TX 31 in downtown, and the visitors center is at the corner of 7th Avenue and S. Beaton Street, just across from the Arts District. The trip should take a little over an hour.

## where to go

**Capehart Communications Collection & The Museum of Telephony.** 409 S. 9th St., Corsicana; (903) 872-0440; www.mindswirl.com/telemuseum. Celebrating communication technology from the 1880s to the 1990s, this 10,000-square-foot former Coca-Cola bottling facility is home to a variety of equipment, appliances, and unique artifacts that detail all aspects of the medium, from phones and magazines to phonographs and film projectors.

Find dozens of switchboards (including ones from the 1800s, and one used by NASA), a 1920s movie sound system, telephone equipment from the USS *Missouri,* and an unusual "potty" phone, plus exhibits on the history of the Western Electric Company. The museum is the private enterprise of Don Capehart and his wife, Rita, who began collecting old telephones and equipment in 1984. Open by appointment and during major town festivities; call for more information.

**Corsicana Visitor Center.** 301 S. Beaton St., Corsicana; (903) 654-4850; www.visit corsicana.com. A restored railroad freight office houses this cheery welcome center, where you can load up on maps, brochures, and local suggestions. This is also the place to pick up the fun, informative Historic Walking Tour and Historic Driving Tour guides, which take you through Corsicana's "roughnecks and wild elephant" story. The center is within walking distance of the Arts District and downtown antiques shops and restaurants. Mon through Sat, 10 a.m. to 4 p.m.

**The Pierce Museums.** 3100 W. Collin St., Corsicana; (903) 875-7642; www.pearce collections.us and www.cookcenter.us. Impressive, well-done (and maybe a little unexpected), the Cook Center at Navarro College houses two significant collections. In one section, find the Pearce Civil War Museum, where photograph, artifacts, creative exhibits, and over 15,000 documents and letters tell the complicated story of that war. Read heartfelt letters from soldiers (and their wives) on both sides of the fight, see stunning battlefield photos, and experience a video recreation of some crossfire. There are also memorabilia from that period, like clothing and a slave bill of sale; rotating exhibits highlight different themes, such as the role of women and spies in the war.

Next, visit the Pearce Western Art Museum, a collection of 228 pieces honoring the American West. Bronze and alabaster sculptures, oil and water color paintings, and works by artists from the National Academy of Western Art and the Cowboy Artists of America evoke the cowboy life, the Native American traditions, and the unspoiled nature of those days.

The center is also home to a Planetarium with a 60-foot-diameter dome; show times vary (and are mainly seasonal), so call (903) 875-7592 for more info. While on campus, ask for directions to the Reading Arrowhead and Indian Artifacts room to check out a collection of over 48,000 original arrowheads. Adults, $8, students and kids under 17, $4. Museum open Mon through Fri, 10 a.m. to 4 p.m., Sat, noon to 4 p.m., closed Sun and select college holidays.

**Pioneer Village.** 912 W. Park Ave., Corsicana; (903) 654-4846; www.ci.corsicana.tx.us/departments/parks/pioneer.php. Get a feel for the days of the settlers and life in Navarro County over the years at this well-maintained collection of historic structures, which was opened in 1958. There's a nineteenth-century Indian trading post, a blacksmith shop, the 1851 Hartwell General Store (stocked with apothecary items), the last slave cabin in the county, and a country doctor's dog-trot-style home, outfitted with furniture and memorabilia. In the old barn, find fascinating photos from county history, like a picture of the fire department circa 1900, vintage wedding and family snaps, and a photo documenting the 1869 election. Check out an exhibit on Bonnie and Clyde (Clyde's uncle lived in the area), and a small museum dedicated to country legend Lefty Frizell, with photos, clothes, memorabilia, and his music playing overhead. (Frizell enthusiasts may want to also visit the commemorative statue located just down the street from the village.) Before leaving, head to the back to view an original cotton gin weighing scale. Adults, $2; students 13 and up, $1; kids under 12, 50 cents. Mon through Sat, 9 a.m. to 5 p.m., Sun, 1 to 5 p.m.

**Walking/Driving Tours.** Various locations; (903) 654-4850; www.visitcorsicana.com. From a nineteenth-century synagogue and 1918 African-American Baptist church to mansions built by railroad and oil barons, Corsicana has a wealth of architectural history. Stop by the visitors center for detailed brochures on a Historic Downtown Walking Tour and a Historic Driving Tour, both of which contain interesting stories about various town happenings and characters, like the tale of how Wolf Brand Chili was founded, and the story of the itinerant rope walker who came to town in 1884, mysteriously died, and was buried in the cemetery under the name "Rope Walker." (You can still see the headstone.)

Along with Temple Beth-El and the First Independent Baptist Church, some of the places featured include the Victorian-heavy Carriage District, where many of the city's top dogs lived in the early 1900s; the Mills Place District, where the mansions range from Tudor to Spanish Colonial styles; the home of G. W. Jackson, an influential leader in education and principal of the first African-American public school in the region (built in 1881); and Petroleum Park, a small site dedicated to the Texas petroleum industry, with the original Hickey # 1 well. In downtown, don't miss the beautifully restored Palace Theater, a 1921 former vaudeville house (Mae West performed here) that's now open for plays, live music, and holiday shows.

**Watkins Wildlife Trophy Room.** 3329 S. 15th St. at I-45, Corsicana; (903) 874-6587. Enter a generic construction office building reception area, open a side door, and suddenly you're surrounded by wild animals. Well, taxidermied ones: An avid hunter, Mr. Watkins has been embarking on safaris and game hunts all over the world for over forty years, and this huge collection contains all of his exotic spoils, as well as those of his kids, grandchildren, friends, and others who have donated their scores. The range is pretty staggering: There are polar, grizzly, and black bears, lions, tigers, elk, rhino, alligator, sable, cheetah, buffalo, and even a black leopard. It's a little unsettling, but at the same time fascinating to be so close to these massive creatures, who seem just as expressive in death as in life. Don't miss the replica of Black Diamond, a circus elephant who ran rampant on the streets of Corsicana in the 1920s, killing a bystander and being killed himself as a result. The collection is free and open Mon through Fri, 8 a.m. to 5 p.m.; just ask for access to the room at reception. There are guide pamphlets there detailing all the animals, but if you'd like a personal tour with Mr. Watkins, call ahead to make an appointment.

# where to shop

**Collin Street Bakery.** 401 W. 7th Ave., Corsicana; (903) 874-7477 and (800) 292-7400; www.collinstreet.com. In 1896, a German immigrant baker named August Weidmann teamed up with a local cotton buyer, W. R. McElwee, to open a bakery and hotel in downtown Corsicana. Downstairs, you could find Original DeLuxe fruit and nut cakes baked using Weidman's old country recipes, with patrons like Will Rogers and circus master John Ringling stopping in for a bite. Most travelers coming though on the railroads would leave with a Collin Street cake in their bag, and when performers from Ringling's circus began asking the bakery to ship the fruitcakes to their friends and family around the world for Christmas, a mail order business was born (and, some say, the tradition of sending a fruitcake for the holidays).

Today, Collin Street still makes cakes to order, but the countless orders are now shipped to over 196 countries—making the DeLuxe the most widely distributed cake in the world. The booming business is one of Corsicana's biggest, and visitors can stop by the main 7th Avenue location to pick up a wide range of baked goods, from all signature fruit and nut cakes to cookies, pies, candy, and breads. (This location also offers some lunch items like salads and sandwiches.) Mon through Sat, 7:30 a.m. to 5:30 p.m., Sun, noon to 6 p.m.

**Downtown Antiques Shops.** Corsicana; (903) 654-4850; www.visitcorsicana.com. Wander the brick-lined streets of the historic downtown to browse about a dozen antiques and collectibles shops. The visitors center has a complete list, but Beaton Street has the highest concentration of spots, including Canterbury Court for English furnishings.

**Navarro Pecan Co.** 2131 E. Hwy. 31, Corsicana; (903) 872-1337; www.navarropecan.com. Texas is known for its pecans, and this plant is one of the largest pecan-shelling units in the world, processing over 50 million pounds of the nut each year. The store stocks all types of flavored and spiced nuts, as well as brittle, candy, jams, and other gourmet treats. Mon through Fri, 8 a.m. to 5 p.m., Sat through Sun, 9 a.m. to 5 p.m.

**Picolos Products.** 316 N. Beaton St., Corsicana; (903) 872-3988; www.picolospickle.com. Another one of Corsicana's signature food products come from this downtown shop, makers of thick, crunchy gourmet pickles since 1988. The original claim to fame is the Sweet & Unique bread and butter pickle, but there are now several other varieties ranging from spicy to sweet, all made using top-grade ingredients. Call for hours.

# where to eat

**3 Sisters Sweets & Eats.** 123 N. Beaton St., Corsicana; (903) 872-0303. Opened in June 2009, this is where Corsicana goes when they want to eat at home, but don't feel like cooking. Find homemade, just-heat-and-serve pastas, casseroles, pies, daily soup specials, and chicken salad, plus an array of baked goods for snacking on in the car. The bakery also does custom-order wedding cakes and other confections. Mon through Fri, 10 a.m. to 6 p.m., Sat, 10 a.m. to 3 p.m. $–$$.

**Black Jack McCanless Steak House.** 105 & 107 S. Beaton St., Corsicana; (903) 872-5641; www.blackjackmccanless.com. When reconstructing a part of the sidewalk outside his soon-to-open steak house back in 2007, Rick Hocker and his crew found something unexpected: a basement filled with remnants of the 1876 Bismark Saloon, including coins, glasses, and old whiskey jugs. The discovery caused a flurry of excitement—TV crews came down from Dallas on the regular—and before he had even opened, Hocker saw close to 10,000 tourists visit his place.

Now, the crowds are coming for a different reason: classic Texas eats with a twist, from jalapeño bottle caps served with ranch dressing, sirloin steaks, and T-bone pork chops to BBQ chicken, Papas Mexican Beer Cheese Soup, and the best-selling chicken-fried hamburger. The Food Network stopped in to check it out, and people are driving in from other towns for a bite. Along with the food, the atmosphere is worth the drive, too, with saloon-style decor and a genuine 1876, 42-foot mahogany bar from a Dodge City hangout of Doc Holliday and Wyatt Earp's. (Hocker found it on eBay.) Live music (mainly country) several nights a week adds to the fun. Restaurant open Mon through Thurs, 4 p.m. to 10 p.m., Fri through Sat, 11 a.m. to 10 p.m.; bar open Mon through Fri until midnight, Sat until 1 a.m. $$.

**Caleb's Diner.** 125 B. Beaton St., Corsicana; (903) 874-5891. Home to the Blue Front Saloon in the 1800s, this corner space became Hashop's Drug in 1905, and the site of a classic soda fountain and lunch spot. Though the name has changed a few times (locals still call it Dee's Place because of the sign on the wall next door), Caleb's is still retro through and through, with red vinyl booths, ice boxes, and memorabilia lining the walls. (It's so perfectly vintage that the Jonas Brothers used it for a photo shoot in 2009.) The soda fountain—one of the oldest in continuous operation in the state—serves malts, shakes, ice cream, and flavored sodas, while the menu's got your burgers, fries, and the like, plus a full breakfast selection. Mon through Fri, 7 a.m. to 3 p.m., Sat, 8 a.m. to 3 p.m. $.

**The Other Place.** 1607 W. 7th Ave., Corsicana; (903) 872-5637; www.eatattheotherplace .com. Consistently voted one of the best places for steaks, desserts and service by the readers of the *Corsicana Daily Sun,* this family-run eatery is a good bet for ½-pound burgers, grilled chicken pastas, crab-stuffed shrimp, and "Luau" pork platters. Desserts are decadent, drizzled with sauces and different every day. Mon through Thurs, 11 a.m. to 9:30 p.m., Fri through Sat,11 a.m. to 10 p.m. $–$$.

**Roy's Café.** 306 N. Beaton St., Corsicana; (903) 874-6791. There's been a diner on this spot since 1932, and the space today probably looks pretty much the same (but for the Fox News on the TV). There actually is no Roy—a man named Roy Justice owned the cafe in 1941 but sold it three years later; for some reason, the subsequent owners have never

## a foodie find

*Every town in this book has a notable restaurant, or four—places creating unique homemade dishes that are well worth the trip. (Full disclosure: I'd gladly drive out of my way for the Tex-Mex in Ennis and Nocona, the sandwiches in Paris and Weatherford, and the scratch-made desserts in most of these towns.) But while a lot of things impressed me about Corsicana, one thing that really stood out was its food scene. At first glance, this might not be the town you'd expect to attract foodies—unlike many of its North Texas neighbors, there's no photo-perfect town square here surrounded by cute cafes and trendy eateries. But dig deeper and you'll find some really delicious eats, many of which have garnered national recognition.*

*At the Two Doors Down Coffee House, owner Todd Jones' s mom and aunt whip up a buttermilk pie that was featured in O Magazine (to say thanks, Jones and his aunt even flew up to New York City to take the staff some fresh pies). Jones also serves great sandwiches on homemade bagels—a dish that took some townsfolk a while to get used to, he says, because bagels were relatively new to town. At Black Jack McCanless, owner Rick Hocker says the majority of his crowd is from out of town, as tales of dishes like chicken-fried hamburgers and perfect steak have spread far and wide. (After noticing a large table of diners taking notes and photos one night, a waiter discovered the crew were from the Food Network—and that they loved their meal.) The town also boasts the oldest soda fountain in continuous operation, where you can still order Blue Bell floats and flavored sodas. And of course, this is to the birthplace of Wolf Brand Chili and the Collin Street Bakery, makers of some of the most widely ordered baked goods in the world (and most likely the originators of the Christmas fruitcake tradition). So when heading to Corsicana, be sure to bring your appetite.*

gotten around to changing the name. This is a tired-and-true locals joint for breakfast all day, chicken-fried steak, sandwiches, and a smattering of Tex-Mex—plus quick refills on the ice tea. A nighttime, sports bar–and–live music outpost of the institution, called Roy's Backporch, opened next door in late 2009. Open Mon through Fri, 6 a.m. to 2 p.m., Sat, 6 a.m. to 1:30 p.m.; closed Sun. $.

**Two Doors Down Coffee House.** 106 W. 6th St., Corsicana; (903) 875-0027; www.two doorsdowncoffee.com. Back in the early 1900s, Todd Jones's great-grandfather helped write the charters for the Mobile and Texaco oil companies out of his law offices at this address. These days, the only black gold found here is gourmet fair- and free-trade coffee sourced from top purveyors, and served hot, cold, or in sweet drinks (like the signature

T.O.D.D., with ice coffee, chocolate, and vanilla). After living in other cities, Jones came back to his hometown and opened this cozy two-room cafe in 2006, and it's the kind of place every neighborhood wishes it had: books line the walls, there are little nooks for reading and chatting, and old records, typewriters, and a piano set the scene. The menu includes lots of lunch-y staples like fresh salads and sandwiches (the latter served on home-baked bagels—a first for Corsicana!), all made here daily by Jones' mother and aunt. But the real stars are the scratch-made desserts, which change daily; the family-recipe buttermilk pie was featured in *O Magazine,* and is usually on the roster once or twice a week (call ahead to check or order one in advance). There's live music and karaoke some nights, monthly "family style" dinners with guest chefs, and a convivial and relaxed atmosphere—making it the kind of place you just might move here for. Mon through Thurs, 7 a.m. to 7:30 p.m., Fri, 7 a.m. to 11 p.m., Sat, 8 a.m. to 3 p.m.; closed Sunday. $.

# day trip 02

## southeast

**water wonderland:**
athens

# athens

An easy, 75-mile drive east along US 175, past Canton and at the cusp of where the plains region becomes the Piney Woods, sits nature-rich Athens. A prominent local lady named the town after Athens, Greece, in the mid-1800s, with the hope that it would become the cultural capital of Henderson County. Its arts scene never really took off, but instead, Athens proved to be strong in natural resources: clay, sand, gravel, and oil are all found in the area, while local farms raise poultry and cattle and produce fruits, dairy, and vegetables—most famously, black-eyed peas. (In recent years, wine has been added to that list, too.) Several lakes dot the countryside, as does the picturesque flora and fauna of East Texas (for more on that, don't miss the East Texas Arboretum). Today, Athens is also home to one of the premier aquatic nature centers in the country, where you can fish, walk wetlands, interact with divers, and see a working hatchery.

Nature may play a big part in Athens' livelihood, but its main claim to fame was entirely man-made. In the 1880s, local potter Fletcher Davis—known as "Uncle Fletch"—started a modest lunch counter at 115 E. Tyler St., along the town square, to help supplement his pottery business. There, he created a sandwich that soon proved popular with the lunch crowd: a ground beef patty placed between two pieces of homemade bread, topped with pickles, onions, and a mix of mayo and mustard. Locals were so enamored of the meal, they raised enough money to send Uncle Fletch to the 1904 St. Louis World's Fair, where

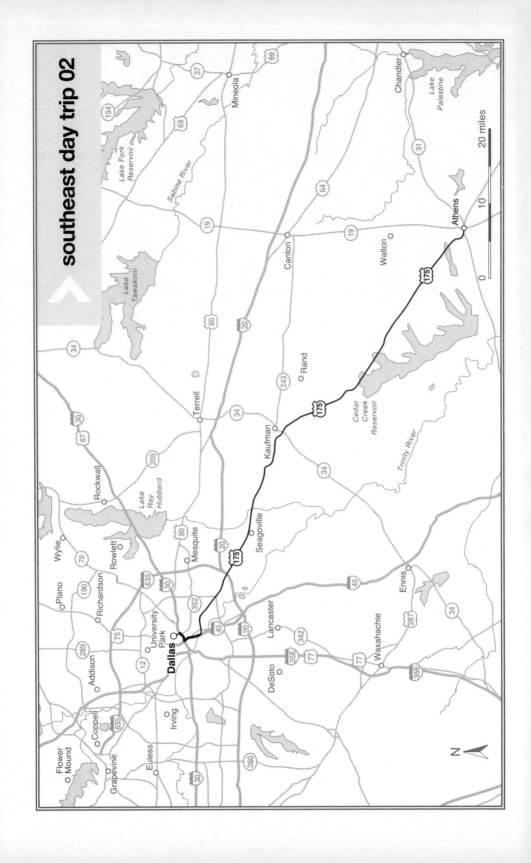

southeast day trip 02

he introduced the world to the hamburger. Extensive research has corroborated Athens' claim to be "home of the original hamburger" (even McDonald's says so); for more on its creation, visit www.originalburger.com.

Sadly, Uncle Fletch's lunch stand is long gone, but you'll find burgers—and lots of other home-cooked treats—at several standout local restaurants, and at the annual "Uncle Fletch Hamburger Cook-Off" every October. In May, don't miss the annual Texas Fiddlers Contest & Reunion, during which hundreds of fiddlers descend on the town square to celebrate the music and compete in various categories.

## getting there

To reach Athens, take US 175 southeast right into town, or I-20 E to Canton, then TX 19 south to Athens. Note that for the few blocks of downtown, US 175 is also called Corsicana Street and that the main town streets are labeled North, South, East, or West, depending on which side of the courthouse they are located.

## where to go

**Athens Scuba Park.** 500 N. Murchison St., Athens; (903) 675-5762; www.athensscuba park.com. When you can't get to the Caribbean or the Great Barrier Reef, hone your diving skills (or learn how to scuba) at this well-maintained aqua center. Once a clay quarry, the spring-fed lake's depth ranges from 20 to 35 feet, and it contains underwater caves and over thirty sunken "wrecks"—from a houseboat and buses to a small airplane—to explore. Camping and night dives are offered on Friday and Saturday. Admission $15 for divers, $5 for nondivers, camping $5, instructors are free for four or more students; call for more info. Open Fri through Sun, 10 a.m. to 6 p.m. in the spring and summer, Sat through Sun, 10 a.m. to 5 p.m. in the fall and winter.

**Athens Welcome Center.** 124 N. Palestine St., Athens; (903) 677-0775 or (888) 294-2847; www.athenstx.org. Load up on maps, brochures, and suggestions from expert local residents. Open Mon through Fri, 8 a.m. to 5 p.m., Sat, 10 a.m. to 4 p.m.

**Berry Farms.** (888) 294-2847; www.athenstx.org. Come May, June, and July, the area around Athens explodes with succulent blueberries and blackberries. Several farms allow you to come pick your own; call the welcome center or visit the Athens Web site for details.

**East Texas Arboretum and Botanical Society.** 1601 Patterson Rd. (off Hwy. 175), Athens; (903) 675-5630; www.eastexasarboretum.org. Specializing in plants, flowers, and trees that are native (or compatible) to the region, this one-hundred-acre complex includes 2 miles of nature trails, a suspension bridge, and several historic homes—including a beautiful 1850s farmhouse—that have been moved here and decorated with period furnishings. Kids will enjoy the numerous life-size playhouses and playgrounds, as well as seasonal happenings like scarecrow contests and hamburger cook-offs. Suggested donation $2; open spring and summer, 7:30 a.m. to 7:30 p.m., fall and winter, 8 a.m. to 6 p.m.

**Henderson County Fair Park Complex.** 3344 TX 31 E., Athens; (903) 677-6354; www .hendersoncountyfairpark.com. From rodeos, barrel racing, and horse, cow, and dog shows to auctions and concerts, there's something happening almost every weekend at this sixty-eight-acre park and 4,500-seat arena—and most of the time, the events are free.

**Henderson County Historical Museum.** 217 N. Prairieville, Athens; (903) 677-3611. A 1896 Fault-Gaunt building houses a jam-packed, two-floor collection of vintage and antique artifacts and memorabilia from the county, including arrowheads and a Civil War flag. Open Fri–Sat only; call for hours.

**NY-TX Zipline Adventures.** 7290 CR 4328, New York, Texas; (903) 681-3791; www .goziptexas.com. Twenty-two miles from the Athens square, in nearby New York, this popu- lar adventure course lets you fly through the hills and trees of East Texas while strapped to a cable. (It's more fun than it sounds.) There are six courses of varying levels, culminating in a 900-foot-long, four-story trail that's the biggest in the state. Open by appointment only.

**Texas Freshwater Fisheries Center.** 5550 FM 2495, Athens; (903) 676-2277; www.tpwd .state.tx.us/tffc. Located about 4 miles from the Athens main square, this is the area's most popular attraction—and one of the best values around. In addition to encompassing a working hatchery (where you can learn about the spawning process), the nature center features over 300,000 gallons of aquariums, housing everything from giant alligators to prehistoric paddlefish, plus miles of wetlands trails and a 1.2 acre catch-and-release fishing pond (they even supply the rods and bait). Most popular are the interactive dive/feeding shows, which take place Tues through Fri at 11 a.m., Sat at 11 a.m. and 2 p.m., and Sun at 2 p.m. Thanks to an underwater speaker system, visitors are able to interact with the diver and ask questions as he or she feeds the fish, some of which stretch to over 6 feet long. Open Tues through Sat, 9 a.m. to 4 p.m., Sun, 1 to 4 p.m.; closed Mon and major holidays; admission $5.50.

**Texas Gospel Music Hall.** 6513 TX 19, South Athens; (903) 675-5217; www.texas- gospelmusichall.com. Fans of traditional bluegrass, country, and gospel music flock to this monthly concert series, started by a former professional gospel singer. The roster of per- formers often includes nationally known acts; check the Web site to see who's coming up.

## where to shop

**The Pea Picker Bookstore.** 108 W. Tyler St., Athens; (903) 675-3488. Booklovers are sure to disappear for hours into this cavernous space, filled floor to ceiling with used tomes of every type, age, and genre. Prices are half-off whatever the cover price—which means you might just pay a quarter.

**The Sweet Pea Collection.** 119 E. Tyler St., Athens; (903) 677-6868; www.sweetpea collection.com. Find shabby chic furniture, slipcovers, home goods, bedding, and more at this upscale-rustic design shop. In the same building, Winnie & Tulula's—billed as "not

## cowpea country

*Athens isn't only home to the hamburger—it's also the black-eyed pea capital of the world. Historically, black-eyed peas were mainly used as feed for livestock, but in 1909, Athens farmer J. B. Henry decided to try to grow large crops of the pea, which were also commonly called "cowpeas." When weevils started getting into his fresh produce, Henry tried drying the peas in the oven to detract the vermin; the dried version could then later be soaked and cooked before eating. The tasty dish took off, and soon the town was crazy for the black-eye pea; a 1919 issue of* Farm and Ranch *magazine claimed that seemingly "the whole population of Athens" was loading sacks of the peas onto their wagons. Over the next couple of decades, several canning plants opened in the county, including Good Luck Peas (to capitalize on the tradition of eating black-eyed peas on New Year's Day for good luck), while Home Folks brand's pickled black-eyes (known as "Texas Caviar") were carried by Neiman Marcus. In 1971, Athens started the Black-Eyed Pea Jamboree, and over the years, the festival's famous cook-off has yielded such creative delicacies as pea enchiladas, "peachyssoise" sauce, cowpea cheesecake, pea wine, and the popular "Peatini" cocktail—which has now been patented. You can experience the festival every fall, after harvest season.*

your mother's antique mall"—stocks an eclectic array of new and vintage treasures. Wed through Sat, 10 a.m. to 6 p.m.

**Wulf Outdoor Sports.** 1220 S. Palestine, Athens; (903) 670-3222; www.wulfoutdoor sports.com. From hunting, fishing, and ATV-ing supplies to clothing, gifts, footwear, and accessories, you can find it at this massive, family-owned emporium. There are also guns, motorcycles, jet skis, and—for the man who has everything—camouflage-patterned armchairs. Open Mon through Fri, 9 a.m. to 6 p.m., Sat, 9 a.m. to 5 p.m., Sun, 1 to 5 p.m.

# where to eat

**Athens Cafe.** 607 E. Tyler St., Ste. 108, Athens; (903) 675-5504. This family-run favorite serves both full American and Mexican menus, so whether you're hankering for burgers, giant baked potatoes, chicken-fried steak or fajitas, you're set. There's also a breakfast menu and daily specials. Mon through Sat, 6 a.m. to 9 p.m., Sun, 6 a.m. to 2 p.m. $.

**Cripple Creek BBQ.** 500 S. Palestine St., Athens; (903) 675-4226. A steady stream of hungry patrons shows up here for the slow-smoked hickory ribs (available in a platter, sandwich, or by the pound) and the "hog wings"—pork shanks served with Texas Toast and sweet-and-sour Mae Ploy sauce. There are also homemade fried pies and apple fritters—and a drive-through window for those who really can't wait. $–$$.

**El San Luis Mexican Cafe.** 300 N. Pinkerton St., Athens; (903) 677-3800. Just a couple of blocks from the main square, past the railroad tracks and surrounded by industrial buildings, sits this temple of down-home Tex-Mex cooking. The small, dinerlike space is super-casual, but both the service and main courses—particularly the generous combo platters—are top-notch. Most combo meals also include a dessert sopapilla, served with squeezable bottles of butter and honey for diners to slather on as they like. Mon through Sat, 7:30 a.m. to 9 p.m., Sun, 7:30 a.m. to 2 p.m. $.

**Flying Gatto Coffee Co.** 222 E. Tyler St., Athens; (903) 670-1002. Set a block behind the town square and visitors center, in a building that, over the years, "has housed everything," this funky coffeehouse serves java, fresh, flavored snow cones (all year long), light bites, and homemade baked goods. Don't miss the cakeballs—palm-sized rounds of moist cake dipped in chocolate that alone might be worth the ride from Dallas. Mon through Sat, 7:30 a.m. to 6 p.m. $.

**Lake Athens Marina Restaurant.** 5401 FM 2495, Athens; (903) 677-8774; www .lakeathensmarina.com. Come Friday night, this is where locals head for fried catfish and burgers, both of which are considered among the best in town. The water-view restaurant is located within the twenty-eight-acre marina complex, which includes an RV camping ground and the only public access docks on Lake Athens. Closed Mon. $–$$.

**Ole' West Bean & Burger.** 1500 E. Tyler St., Athens; (903) 675-8100. A stone fireplace, wooden tables, and a wall of graffiti set the scene at this barn-shaped restaurant located a short drive away from the square. Favorites include the fresh, ½-pound burgers (served with hand-cut fries), as well as the daily specials and comfort foods like corn dogs, hush puppies, and Frito Pie. $–$$.

## where to stay

**Oak Creek B&B.** 9004 CR 2800, Athens; (903) 675-5509; www.oakcreekbnb.com. Enjoy a full homemade country breakfast, private cottages, hammocks, on-site nature trails, and a fishing pond at this romantic retreat, where the peaceful feel comes courtesy of a no-kids policy. There's also a fire pit where you can cook your own dinner; you bring the food, they provide everything else. $–$$.

**Tara Vineyard & Winery.** 8603 CR 3914, 1.5 miles off US 175 between Dallas and Athens; (903) 675-7023; www.tarawinery.com. Opened in 2009, the inn at this beautiful working winery features three vineyard-view rooms (one with a private Jacuzzi bath), plus balconies, sitting rooms, terraces, and a game room set about the late-nineteenth-century property. Relaxation is key: There are no phones, TVs, or alarm clocks in the rooms (though there is a Direct TV-equipped game room, and free Wi-Fi), and guests enjoy live music on the weekends from Austin-based bands. Breakfast is included. $$.

# day trip 03

## southeast

**east texas star:**
palestine

# palestine

Drive about 115 miles southeast of Dallas and you'll be heading toward the Piney Woods region, an area lush with magnolia, cypress, oak, and pine trees. This is the land of four seasons, where the fall foliage blazes bright, and, come spring, the azaleas, wisteria, and dogwoods are in full bloom. Just this side of the Piney Woods border sits Palestine, a town that the railroads built, and that a dedicated citizenry have preserved. You'll find noteworthy architecture, quirky shops, some interesting new developments, and a healthy dash of small-town charm. But most of all, you'll be surrounded by scenic natural beauty, in the official home of the Texas Dogwood Trails.

Palestine (that's "pal-uh-steen," if you please), actually boasts a number of distinctions. For one, it's one of the oldest towns in Texas, beginning as a grist mill and trading post in the 1830s before officially becoming a town—and the seat of Anderson County—in 1846 (shortly after Texas was annexed to the United States). The local representative to the new state legislature was given the honor of naming the new town, and he chose Palestine to commemorate the place in Illinois from where his family had emigrated.

The town grew steadily over the next few decades, building a courthouse square surrounded by shops and nearby residential neighborhoods. But things really took off in 1872, when the International & Great Northern railroad came to town. The importance of the railroad for Palestine can't be overestimated: It brought in new residents and merchants,

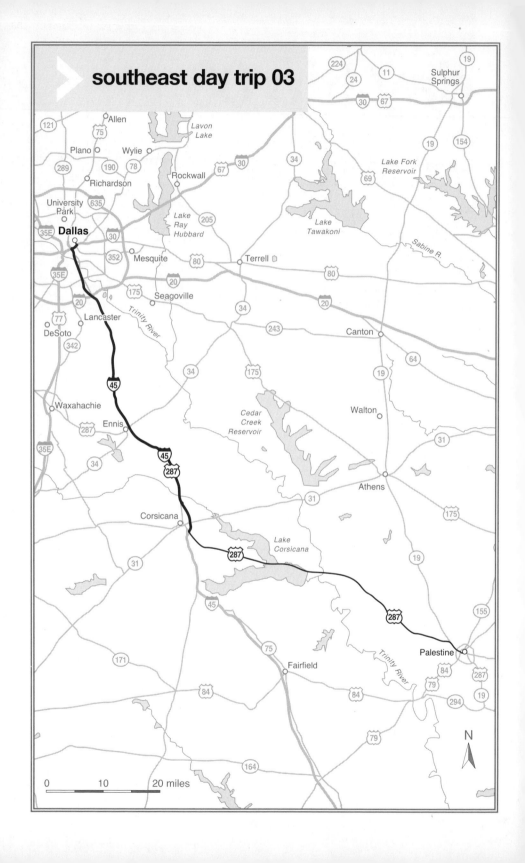

# southeast day trip 03

helped establish the town as a transportation hub, and even changed the layout of the city. Because the railroad bypassed the hilltop courthouse square and put its tracks, stores, and offices on flatter land a mile west, a new commercial center emerged; the area around the train hub was soon hopping with shops, saloons, and hotels, creating a New Town, while the courthouse area was labeled Old Town—designations that still exist today. (Because of this, Palestine doesn't have the typical central square setup seen in many North Texas towns.) At its height, over one hundred acres within the city limits were dedicated to the rail yards, and several lines converged here. (The railroad continues to hold land here today.)

The transport and shipping industries, along with a smattering of grist and cotton mills, kept the town growing into the new century. In 1928, oil was discovered east of Palestine, and a new industry began. Between the two enterprises, Palestine was able to avoid the worst of the Depression, and continue to thrive. After changing hands several times over the decades, the railroads left town in 1982, taking many jobs with them. Today, the town of just over 18,300 boasts a diverse economy of everything from oil and gas offices and a beef-packing plant to a NASA Scientific Balloon Facility. Tourism, though, remains one of the main draws, as thousands of visitors arrive a year to walk the Dogwood Trails in April, attend the Oktoberfest, hunt for antiques, and visit the famous, 110-plus old Eilenberger's Bakery for some Texas Pecan Cake. Because there was relatively little industrial change over the years here, Palestine boasts an impressively large number of historic homes and structures (most of the buildings in town are from the 1870s–1920s), giving it a charming feel. While a new bar or winery may occupy the old spaces, locals are thoughtful with their restorations—ensuring that Palestine's rich history lives on.

## getting there

To reach Palestine, take I-45 south to Corsicana, then veer left onto US 287; this will head southeast right into town—where it is also called Spring Street. The trip should take about two hours. Note that when locals refer to "The Loop," they are talking about TX 256, which rings the city.

## where to go

**Anderson County Courthouse.** 500 N. Church St., Palestine; (903) 723-3014; www.visitpalestine.com. Craftsmen from Italy helped create this stunning neoclassical structure, replete with double spiral staircase and stained glass panels in the dome. Drive by for a look or, for a unique experience, book an appointment to see the historic courtroom and meet a judge with a private collection of historic artifacts; contact the convention and visitors bureau for details.

**Columbia Scientific Balloon Facility.** 1510 E. FM 3224, Palestine; (903) 729-0271. Since the 1960s, the Columbia Scientific Balloon program has launched over 2,200 giant, unmanned balloons for scientific explorations, primarily out of permanent facilities in New

Mexico, Australia, Antarctica—and Palestine, Texas. This particular facility, which is over-seen by NASA, launches balloons as large as 300 feet in diameter to study the atmosphere, near space, earth science, and more. Tours can be arranged by appointment; call the facility or the Palestine convention and visitors bureau for more info.

**Davey Dogwood Park.** 210 N. Link St., Palestine; (903) 723-3014; www.visitpalestine .com. Feel yourself starting to exhale at this peaceful 200-acre park, where meadows, streams, rolling hills, and fragrant forests showcase the beauty of East Texas and the Piney Woods. The park is one of the featured sites of the annual Texas Dogwood Trails Festival from late March to early April, when the area's famous dogwoods are in bloom. Picnic areas and scenic viewpoints are scattered throughout. The park is located just north of town along N. Link Street (which is also called FM 3309). Take that road north to N. Queen Street for the park entrance.

**Historic Neighborhoods.** (903) 723-3014; www.visitpalestine.com. From the highest point in town (the Courthouse Square) and beautiful historic homes to an 1880s church with over 300 stained glass windows, Palestine has a wealth of historic structures and neighbor-hoods. (In fact, most of the architecture in town is from the 1870s to 1920s, and there are four National Historic Registry–approved areas.) The visitors bureau stocks free Historical Driving Tour Guides for the north and south sides, which contain a mountain of information on architecture and town history. Some of the main areas to check out include the Court-house Square, home to the majestic city building; the Downtown (different from the square), where grand brick structures that once housed saloons and mercantiles are now home to antiques boutiques and specialty shops; and the quaint, creek-side Old Town, once the site of warehouses, farm stores, barns, and the cotton mill (and today, fun boutiques and a funky bar). The residential neighborhoods are worth a look, too: stately Victorians, Queen Annes, and Greek Revival mansions, traditional prairie-style homes, and beautiful Craftsman bungalows line the shady streets, and are a treat to check out from the outside.

**Museum for East Texas Culture.** 400 Micheaux Ave., in Reagan Park, Palestine; (903) 723-1914; www.museumpalestine.org. In 1916, this distinctive Tudor-Gothic-style build-ing adorned by stunning brickwork opened as Palestine's new high school. After serving decades of students, the building was set to be demolished in the 1980s when concerned citizens stepped in, turning it instead into a museum honoring Anderson County history. The two floors of former classrooms, gymnasiums, and auditoria now house all manner of memorabilia, curios, and antiques, divided into various themes. Explore rooms celebrating railroad history (complete with the counter and desk from the now-demolished Palestine Railroad Depot), the fire department, early-twentieth-century education and African-American heritage. There's antique medical and dental equipment, photos, and, in the basement, an original historic cabin. On the top floor, a small gallery features rotating exhib-its from local artists. (On a side note, the adjacent Reagan Park hosts free Classic Movies in the Park night on the first Saturday of the month; call the visitors bureau for details.) Adults, $2; Mon through Sat, 10 a.m. to 5 p.m.

**Palestine Community Forest.** Access from intersection of TX 19 and US 287 a few miles northwest of town, Palestine; (903) 723-3014; www.visitpalestine.com. Sumac, sweetgum, and plenty of pine trees cover these 700 acres, where scenic drives lead to four lakes. Enjoy fishing, boating, and picnicking among the flora.

**Palestine Convention and Visitors Bureau.** 825 Spring St., at the junction of US 84 and US 287/TX 19, Palestine; (903) 723-3014 or (800) 659-3484; www.visitpalestine.com. A restored historic train depot is now filled to the brim with maps, brochures, and staffers to help get your visit started. This is also the place to pick up pamphlets on the historic driving and walking tours, as well as get help setting up some of the by-appointment-only activities listed below. Mon through Fri., 8 a.m. to 4 p.m., Sat, 10 a.m. to 4 p.m., Sun, noon to 4 p.m.

**The Palestine Police Museum.** 511 N. John St., Palestine; (903) 731-8468. This small collection, housed in the Palestine Police Department building, honors the history of law enforcement in town, dating back to the first constable appointed in 1871. Peruse photos, uniforms, badges, vintage equipment, and memorabilia like the longest gun carried in the history of the department (an eight-and-three-fourth-inch Colt 45 Caliber Anaconda revolver). Free; open Tues through Fri, 1 to 5 p.m., Sat by appointment.

**Texas State Railroad.** Park Road 70, US 84 East, Palestine; (903) 683-2561 and (888) 987-2461; www.texasstaterr.com. Families, railroad history enthusiasts, people looking for a unique experience—they all come from far and wide to this special part of Texas heritage. Founded in Rusk in 1881, and expanded to Palestine in 1909, the Texas State Railroad was an East Texas line that helped move hardwood and iron products within the region and, through connection to other lines, to cities as far as Austin. Once the line stopped operating in 1913, the tracks were leased to other routes, until service stopped all together in 1969. In 1976, the depots in Rusk and Palestine—and the rail line in between—were opened to the public as a part of a historical park, where today, visitors can view antique engines, learn about rail history, and ride the vintage steam and diesel rails between the two towns (the starting /ending points alternate between the depots, so check the schedule).

Roundtrip journeys between Palestine and Rusk take place most Fridays and Saturdays; the trip takes 1.5 hours each way, plus a lunch break at the other end, for a total of 4.5 hours. Shorter dinner and themed rides are held throughout the year—along with events in the park, like family barbecues with live music—so visit the Web site for more information. (The Palestine depot park also houses campgrounds and RV hookup sites.) Train ride prices vary depending on type of engine (steam or diesel) and location of seat (indoor or open air); open year-round. The park is located approximately 2 miles east of Loop 256, on US 84.

# where to shop

**Downtown Historic District.** (903) 723-3014; www.visitpalestine.com. Also called New Town—though most of the buildings are from the late-nineteenth and early twentieth centuries—the brick-lined streets between Crawford and Spring and Queen and Sycamore contain numerous unique shops. Hours are generally 10 a.m. to 5 p.m., but many retailers are closed Sun through Tues, so call ahead if looking for somewhere specific. Some standouts include:

**City Shoe Shop** (110 W. Main St.; 903-729-3041). This second-generation shoemaker still creates custom shoes and cowboy boots—and fixes well-worn ones, as well.

**Duncan Depot Antiques** (106 W. Main St.; 903-723-2899). Considered one of the best by seasoned antiques hunters, this large multivendor space stocks furniture, collectibles, jewelry, and memorabilia, and also boasts an extensive collection of (not-for-sale) vintage pharmacy pieces.

**Old Magnolia Mercantile** (120 W. Oak St.; 903-729-1200). Lots more antiques and knickknacks from a variety of dealers, plus a café and coffee shop in the middle (see "Where to Eat"). Don't miss the large collection of international beer bottles.

**Silver Lady** (115 W. Oak St.; 903-729-0600). The place in town for jewelry, tabletop and glassware, collectibles, and other gifty items.

**Star of Texas Antiques** (107 W. Oak St.; 903-723-6363). A one-time silent movie house and vaudeville theater now houses a lovely selection of American antiques furnishings, lots of great old photos, and two floors of books, some dating back a century or more.

**Texas Art Depot** (301 W. Oak St.; 866-725-1940). There's more than just two floors of art at this thirty-year-old family-run business, located in a converted old hotel. On the ground floor there's custom framing and art works, then upstairs, find hundreds more paintings, plus a winery/tasting room where you can sip the house-blend "Granny Muffin" wines while perusing the art. The store also does a brisk online business, shipping art work all over the world (www.texasartdepot.com).

**Eilenberger's Bakery.** 512 N. John St., Palestine; (800) 788-2996; www.eilenbergerbaker .com. For over 110 years, this bakery has been hand mixing, baking, and decorating fruit and nut cakes using the same recipes brought over from Germany by founder F. H. Eilenberger's parents. The company does a thriving mail- and Internet-order business for their signature Texas pecan and fruit cakes, but this retail store—attached to the main bakery—is the only one. Mon through Fri, 7 a.m. to 4:30 p.m., Sat, 8 a.m. to 2 p.m.

**Old Town Palestine.** 302 E. Crawford, 2 blocks west of the Courthouse, Palestine; (903) 731-4434; www.oldtownpalestine.com. Once the agricultural center, dotted with mills and barns, this picturesque area's restored buildings now house shops, restaurants, and even a candle factory. Stroll around the small neighborhood, which also contains a creek and the cute Saw Mill Hollow Park, where some of the Dogwood Trails festivities take place. Stores to check out include Mercantile on the Creek (215 E. Crawford St., 903-729-1200), for country-retro vintage furniture, gifts, and gourmet food; and Mary Jean's Artifacts (302 E. Crawford St.; 903-731-4434), a 3000-square-foot tin barn now offering an eclectic selection of gifts, jewelry, clothing, and home decor. Owner Mary Jean Mollard is something of a driving force in town (she also owns The Redlands Inn and restores historic buildings), and she's a fountain of knowledge on local and regional history, and present-day developments and activities.

# where to eat

**Amore.** 400 N. Queen St., Palestine; (903) 729-1475; www.redlandshistoricinn.com. Set on the ground floor of The Redlands Inn, this sunny spot is a good bet for Italian standards like manicotti, Chicken Marsala, and penne, as well as salads and buttery garlic bread. The owners are from Italy (they also have an eatery in Fort Worth), and preside over a friendly wait staff and a convivial atmosphere. Opened in 2009, this has become a fast favorite with the downtown office lunch crowd and special occasion evening diners. $–$$.

**Little Mexico.** 2025 W. Oak St., Palestine; (903) 723-3143. One of the oldest restaurants in town still draws a crowd of die-hards for their standard Tex-Mex fare, which includes fajitas and enchiladas. Good for families. $.

**Madeline's Tea Room.** 909 FM 2419, Palestine; (903) 731-7095; www.madelinestearoom .com. Located in a house about 2 miles outside of town, at the corner of US 287 south, this ladies' scratch-made favorite is famous for its chicken salad, made with apples, walnuts, celery, and house dressing. Salad plates and daily specials (which include pastas and quiches) all come with soup, scones, lemon curd, and Devonshire cream. ("Light" plates come with a muffin and fruit.) Naturally, there are also teas served by the pot and fresh daily desserts. Wed through Sat, 11 a.m. to 2 p.m. $.

**Old Magnolia Coffee Shop.** 115 W. Main St., Palestine; (903) 729-4411. Tucked inside the Old Magnolia Mercantile antiques mall (see "Where to Shop" above), this comfortable coffee bar and luncheonette serves a full roster of caffeinated drinks—straight and flavored—plus spuds, salads, wraps, and specials like stuffed avocados in the restaurant section. There are couches and tables near the coffee bar, and Wi-Fi, making this a popular downtown hangout. $.

**Shep's Bar-B-Q.** 1013 E. Palestine Ave., Palestine; (903) 729-4206. Folks line up for the smoky, moist ribs at this causal spot, which are made with a sweet-and-spicy rub. You'll also find all the other 'cue staples, like brisket and sides. Mon through Thurs, 11 a.m. to 7 p.m., Fri through Sat, 11 a.m. to 8 p.m. $.

# where to stay

**Elmwood Gardens.** 680 Anderson CR 446, Palestine; (903) 724-5619 or (903) 549-2716; www.elmwoodgardens.com. One of East Texas's most popular wedding venues is also a lovely B&B. Rooms are set in historic dog-trot houses or cottages, and are strewn around the four-acre property, which is dotted with lush water gardens. Antique furnishings, home-made quilts, and a lack of phones or TVs keep the setting comfy and relaxing (and it's easy to avoid the inevitable wedding or bridal photo shoot). Rates include a country breakfast. $$.

**Fig Tree Manor.** 203 Erwin St., Palestine; (903) 729-3457. Consistently voted the top B&B in the area, this four-room charmer is nestled in the Old Town section, surrounded by lush foliage and blissful silence. Borrow a bike for a ride along the Dogwood Trails, take a dip in the lap pool or spa, or just laze on the porch to enjoy the scenic views. Two of the suites have private baths, while all boast a hand-picked decor that might include a claw-foot tub or ornate wrought iron bed frame. $$.

**The Redlands Historic Inn.** 400 N. Queen St., Palestine; (800) 550-5445 and (903) 729-2345; www.redlandshistoricinn.com. Built in 1914, and listed with the National Register of Historic Buildings, this corner structure was created as an elegant hotel for travelers arriving on the railways. From 1919 to the 1950s, it then housed the headquarters of the International & Great Northern Railroad, before lying empty for many years. The current owners have spruced it up to resemble its turn-of-the-century beginnings, though along with the antiques, rooms also feature modern touches like HD cable TV. The inn offers both short- and long-term accommodations, so most all the rooms are apartment-style, with kitchen-ettes, living areas, and a homey decor. (Some have balconies, too.) $$.

**Sabor a Pasion.** 110 Anderson CR 406, Palestine; (903) 729-9500; www.saborapasion .com. Less than five minutes outside The Loop (TX 256), you'll find a twenty-five-acre, hill-top country house complete with deer in the back pasture, elegant en-suite rooms—and a gourmet chef. Named one of the Top 20 chefs in New Zealand, Simon Webster is both personal chef and innkeeper to guests here, along with his wife, Beki. Upon arrival, you'll enjoy a taste of his culinary prowess with a special treat, while the daily breakfast is cooked to order; dinner is available Friday and Saturday by reservation, and might include some-thing like Thai Prawn Tamales or wood-fired pizza. (Cooking classes can also be arranged.) Rooms are simple and bright, with queen beds, CD players, and sofas (a phone and TV are only in the lounge). $$.

# worth more time

If time permits, head just out of town into the East Texas countryside for a visit to a vineyard or winery. At the **Texas Vineyard & Smokehaus** (2442 Anderson CR 2133, Palestine; 903-538-2950; www.texasvineyard.org), owners Rafael and Cheryl Hernandez will warmly welcome guests with a tour of the grounds, which include a tasting room, bistro, lavender field, and vineyard; or just sit on the balcony, munching on appetizers and sipping wines made in Texas, from Texas grapes. (Their sangria is also a killer.) Hours vary seasonally, but generally they are open Wed through Sun, from noon to 9 p.m. in the summer, and noon to 6 p.m. in winter. The vineyard is located about 5.5 miles from the Hwy. 256 loop.

At **Sweet Dreams Winery** (2549 CR 44, Palestine; 903-549-2027; www.sweet dreamswinery.com), the wines are made "in the tradition of times past," and include such sweet-sounding varieties as Bumble Bee Kiss (honey raspberry), Texas moonlight (Muscadine), and Midnight in Texas (blackberry, blueberry, and wild grape.) Tastings are available every Sat from 11 a.m. to 8 p.m.; hours may vary in January and February.

# south

# day trip 01

south

**bluebonnets and polka:**
ennis

# ennis

Texas's Czech history is alive and well 33 miles down I-45, in the city of Ennis. And so are the bluebonnets: A 40-mile stretch of grassland here is so lush with the azure flowers in season, that the town has been designated the "Official Texas Bluebonnet Trail" by the state legislature. Every year, festivals celebrating these two things—the Old World heritage and music of the Czech community and the dazzling bluebonnet fields—draw close to a million tourists to Ennis, where the regular population hovers at about 19,000. But look beyond the hoopla and you'll find a place that's much more than its main claims to fame—a classic small town where football is king, the eats are homemade, there's still a working drive-in, and where you can easily while away an afternoon.

Ennis was literally founded by the railroad: In 1871, the Houston and Texas Central Railroad picked up 647 acres of land in this part of Ellis County, with the goal of building their northern terminus. The town itself was formally established the next year and named for Cornelius Ennis, a noted railroad executive and one-time mayor of Houston. With the trains in town, Ennis became an agricultural and commercial hub throughout the late 1800s and early twentieth century, as well as a major producer of cotton. Many of the Czech and Slovak immigrants who settled here in those times were farmers, and their legacy lives on in the area today.

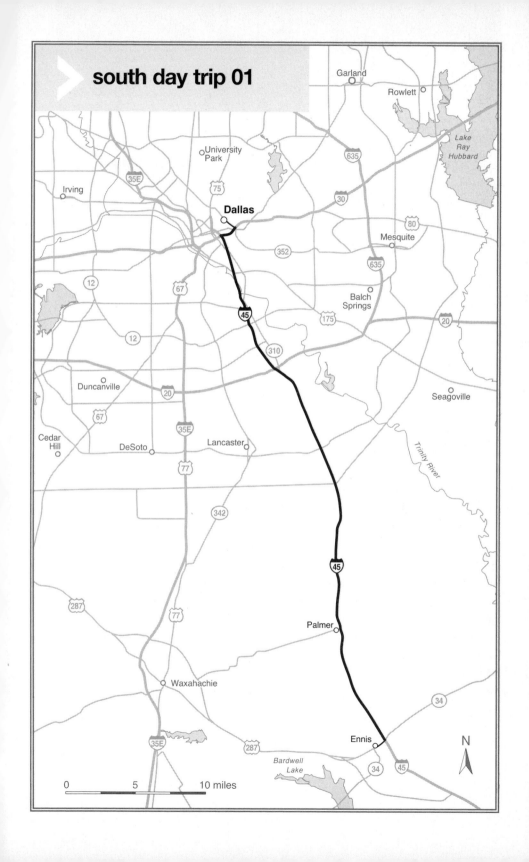

Garland

Rowlett

University
Park

35E

Irving

75

Dallas

635

Lake
Ray
Hubbard

80

Mesquite

12

67

352

45

635

Balch
Springs

175

310

20

12

310

20

Duncanville

20

Seagoville

67

35E

Cedar
Hill

DeSoto

Lancaster

77

Trinity River

342

287

77

45

287

77

Palmer

Waxahachie

34

35E

287

Ennis

34    45

Bardwell
Lake

N

0          5          10 miles

Once the cotton boom ended, Ennis, like many towns, looked to diversify. These days agriculture still plays an important role, along with over forty other industries, from call centers to robotics companies. The local high school is ranked among the Top 100 schools in the United States, and its football team, the Lions, are four-time state champs. (Visit the town during football season and you'll see plenty of people decked out in maroon-and-white.) The red brick historic buildings of downtown are slowly filling with shops and businesses—most of them unique and locally owned—and while you wander around down-town, you can still hear the whistle of the train as it comes through Ennis.

## getting there

To reach the historic downtown and the visitors center, head south on I-45 about 33 miles to exit 251-B. Make a right at Ennis Avenue, which will lead into town. (Note that East Ennis Avenue becomes West Ennis Avenue once you pass US 287.) Tip: When driving down I-45, be sure to follow the speed limits around the town of Palmer, notorious for its speed traps.

## where to go

**Czech Museum.** On TX 34 East; open by appointment only, so call for exact address and to reserve a time, (972) 878-4748. View memorabilia, photographs, dolls, costumes, and decorative items celebrating Ennis's Czech and Slovak heritage. The museum is located in the Sokol Hall Activity Center but is only open by appointment, so be sure to call ahead.

**Ennis Convention and Visitors Bureau.** 2 E. Ennis Ave., Ennis; (972) 878-4748; www .visitennis.org. Located in the historic train depot, this cheery visitors center can load you up with brochures and maps for driving and walking tours. While there, check out some of the local memorabilia on display and pick up a beautiful Czech-style painted egg created by a staff member. Mon through Fri, 8 a.m. to 5 p.m. Open seven days a week in April during the Bluebonnet Trails (except Easter Sunday).

**Ennis Railroad and Cultural History Museum.** 105 NE Main St.; (972) 875-1901. Built in 1915, this building next door to the visitors center originally served as a restaurant and another part of the train depot. Since 1992, it's been home to a charming railroad and local history museum, staffed by volunteers. Check out a large collection of train memorabilia, plus dioramas, a large display of vintage Czech crystal and railway china, small exhibits on local military history and more. Adults, $2, children under 12, free. Mon through Sat, 10 a.m. to 4 p.m., Sun, 1 to 4 p.m.

**Festivals and Trails.** Hundreds of thousands of visitors a year attend Ennis's annual fes-tivals and drive its scenic bluebonnet trails. The visitors bureau and its Web site can offer details on festival dates and times, as well as maps for the bluebonnet trails. Note that dur-ing bluebonnet season (the month of April), the visitors bureau office is open seven days a week to accommodate the over 500 visitors a day who are stopping by; during this time, you can also check their Web site for up-to-the-minute info on blooming patterns and where to find the best photo ops.

One of Ennis's main events is the National Polka Festival (www.nationalpolkafestival .com), one of the largest in the country and an Ennis tradition since 1966. Typically taking place over three days in May, the festival includes dancing, parades, live music, traditional food, and dozens of vendors, as well as a "Polkafest Run" and children's activities. Though smaller in scale, the Ennis Czech Music Festival brings an array of acts to town (usually in February), while the famous Ennis Bluebonnet Trails Festival takes place toward the middle of April, during the height of the flower's season.

**Galaxy Drive-In Theater.** 5301 N. I-45, at exit 255/FM 879; (972) 875-5505; www.galaxy driveintheater.com. Take a trip back in time with a movie under the stars at one of the few drive-ins left in the area. Every night, the Galaxy screens two first-run movies (the same as you'd find at the multiplex) back to back, and for the price of one; adults pay $6, kids 5 to 11, $2 (free for the under-5 set). No outside food or drinks are allowed, but the snack bar prices are pretty reasonable, too. The theater is located off I-45 just north of Ennis (you can see it from the highway).

**Texas Motorplex.** 7500 W. Ennis Ave.; (972) 878-2641; www.texasmotorplex.com. With its top-rated drag racing facilities, this speedway draws over half a million fans a year. (It's also home of the world speed record of 333.95 mph.) Check the Web site for a calendar of upcoming events.

# where to shop

**Historic Downtown.** Along Knox, Brown, Main, Dallas, and McKinney Streets in downtown, Ennis. Wander the red brick streets of the historic downtown to browse an array of gifty places. There's no central courthouse to base things around, but the shops are mainly concentrated along the above streets, all within walking distance of the visitors center. Parking is free along any of the downtown streets.

Some of the don't-miss destinations include **Good Time Charlie's General Store** (114 W. Knox; 972-875-9737), which is packed to the rafters with everything from antiques collectibles to 1970s lunch boxes, old LPs, vintage guitars, comic books, and pretty much anything else you can think of. At **ByGones** (106 S. Dallas), owner Sharon Fisher describes her eclectic stock as "just stuff . . . but better than antiques," while at The Farm House (105 NW Main, 972-875-3855), you'll find a stylish, shabby-chic space furnished with antiques, and carrying clothes, children's items, jewelry, and upscale girly gifts. Places for Czech crystal and European antiques include **H&H Gifts** (101 SW Main, 972-875-2791) and **Czech Heritage Shoppe & Antiques** (219 W. Ennis Ave, 972-878-2929).

## where to eat

**4 Goodness Cakes.** 212 W. Brown St., Ennis; (214) 707-6617. Opened in late-2008, this sweet bakery uses owner Gail Peyton's grandmother's recipes for such treats as Italian cream, pink velvet and banana cupcakes, and perfect chocolate chip and old-fashioned sugar cookies. Tues through Fri, 10 a.m. to 5 p.m., Sat, 10 a.m. to 3 p.m. $.

**El Mexicano Grill.** 219 W. Ennis Ave., Ennis; (972) 875-9008. Sit on the spacious patio or in the pleasant dining room for fresh-made Tex-Mex, including flavor-packed cactus soft tacos, tomatillo-covered enchiladas, potent margaritas, and mixed-grill fajitas. The friendly, family-run place starts off every meal with chips and two kinds of salsa—hot and cold. Breakfast taquitos, burritos, and omelets are served until 11 a.m. While waiting for the food to arrive, head through the door in the back of the dining room, a back entrance to the Czech Heritage antiques furniture shop. Sun through Thurs, 7 a.m. to 10 p.m., Fri through Sat, 7 a.m. to 11 p.m. $.

**Firehouse Grill.** 219 SW Main St., Ennis; (972) 875-8353. "We do everything but grow it!" says owner Aline Whatley about the food at the family-friendly restaurant she (a tax prep accountant) opened with her husband, Jimmy. Located near a firehouse, the place kind of took on that theme organically: The owners had originally put up a few firefighter-related posters and memorabilia, as well as a small tribute to Jimmy's father, a fallen Dallas police-man, but soon people were bringing in their own related items, donating uniforms, badges, and even a fire hose. The decor provides a colorful background to the tasty, refined pub grub, including pan-seared crab cakes, onion ring "tanglers," and sweet potato fries to start, followed by burgers, seafood, and rib eye, T-bone, or New York strip steaks. Entrees all come with a choice of sides, like mac and cheese or fried squash, but save room for the

## crazy for kolache

*Drive through North Texas, particularly towns south of the Metroplex, and you'll notice countless Interstate-side signs beckoning you to stop for a fresh kolache. Originally from central Europe, these tasty pastries come stuffed with sweet fill-ings like blueberries, poppy seeds, or apricot, or savories like sausage or cream cheese. Popular for breakfast or lunch, the baked treats are more moist, chewy, and dense than flaky—think stuffed roll over a croissant—and are served both warm and room temperature. In towns like Ennis and West (located on the way to Waco), highway drivers stop in droves to load up by the freshly baked dozen, while in Caldwell, Texas (set further south, near Bryan-College Station), the annual Kolache Festival draws hungry crowds.*

homemade pie or caramel-topped brownie "explosion." Mon through Thurs, 11 a.m. to 9 p.m., Fri through Sat, 11 a.m. to 10 p.m. $$.

**Kolache Depot Cafe & Bakery.** 114 W. Brown St., Ennis; (972) 878-2227; www.kolache depotbakery.com. Also known as Brown Street Cafe (the two places are in one space), this casual Ennis icon is best known for its Czech kolache pastries, baked fresh daily and stuffed with an assortment of fruits, meats, or cheeses. (A small second outpost attached to a gas station at the intersection of I-45 and Ennis Ave. sells just the kolaches to a snacking Interstate crowd.) For something more substantial, there are burgers, sandwiches, and wraps available on nearly a dozen types of bread, soups and salads, "overstuffed spuds," and hot brisket plates—all made with fresh ingredients and signature "Czech-Tex" flavors. Daily, 6 a.m. to 2 p.m. $.

**Wildflower Cafe.** 211 W. Knox St., Ennis; (972) 878-6868. This quaint tearoom, a favorite with the lunch crowd, is tucked into the middle of a home decor store. After filling up on sandwiches, salads, and sweet tea, take a second to browse the stock—particularly the paintings by LaJuan Schlegel, an acclaimed artist who works out of a studio in the back of the store. Schlegel's depictions of bluebonnets and floral landscapes have become something of an Ennis calling card, and are depicted on postcards, prints, and posters. $.

# day trip 02

south

**movie town, texas:**
waxahachie

# waxahachie

Take I-35 E south for less than 30 miles, and suddenly, you're in the past. The seat of Ellis County, Waxahachie boasts over 275 structures and sites recognized by the National Register of Historic Places—that's over 20 percent of the official historic sites in all of Texas. As a result, over the years "The Gingerbread City" has been a go-to spot for filmmakers looking for a photo-ready period location. Over thirty movies and TV mini-series have been shot here, including Oscar winners like *Bonnie and Clyde, Tender Mercies,* and *Places in the Heart.* Along with its man-made beauty, Waxahachie is also the official "Crape Myrtle Capital of Texas," for its wealth of pink, purple, and fuchsia blooms. All the more reason why for this day trip, a camera is a must.

At the center of Waxahachie's architectural fame is the Ellis County Courthouse, an elaborate nineteenth-century confection of turrets and spires that was a testament to the town's prosperity. Established as the county seat in 1850, and officially incorporated in 1871, *Waxahachie*—a Tejas Native American word for "buffalo creek"—became a bustling place, home to settlers from the southern United States as well as German, Czech, and Hungarian immigrants. The surrounding black loamy soil proved perfect for growing crops like corn and cotton, and once the railroad came in 1879, the town became a major trade hub; by 1907, several railroad lines crisscrossed here, there were numerous mills and gins, and the number of cotton bales sold boomed to over 105,000 by 1910—making it the

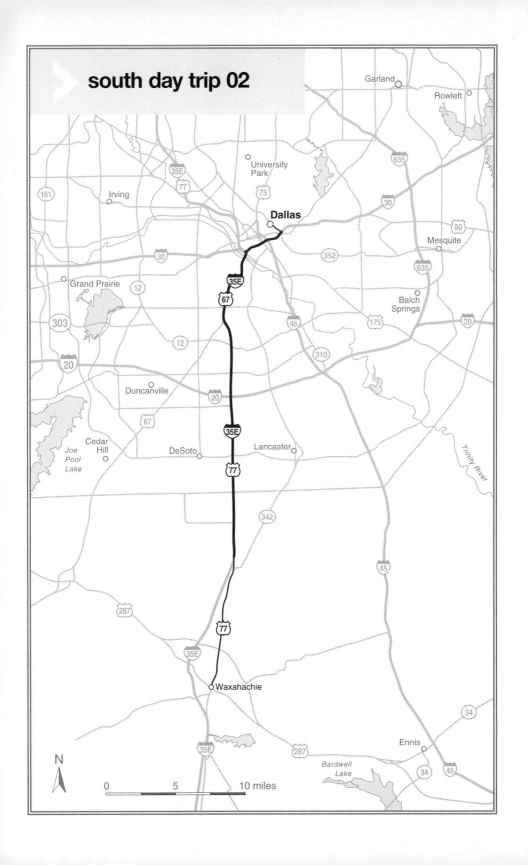

**south day trip 02**

largest cotton producing area in the nation. Residents enjoyed seeing the top acts of the day at the Opera House, there were several colleges (and saloons) in town and, in 1913, even a hot springs spa resort.

All this money meant houses for the influx of residents, both wealthy and working class. Victorian houses cover several neighborhoods, while unique shotgun-style homes can still be seen in the historically African-American Wyatt Street area. Despite several major fires in the late 1800s and early 1900s (and one massive cattle stampede on the Courthouse Square in 1902), Waxahachie has managed to hold on to a large number of its historic buildings. At first, this was most likely due to the fact that, since the decline of the cotton industry in the 1930s, the town's growth has been relatively slow (today's population is around 26,000), but in the last few decades, dedicated work by local preservation and historical societies has helped keep alive Waxahachie's picture-perfect look. Several notable events throughout the year, like the Gingerbread Candlelit Home Tour and the Crape Myrtle Festival, keep the crowds coming.

## getting there

To reach the historic downtown, head south on I-35 E to exit 399A, then take S. Rogers Street/FM 66; this will merge with US 77, which becomes Elm Street in downtown (then Ferris Avenue just north of downtown). The Waxahachie Chamber of Commerce is located 4 miles from the historic downtown (and is only open during the week), so the Heritage Visitors Center (see below) is the best bet for brochures and driving tour maps. If you would like to contact the chambers in advance of your trip, call (972) 937-2390 or browse their site at www.waxahachiechamber.com; the site has attraction details and a few downloadable maps.

## where to go

**Ellis County Courthouse.** 101 W. Main St., Waxahachie; (972) 825-5011. Located at the intersection of Main and Rogers Streets, in the middle of the town square, this 1895 Richardsonian Romanesque structure is one of the 100 most photographed buildings in the state. In his book, *Texas,* James A. Michener describes the courthouse as "a fairy tale palace"—a fitting summary for a building loaded down with battlements, spires, sky-high turrets, and a working clock tower with 800-pound bell. Inside, you'll find carved wood, Corinthian columns, detailed molding, pine floors, ornate windows, and evidence of the over 2 million bricks used to build the place. Designed by noted architect James Riley Gordon, and made up with a mix of gray and pink granite, Texas limestone, and Pecos Red sandstone, the courthouse was state of the art when it opened, and it's interesting to see the creative touches used by the builders.

After a recent multimillion dollar renovation, the courthouse is open for business Mon through Fri, 8 a.m. to 5 p.m.; visitors are welcome to look around, but do keep in mind that this is a working courthouse. A few guided tours are given during the year, usually during major festivals; contact the visitors bureau for details. Detailed write-ups about the structure, including the architectural details, are available at the Heritage Visitors Center.

**Ellis County Museum and Heritage Visitors Center.** 201 S. College St., Waxahachie; (972) 937-0681; www.rootsweb.ancestry.com/~txecm. Learn about the rich history of the county, and Waxahachie in particular, through a large collection of memorabilia. People have been donating items to the historical society for over forty years, so the resulting archives span everything from textiles (clothing, quilts, bedding) to medical equipment, firearms, old signage, and cotton industry relics. (And not even everything in the collection is on display.) The museum is also home to a visitors center where you can pick up walking and driving tour maps. Mon through Sat, 10 a.m. to 5 p.m., Sun, 1 to 5 p.m.

**The Munster Mansion.** 3636 FM 813, Waxahachie; www.munstermansion.com. This private home has been designed to exactly replicate the mansion from the 1960s TV show, *The Munsters*—from the exterior right down to the coffin phone, electric chair, and open-sesame staircase inside. Reportedly haunted (for more on that, see the Web site), the home is only open to public once a year (usually around Halloween, naturally), but there's talk about extending that to other dates. For now, drive by to take a gander, and a picture (but please stay outside the gates, as it is the McKee family home). Take US 77 north to US 287, head east briefly to Brown Street/FM 813, then take that north. You will wind through a few residential subdivisions before coming upon the mansion on the right.

**Waxahachie Creek Hike & Bike Trail.** Starting at Getzendaner Memorial Park, 2 blocks south of W. Main St. (Bus. US 287), along N. Grand Ave. This scenic 4-mile trail meanders alongside the creek, leading from the main downtown park through the woods and historic cemetery, before ending at Lion's Park. A great place for busting out the bikes, or just taking a walk.

**Waxahachie Driving and Walking Tours.** With five historical districts—the Ellis County Courthouse District, West End Historic District, Oldham Avenue Historic District, Wyatt Street Shotgun Houses District, and North Rogers Street Historic District—Waxahachie has a lot to explore. Stop into the Heritage Visitors Center (see above) to pick up detailed maps for a downtown walking tour and residential neighborhood driving tours; the brochures are filled with interesting facts about the structures, as well as detailed directions. Though most of the homes are private, some are opened at various times a year, like during the Gingerbread Trail Home Tour and Candlelight Home Tour; the Chamber and Heritage Visitors Center will have the latest info on dates and times.

Other popular Waxahachie car-view tours include the Crape Myrtle Driving Trail. Thanks to this flower's long blooming season, you can spot the buds most of the year, but the peak amount are usually on display in spring and early summer. (The annual Crape Myrtle Festival is usually in July.) A downloadable trail map is available at the chamber's Web site.

# where to shop

**Historic Downtown.** Streets surrounding the courthouse, at Main and College Streets, Waxahachie; www.downtownwaxahachie.com. The best concentration of independent stores in town are centered around the courthouse. Wander the street to check out unique gifts, clothing, and antiques purveyors.; most are open until 5 p.m. seven days a week. Among the standout shops is the **Gingerbread Antique Mall** (310 S. College St.; 972-937-0968), where over twenty dealers peddle antiques and collectibles from all over the world, with a large selection of Victorian, Mission, and primitive items. On the second Saturday of each month, from 10 a.m. to 2 p.m., Gingerbread holds an "Appraisal Day," during which experts will appraise your attic finds for free. At **Old Town Village Antiques & Uniques** (307 S. Rogers St.; 972-938-9515), browse three floors of goods from over sixty dealers, while tunes from the 1950s and '60s keep the atmosphere upbeat.

Visit the Downtown Waxahachie Web site for a complete list of retailers.

# where to eat

**The 1879 Chisholm Grill.** 111 S. College St., Waxahachie; (972) 937-7261; www.chisholm grill.com. This two-story Victorian has been the site of a restaurant since the 1920s, though the current incarnation began in 2008. Old-fashioned home-cooking is still the name of the game, with Mom's Meatloaf, spaghetti and meatballs, daily quiches, and a lengthy menu of sandwiches, salads, and appetizers. Of course, there are also dozens of grilled or fried chicken options and juicy premium Black Angus steaks, plus a rotating selection of baked-here cobblers, pies, and puddings. Tues through Fri, 11 a.m. to 9 p.m., Sat, 8 a.m. to 9 p.m., Sun, 8 a.m. to 4 p.m. $$.

**Catfish Plantation.** 814 Water St., Waxahachie; (972) 937-9468; www.catfishplantation .com. "Serving souls and spirits" is the tagline of this Cajun- and Creole-spiced downtown restaurant—a reference to its status as one of the most haunted eateries in Texas. Investigated by several national paranormal expert organizations (as well as media like the Travel Channel), the spot is apparently home to a gaggle of Waxahachie residents from times past—including one of the home's previous owners, and a man who likes to flirt with the ladies. Whether you believe or not, the popular restaurant is a must-visit for its unique atmosphere (it's set in a pink-colored historic home) and it's tasty menu. Best-sellers include apps like colossal onion rings, sweet potato fries, and Cajun hush puppies; chicken-fried steak sandwiches; main plates like blackened catfish and southern fried chicken; and homemade cobblers and bread pudding. Wed through Sat, 11 a.m. to 9 p.m., Sun 11 a.m. to 8 p.m. $–$$.

**College Street Pub.** 210 N. College St., Waxahachie; (972) 938-2962; www.collegestreet pub.com. England meets Texas at this lively local hangout, where the drinks are flowing, the flatscreens are tuned to the game, and there's live music from regional bands. The menu ranges from salads, sandwiches, burgers, and typical pub grub (nachos, chicken wings, lots of fried goodies) to British-inspired fare like bangers and mash and fish and chips. The pub is also home to the self-proclaimed "greatest jukebox in town." Mon through Thurs, 11 a.m. to 10 p.m., Fri through Sat, 11 a.m. to midnight, closed Sunday. $–$$.

**The Dove's Nest.** 105 W. Jefferson St., Waxahachie; (972) 938-3683; www.thedovesnest restaurant.com. Since opening in 1992 as a tiny tearoom in the back of gift shop, this family-run restaurant has launched an award-winning cookbook, been lauded in Texas newspapers and magazines, and expanded into a 1913 former hardware store building. There are still gifts and antiques for sale, but the main draw is Chef Aaron Neal's "new Southern" cuisine, including daily gourmet pizzas, chicken-apricot salad sandwiches, tuna and wild rice salad, and chocolate bourbon pecan pie—washed down with homemade orange-spiced ice tea. Mon through Sat, 11 a.m. to 2 p.m. $.

**Two Sisters Lunchbox Cafe.** 308 S. Rogers St., Waxahachie; (972) 923-4463; www.two sisterscupcakes.blogspot.com. There are soups and six tasty sandwiches—each topped with a pickle and chips—to choose from at this lunch spot tucked into the My Father's Antiques store, but the real stars are the colorful scratch-made cupcakes. The offered flavor changes daily, but the sisters' roster runs to dozens of unique combinations, like PB&H, s'mores, grasshopper, Dreamsicle, piña colada and lemon gingersnap. Tues through Sat, 10 a.m. to 2 p.m. $.

# where to stay

**The Chaska House.** 716 W. Main St., Waxahachie; (972) 937-3390; www.chaskabb .com. The six deluxe rooms at this inn pay tribute to different writers with their varying decor, from the antebellum grandeur of the Margaret Mitchell suite to the Jazz Age–style of the Scott Fitzgerald and the Renaissance touches in the Will Shakespeare. It's all done with class and a touch of whimsy, though—not kitsch—in keeping with the focus on relaxed luxury. The house itself is a 1900 Revival-style mansion located a few blocks from downtown. $$–$$$.

# day trip 03

south

# waco

Ninety-six miles south of Dallas, or just about two hours when cruising down I-35, is a city of surprises. If you're like many Metroplexers, Waco may just be a sign you pass on the way to Austin, or a place you've heard about on TV (and not always in the best context). But in fact, this city of about 120,000, home to Baylor University, is both picturesque and interesting—a pleasant greenbelt along the Brazos River that's packed with things to do. There's a noteworthy zoo, a working heritage community, mammoth sites, and an array of independent stores. Plus, no matter what your interests—be it Victorian British poets or Texas-born icons like Dr. Pepper and the Texas Rangers—there's a museum here that's got you covered.

While many Texas towns can trace their roots to the 1800s, Waco's got some proof of what was going on here a few thousand years earlier. Set at a low-level point along where the Balcones Fault escarpment was cut by the Brazos River millions of years ago, this part of North Texas was home to mammoths, which came from the west, and mastodons from the east. In recent years, important discoveries have been made of mammoth skeleton, as well as the skeletons of a 10,000-year-old man and child. (See the "Where to Go" section for more info.) Several hundred decades later, the area became home to the Huaco Indians, from whom the name "Waco" is derived. Settlers began arriving in the 1830s, setting up residence along the Brazos River, and the town was officially incorporated in 1856.

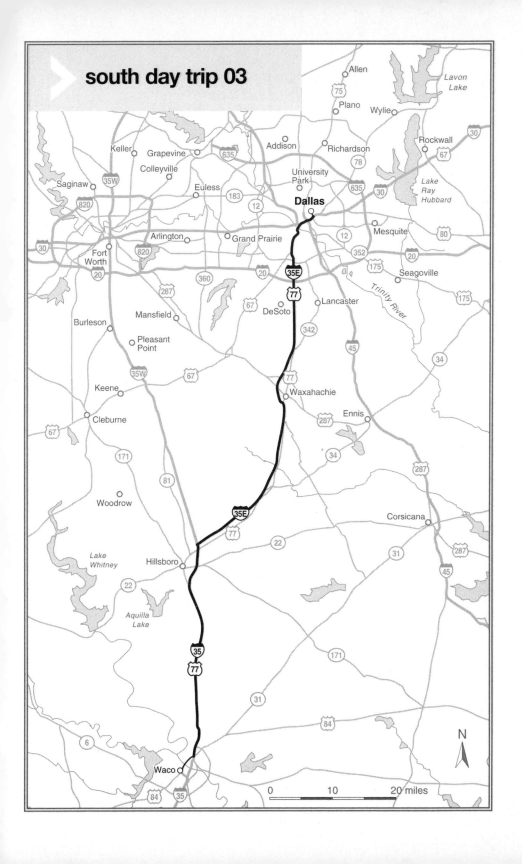

south day trip 03

Though the Civil War left it badly affected, the rise of the Chisholm Trail helped it mend, as the cowboys who were driving cattle northward past the Brazos made the town a commercial stop. By 1870, Waco had a 475-foot suspension bridge—built with 2.7 million local bricks, it was the first bridge to cross the Brazos, and helped to drive the cattle trails right through town. The bridge is still an important part of the town landscape and a site of many festivals and events; Indian Springs Park sits on the west bank of the river, Martin Luther King Jr. Park on the east, and a Riverwalk connects the bridge to the Waco tourist info center and several attractions.

Throughout the early 1900s, Waco continued to grow, becoming a railroad and commerce hub and a major cotton center; the first Cotton Palace Pageant was held here in 1894 and still takes place every April. The boom gave Waco a lot of honors—first skyscraper west of the Mississippi (the still-standing Alico Building), the oldest continually operated university in Texas (Baylor, founded in 1886)—and helped create its leafy neighborhoods and historic buildings. Unfortunately, much of that was damaged in 1953, when an F5 tornado—the tenth-deadliest in U.S. history—touched down in town. Because of the bluffs around the Brazos River, Waco is typically protected from extreme weather and remains mild all year long, but on that May day, freak winds propelled the tornado directly into town, where it killed 114 people, destroyed hundreds of homes and businesses, and damaged a few hundred more, including the Dr. Pepper Bottling Plant. (The Suspension Bridge survived.) While Waco pulled itself together after the event, the effects of the tornado are considered among the main reasons why the city didn't grow as substantially in following years as nearby places like Austin.

Then came the 1990s: Whoever said that all publicity was good publicity probably didn't live in Waco in that decade. During the standoff, raid, and subsequent tragedy at the Branch Davidian cult compound in 1993, the international media descended on the town, and the name "Waco" became, for a time, synonymous with those bizarre and controversial happenings. No matter that the compound was actually some ways out of town. ("They would show these reporters standing in the middle of a flat, empty field, and underneath them it would say "Waco, Texas" on the screen—when they were nowhere near the city," a local griped recently.) A similar misconception occurred during the presidency of George W. Bush, whose "Western White House" in Crawford, Texas, was 20 miles from Waco. Again, reporters made the city their base—but often showed footage of brush clearing out in the countryside.

Happily, these days Waco is making a name for itself in other ways, thanks to an influx of businesses, a nationally recognized zoo, and a lot of pleasant, quality-of-life touches that are attracting residents. A free trolley runs from downtown to Baylor, there are lots of activities taking place in the riverside parks, and the lush Riverwalk will be expanded in 2010. (On the celebrity font, Steve Martin, Jessica Simpson, and Jennifer Love Hewitt were all born here.)

# getting there

For a closer look, take I-35 south for about 96 miles. Most of the main attractions, including the Dr. Pepper Museum, Cameron Park Zoo, and museums at the Baylor campus can be reached by taking exit 335B; the downtown is on the west side of the highway, Baylor on the east. Note that in town, I-35 is also sometimes referred to as Jack Kultgen Highway.

# where to go

**Armstrong Browning Library.** 710 Speight, on the Baylor University Campus, Waco; (254) 710-3566; www.browninglibrary.org. An elegant, Italianite structure on the Baylor campus houses the personal collection of Dr. A. Joseph Armstrong, head of the university's English Department from 1912 to 1952. Dr. Armstrong spent years studying the lives and work of nineteenth-century poets Robert Browning and Elizabeth Barrett Browning, most famous for their love letters, and this special archive—the most extensive in the world—is the result. Find furniture and memorabilia from the Brownings' home (donated by their descendants); artwork and sculptures depicting the poets and their friends or created by their son, Pen, a celebrated artist; and countless books, letters, manuscripts, and research materials. The library is also known for its sixty-two stained glass windows, believed to be the largest group of secular stained glass anywhere. The panes are located in the main foyer, the research hall, and several alcoves, and most celebrate specific Browning poems. Tip: Ask a library staffer to let you onto a little balcony on the administration floor, which offers the best views of the grand foyer windows. The beauty of the building and the romance of the Brownings' story have made this a popular choice for weddings, but the library gets so many requests it has had to severely restrict the number. Free. Mon through Fri, 9 a.m. to 5 p.m., Sat, 9 a.m. to noon.

**Cameron Park Zoo.** 1701 N. 4th St., Waco; (254) 750-8400; www.cameronparkzoo.com. Touted by *Wildlife Conservation Magazine* as the "best zoo in the U.S.," this gem is tucked away on 52 acres of the 416-acre Cameron Park, in a relatively undeveloped area bordering the Brazos River. The focus here is on recreating natural habitats with lush foliage, traditional shelters, and not a lot of cages, and on letting visitors get as up-close-and-personal as possible. Kids can interact with otters while sliding down a glass tube through the otter area, while everyone can spy giraffe, elephants, and rhino on the "African Savannah," check out primates on Gibbon Island, and walk though an underwater world in the Brazos River Country exhibit. The recently added Asian Forest section houses a Komodo dragon and several orangutans, which can be spotted swinging from treetops and jumping around on giant hammocks. (In a show of allegiance to his new hometown, one of the orangutans loves—what else?—Diet Dr. Pepper.) There are also natural trails, a Tree Top Café, and a large play area with fountains and tree houses. Adults, $9, children under 12, $6. Mon through Sat, 9 a.m. to 5 p.m., Sun, 11 a.m. to 5 p.m., closed on Thanksgiving, Christmas, and New Year's Day, and the last Friday and Saturday in June.

**Dr. Pepper Museum.** 300 S. 5th St., Waco; (254) 757-1025; www.drpeppermuseum .com. If you're new to Texas, you might have noticed that the state is a little obsessed with a certain beverage (and it's not beer). The oldest major soft drink in America, Dr. Pepper was created at the Old Corner Drug Store in Waco by Dr. Charles Alderton, in 1885—scooping Coca-Cola by one year. Back then, the drink was even known as "Waco"—as in, "Gimme a shot of Waco." Built in 1906, this building housed the Artesian Manufacturing and Bot- tling Company—the first Dr. Pepper manufacturing facility—and was turned into a museum in 1989. Inside, you'll find an homage to the soft drink in general, and Dr. P in particular: vintage cans, antique freezers and soda machines, memorabilia, videos of commercials spanning several decades, and much more. Workshops throughout the year allow kids to create their own soda idea, and teach them about marketing and enterprise. Of course, there's also a gift shop and a soda fountain serving floats, malts, and "fresh" Dr. Pepper. Adults, $7, kids, $3. Mon through Sat., 10 a.m. to 4:15 p.m., Sun, noon to 4:15 p.m.; soda fountain and gift shop open until 5 p.m. Hours are extended during high season, so call ahead to confirm.

**Historic Homes.** (254) 753-5166; www.historicwaco.org. The Historic Waco Foundation manages four beautiful historic homes in town, all of which are open for tours on Sat to Sun., 2 to 5 p.m., and by appointment. (The East Terrace house is also open Tues through Fri. 11 a.m. to 3 p.m.) The properties include the 1870s McCulloch House, once the cen- ter of Waco's social scene; and the Greek Revival Earle-Napier-Kinnard house, with its Victorian-era Teeling Playhouse. Call or visit the site for more info. Admission to one house is $3 for adults, $2.50 for seniors, and $2 for students; each additional house is an extra $2 per person.

Another historic home, the Earle-Harrison House and Pape Gardens, is operated by the G. H. Pape Foundation. The only restored Greek Revival–style antebellum house in Waco that's open to the public, this striking property was once the home of a Confederate general, before facing demolition in the 1970s. Now faithfully preserved, the grounds include a five-acre botanical garden complete with lily pond, herb and vegetable gardens, and a 75-foot rose arbor. The house and grounds are open by appointment, Mon through Thu, 8 a.m. to 8 p.m., and on the first Sunday of each month; admission is $5 for a guided tour. Call (254) 753-2032 or visit www.earleharrison.com for details.

**Homestead Heritage.** Halbert Lane, Elm Mott; (254) 757-9600; www.homesteadheritage .com. To reach this attraction just north of Waco, take exit 343 off I-35 and head west on FM 308. Go 3 miles to FM 933, turn north, and travel 1.5 miles to Halbert Lane. Turn west on this street, which takes you the visitors center.

Get a glimpse into another world at this 510-acre homesteading community, where residents live and work in a traditional manner. Watch artists creating pottery, quilts, baskets, and furniture in the crafts center, see wheat being ground in the 1830s gristmill, and take a walking tour of the farm and ranch. The popular deli and bakery serves fresh, homemade dishes including soups, salads, and sandwiches, plus burgers, sausages, and brisket made with all-natural, grass-fed beef. The bread and buns are made on-site using stone-ground flour, as are the delicious pies and pastries; all are available to take home. (The fresh ice cream is best eaten here.) Homestead also hosts some notable festivals throughout the year, including an annual Labor Day Sorghum Festival and the Craft & Children's Fair, complete with carriage rides, barn raisings, apple-cider pressing, and much more; dates vary, so check the Web site for details.

**Mayborn Museum Complex.** 1300 S. University Parks Dr., Waco; (254) 710-1110; www.maybornmusum.com. Families will find lots to explore at this well-done complex on the Baylor campus. In the main building, there are sections on natural history, with animal skeletons (check out the 75-million-year-old sea turtle!) and exhibits on various habitats; rooms that take you through local history, from the dino days (complete with a 28-foot-long model of a Pilosaur and a replica of the mammoth site) to the time of the Native Americans and pioneers; and sixteen themed Discovery Rooms, where kids can get more hands-on (don't miss walking through the giant model of a heart). One cool touch: the museum offers cell phone audio tours for certain sections; ask for details. Outside, stroll past and into fifteen original wood frame buildings in the Historic Village, which offers more insight to the area's early days. Adults, $6, kids under 12, $4. Free the first Sunday of the month. Mon through Wed and Fri through Sat, 10 a.m. to 5 p.m.; Thurs, 10 a.m. to 8 p.m.; Sun, 1 to 5 p.m.

**Texas Ranger Hall of Fame and Museum.** 100 Texas Ranger Trail (exit 335B of I-35, at University Parks. Dr.), Waco; (254) 750-8631; www.texasranger.org. Identified by their signature cowboy hats and silver star badges, the elite Texas Rangers, the state's oldest law enforcement agency, are tasked with solving crimes and tracking down fugitives. This fascinating museum's various galleries focus on different aspects of Ranger history, as well as police work in general. Check out police equipment from the early days to the present; sections on famous cases tackled by the Rangers; historic firearms (including guns found on Bonnie and Clyde after their shoot-out with the Rangers); and exhibits on Women and the Rangers. There's also an extensive back room with movie- and TV-related Ranger memorabilia, from vintage movie posters to the *Walker, Texas Ranger* hat. Adults, $6, kids, $3; Daily, 9 a.m. to 5 p.m., closed major holidays.

**Texas Sports Hall of Fame.** 1108 S. University Parks Dr., Waco; (254) 756-1633; www.tshof.org. Fans of professional, college, and high school sports will cheer this tribute to Texas teams and distinguished athletes. You can watch classic replays in the Tom Landry Theater, learn university fight songs, see a Heisman Trophy up close, browse tons of photos and memorabilia, trace the evolution of the tennis racket, and see items from the inaugural game of the new Cowboys Stadium. The Hall of Fame tributes are divided into three sections: the Texas Sports Hall of Fame, honoring professional athletes (Texas was the first state to have such a facility), the Texas Tennis Hall of Fame, and the Texas High School

Football Hall of Fame. Adults, $6, students (K through college), $3. Mon through Sat, 9 a.m. to 5 p.m., Sun, noon to 5 p.m.

**Waco Mammoth Site.** 6220 Steinbeck Bend Rd., Waco; (254) 750-5980; www.waco mammoth.org. Take exit 335C off I-35 and head west on Martin Luther King Boulevard (which turns into Steinbeck Road) to get to this unique site, which opened to the public in late-2009. In 1979, a large bone was discovered in a ravine near the Bosque River, and that was just the tip of the iceberg. Thirty years of excavation have revealed the largest known concentration of Pleistocene mammoths dying from the same event, and the only recorded discovery of a nursery herd. Visitors can walk along bridges in the dig shelter to spot the giant remains below. Shaded with cedar, mesquite, and oak trees, the wooded one-hundred-acre park also include scenic trails and rest areas. Adults, $7, kids 3 to 12, $5, under 3, free. Tues through Fri., 11 a.m. to 5 p.m., Sat, 9 a.m. to 5 p.m., Sun through Mon, closed.

**Waco Tourist Office.** 106 Texas Ranger Trail, next to the Texas Rangers Museum; take exit 335B off I-35; (254) 750-8696 or (800) 922-6386; www.wacocvb.com. Get a big Waco welcome at this visitors center, along with brochures, maps, and help planning itineraries. Waco has a very well-organized and informative Web site, as well (you can even chat with a "Waco Specialist" online), so be sure to check that for more info. Mon through Sat, 8 a.m. to 5 p.m., Sun, 10 a.m. to 5 p.m.

# where to shop

**Bloom & Bee Swanky.** 210 S. 5th St., Waco; (254) 753-2292; beeswanky.blogspot.com. Voted as one of the Top 45 Stores in Texas by shopacrosstexas.com, this stylish home-furnishings boutique showcases owner Amy Bradshaw's vintage and vintage-inspired finds, along with new products like fragrance and apothecary items. The stock might include reupholstered vintage chairs, rings and heart-shaped pendants made from recycled antique flatware, and soft, decorative pillowcases created from repurposed French grain sacks. There are also antiques, Fenton glass and collectibles, gourmet foods, linens and bedding, and a selection of one-of-a-kind clothing. Mon through Sat, 10:30 a.m. to 5:30 p.m.

**The Shops of River Square Center.** At 2nd and Franklin Streets in downtown, Waco; (254) 757-0921; www.shopsofriversquarecenter.com. A one-hundred-year-old former hardware building has been turned into Waco's hippest retail hub. Find a cafe, a hair salon and, downstairs, the Spice furniture and home decor store, which has drawn customers from as far as Dallas and Austin with its well-curated mix of wares. Upstairs, dozens of indie designer booths are housed under one roof. Browse trendy Lucky Lady cowboy boots, Kaboodle handmade pendants, Girl Next Door vintage and reworked clothing and furniture, and bespoke shoes and bags by Zoe Rios. Mon through Sat, 10 a.m. to 6 p.m., Sun, noon to 5 p.m.

**Show and Tell Antiques.** 1525 Morrow Ave., Waco; (800) 486-5372; www.showandtell waco.com. Since 1972, discerning customers and collectors have been heading here for high-quality art, cut and pattern glass, silver, china, and stemware. The shop specializes in nineteenth-century art glass and Early American pattern glass, but there's a wide array of diverse pieces. Tues through Sat, 10:30 a.m. to 4:30 p.m., and by appointment.

**Sironia.** 1509 Austin St., Waco; (254) 757-7467; www.shopsironia.com. With Amelia's restaurant in the middle and over forty individual designer booths spread out over two floors, this upscale spot has become a one-stop-shop for unique goods. Find children's toys at Once Upon a Time, contemporary clothing and accessories at Panache, custom jewelry at The Design House, and antiques and gifts at Designs by Betsey, plus lots of stationery, candles, beauty products, and fashions throughout. Tues through Sat, 10 a.m. to 6 p.m.; cafe Tues through Sat, 11 a.m. to 2:30 p.m.; closed Sun through Mon.

## where to eat

**Buzzard Billy's Armadillo Bar & Grill-O.** 100 N. Jack Kultgen Fwy. (I-35), Waco; (254) 753-2778; www.buzzardbillys.com. Part of a four-restaurant chain through the Midwest (this is the only Texas location), Billy's serves Cajun-Creole dishes and a wide array of beers in a funky atmosphere. Experiment with fried Louisiana alligator tail, or stick to classics like crawfish étouffée, red beans and rice with sausage, chicken, or shrimp Creole and jambalaya. There are also lots of tasty appetizers, spicy soups, and gumbo, hearty chicken salad, po' boys, and creative pastas made with Creole herbs or Jamaican jerk flavors. The casual spot boasts a deck overlooking the Brazos River, and staffers will dole out rolls to

## the candy connection

*Dr. Pepper isn't the only sweet thing that calls Waco home: The city also produces all the Snickers bars for the United States. The Mars company, makers of the nutty bar, has eight plants in the country, each producing different treats, from Milky Way bars (made in Pennsylvania) to M&Ms (made in New Jersey). While the Chicago plant makes the Snickers minis, and the Georgia location the new Snickers Marathon, Waco is the only place to make the original Snickers—the country's number one candy bar. Unfortunately, the plant is not open to visitors (they are nuts about cleanliness and quality control), but you'll find the locally made treats at most Waco events and festivals. Rumor has it that when the White House press corps and staff were in town with former President George Bush (his Crawford Ranch is near town), they would often get sent bars fresh off the line.*

feed the turtles. Mon through Thurs, 11 a.m. to 10 p.m., Fri through Sun, 11 a.m. to 11 p.m. $–$$.

**Elite Circle Grille.** 2132 S. Valley Mills Dr., Waco; (254) 754-4941; www.elitecirclegrille .com. "Where the elite meet to eat," was the slogan of this cafe back in the early- and mid-1900s, a tongue-in-cheek reference to the fact that everyone from truckers to bankers could be found at its counters. Opened in 1919 in downtown Waco (the current location on the Circle, now at exit 333A off I-35, opened in 1941), the restaurant was founded by a family from Sparta, Greece, who continued to run it until 1985. Several notable things happened at the Elite: It was the first restaurant in town to use refrigeration, the first to have air-conditioning, and in the 1950s, it was a favorite of a young private stationed at nearby Fort Hood—some kid named Elvis Presley. Now refurbished to honor its heritage, the Grille serves attractively presented dishes like fajita nachos, Shiner Bock beer-battered onion rings, several fish and steak entrees and lunch-friendly salads, chicken sandwiches, and burgers. The atmosphere may be a tad more refined than in the early days, but this is still a casual and popular local favorite. Sun through Thurs, 11 a.m. to 10 p.m., Fri through Sat, 11 a.m. to 11 p.m. $–$$.

**George's.** 1925 Speight Ave., Waco; (254) 753-1421; www.georgesrestaurant.com. Anyone who grew up in Waco, attended Baylor, or has even driven regularly between Dallas and Austin on I-35 is sure to know this mainstay, where the beer and chicken-fried steak have been flowing since the 1930s. Originally called "Harry B's," then switched to "George's" in the 1960s, the casual eatery has in recent years increased its profile (they've catered to senators, governors, and former President Bush's staff out in Crawford), but the vibe is still collegiate and the eats still fried and juicy. In addition to a full breakfast menu, find wings, jalapeño poppers, Tex-Mex classics, seasoned shrimp, steaks, stuffed baked potatoes, and an array of creatively topped burgers. There are also lunch specials, and homemade key lime pie, bread pudding, and cobbler for dessert. If you're not the one behind the wheel, try the student favorite "Big O"—beer served in a giant fish-bowl glass. George's has been immortalized in songs by country singer Pat Green (a Waco native) and continues to host live music every Saturday night. Mon through Sat, 6:30 a.m. to midnight, closed Sunday. $$.

**Siete Mares.** 1915 Dutton Ave., Waco; (254) 714-1297; www.elsietemares.net. Look past an unimpressive exterior and very casual interior and you'll find creative, fresh fare that, according to *Texas Monthly* magazine, will "impress even the most jaded out-of-towner." (It was also the favorite of the White House staff and Press Corps when they were in town with President Bush.) Veracruz-style seafood is the specialty, with exotic choices like octopus marinated in lime and white wine, and eight types of seafood mixed with frog legs and rice, with chipotle sauce. Seviche, crab-stuffed avocados, marinated pork tacos, and a tangy yellow house salsa are other standouts. Tues through Sat, 11 a.m. to 2 p.m. and 5 to 10 p.m. $$.

**Uncle Dan's BBQ.** 1001 Lake Air Dr., Waco; (254) 772-4744; www.uncledansbbq.com. Another local haunt, Uncle Dan's has been serving "barbecue as tender as a mother's love" since 1978. Find all the staples, including brisket, smoked ribs, catfish and chicken-fried steak, with sides like mac and cheese, mashed taters, huge baked potatoes, and four kinds of beans. The smokehouse hamburgers are also popular, and most of the meats are also available as a sandwich. Non-carnivores have a selection of salads, cobblers, and pies. A to-go window makes take-out a breeze. Mon through Sat, 11 a.m. to 8:30 p.m. (To Go window open until 9 p.m.) $.

## where to stay

**The Cotton Palace B&B.** 1910 Austin Ave., Waco; (254) 753-7294 and (877) 632-2312; www.thecottonpalace.com. A 1910 Arts and Crafts–style house has been beautifully restored to house a three-story B&B, set on a picturesque street just minutes from downtown. The seven individually decorated rooms and suites include private baths, posh linens, and cable TV, while some boast whirlpool tubs. Everyone enjoys a full homemade breakfast (selections might include lemon soufflé pancakes or scratch-made cream cheese bread) as well as complimentary drinks and a "bottomless" cookie jar all day. $$.

**Hilton Waco Hotel.** 113 S. University Parks Dr., Waco; (254) 754-8484; www.waco.hilton .com. Located just across from the Shops of RiverSquare Center and the warehouse entertainment district, this chain link offers easy access to area attractions, the Brazos Riverwalk, and Indian Springs Park. Expect all the amenities typical of the chain, including an outdoor pool and on-site restaurant. $$–$$$.

**The Livingston at Heritage Square.** 330 Austin Ave., Waco; (800) 651-1664; www.the livingston.com. Drawing on her background as an interior designer and editor for several national home design magazines, owner Mary Baskin has created a lovely hidden gem in the heart of downtown. The inn offers five one-, two-, or three-bedroom suites, all with fully equipped kitchens, washer and dryer, flat-panel TVs, and free Internet. Each apartment-sized suite is decorated in a style evoking a different city's neighborhood—New York's Upper East Side, London's Richmond Hill, Paris' St. Germain—but it's all done with high-end furnishings and a discerning eye, so the result is glossy, not kitschy. $$.

# day trip 04

**girlfriends' getaway:**
salado

# salado

Set along the beginning of Texas's rolling Hill Country, just off I-35 between Waco and Austin, Salado is doable for a day trip, but also a charming spot for an overnight getaway. Boasting an illustrious history, the village in recent years has established itself as a haven for artists, antiques stores, and tearooms, and as a result has become a popular spot for weddings, bridal parties, and girlfriend weekends. Though it's located deep in the heart of Texas, the town remains a little quirky—an enclave where you're more likely to find wine-and-gallery walks, lunching ladies, and an annual Chocolate & Art Festival than BBQ and football games.

Salado's sophisticated tastes can likely be traced back to its roots: The creekside village was founded in 1859 as a place for Salado College, which became one of Bell County's finest schools. The town developed into both an agricultural and industrial center, growing to become the second biggest settlement in the county by the 1880s; at the time, you could find three cotton gins, seven churches, fourteen stores, and the county's first bridge—a wire cable suspension version—in town. Close to two lakes and a river, Salado was also the site of a main stagecoach stop on the cattle trails between San Antonio and Missouri, and its still-operating Stagecoach Inn is the longest continuously running hotel in Texas.

Once the college closed in the late 1880s, the old stone buildings were taken over until 1913 by Thomas Arnold High School, a private school that counted a Rhodes Scholar among its graduates. Though the town population dipped drastically pre– and post–World

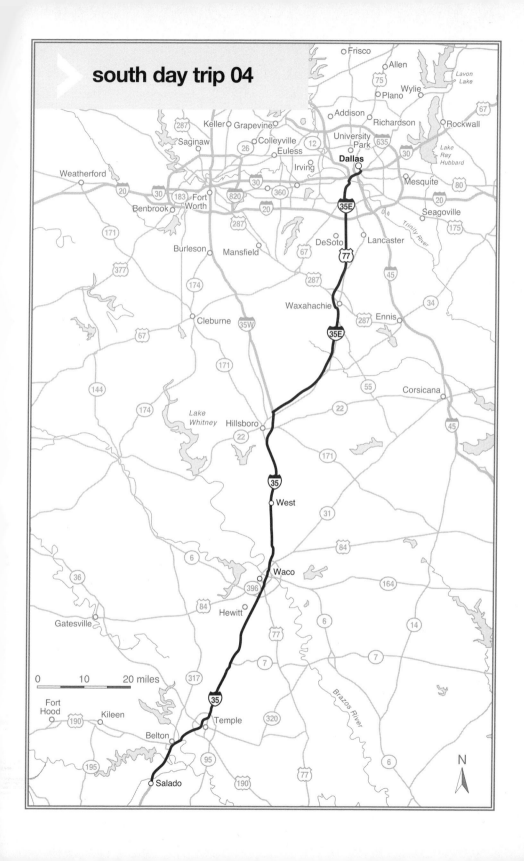

south day trip 04

War II, Salado held on to its history, making sure to preserve it for generations to come. In 1966, Salado Creek was designated as the state's first Natural Landmark, and today, the town has twenty-three Texas Historical Markers and eighteen buildings on the National Register of Historic Places. One interesting side note: For 120 years, Salado functioned without a local city government. In 2000, however, when faced with the prospect of being annexed by nearby Belton, residents voted in favor of incorporation and elected their first mayor. (If you want to meet her, head to the home decor store Charlotte's of Salado—she's the owner.)

## getting there

To reach Salado's historic district, head south on I-35, following the signs for the town; Salado is about 145 miles south of Dallas. When coming from the north, you will take exit 284 on to Thomas Arnold Road and turn left, doubling back under I-35 to head east into town. Thomas Arnold Road ends at Main Street.

## on the way

Along the way, you may want to stop and refuel—the car, and yourself—in West, Texas, located a little over halfway to Salado. Take exit 353 off I-35, head under the highway to the northbound service road, and pull into the famous **Czech Stop and Little Czech Bakery** (254-826-4179; www.czechstop.net). Outside, there are gas pumps; inside, home-baked goodness in the form of pound cakes, fried pies, cookies, cupcakes, nut brittle, and fresh loaves of bread. Most popular are the kolaches, Czech pastries filled with fruit, sausage, poppy seeds, and more. Open twenty-four hours a day, seven days a week.

## where to go

**Central Texas Area Museum.** 423 S. Main St., Salado; (254) 947-5232; www.ctam-salado.org. Learn about the history and development of the region and its early frontier settlers at this museum, which is housed in a century-old rock structure near Salado Creek. The museum is also the site of an annual gathering of all the Scottish clans of Texas, as well as a resource for people researching their genealogy. Open Tues through Sat, 10 a.m. to 5 p.m. Admission by donation.

**Mill Creek Inn & Golf Course.** 1610 Club Circle., Salado; (254) 947-5698; www.millcreek-golf.com. Play a round or two on courses designed by top golf architect Robert Trent Jones Jr., under shade of elm and oak trees. Greens fees range from $25 to $55, depending on the time of day, season, and day of the week; tee times must be reserved in advance over the phone. The club strictly enforces a dress code of collared or golf shirts for men (must be tucked in), appropriate golf attire for women, and no denim for either. Condo-style accommodations are available at the inn.

**Salado Silver Spur Theater.** 108 Royal St., Salado; (254) 947-3456; www.saladosilver spur.com. Not your typical regional theater, the Silver Spur's calendar has a little something for everyone: well-known dramatic plays like *Steel Magnolias,* original melodramas, live variety shows with vaudeville-style acts and slapstick galore, and even silent movies accompanied by live music.

**Salado Visitors Center.** 881 N. Main St., Salado; (254) 947-8634; www.salado.com. Stop by this cute wooden bungalow at the far end of Main Street to pick up brochures, browse menus, or just sit a spell on the porch. Regular hours are Mon through Fri, 8:30 a.m. to 4:30 p.m., but volunteers often man the office on weekends during high season; call ahead to confirm.

**Tablerock Festival of Salado.** 409 Royal St., Salado; (254) 947-9205; www.tablerock .org. Started in 1979, this nonprofit arts organization is named for a limestone table–shaped monolith set near Salado Creek that was once a meeting place for local Native Americans. Throughout the year, the group presents musical and theatrical performances at the rock and adjacent Goodnight Amphitheater; poetry readings, holiday plays, "Fright Trail" ghost walks, and a show detailing the legends of Salado are among the regular events.

## where to shop

Over sixty boutiques, antiques stores, galleries, and design stores line Main Street and the side roads in old Salado; a detailed shopping guide is available at the visitors center. Some notable spots include:

**Antique Rose of Bell.** 402 N. Main St., Salado; (254) 947-3330. American and European antiques, pottery, vintage jewelry, collectibles, and more are displayed throughout this late-Victorian-style home, built in 1885. Open weekends and holidays from 10 a.m. to 5 p.m., and by appointment.

**Charlotte's of Salado.** 8 Rock Creek, Salado; (254) 947-0240; www.charlottesofsalado .com. Sip on complimentary house-blended coffee while browsing rooms packed with furnishings, housewares, floral arrangements, and gifty knickknacks. The atmosphere is very relaxed and welcoming, so if you have any questions about Salado or want recommendations, feel free to ask store owner Charlotte Douglass, who's served as both the town's mayor and chamber of commerce chairwoman. Mon through Sat, 9:30 a.m. to 5:30 p.m., Sun, 10:30 a.m. to 5 p.m.

**Mud Pies Pottery.** 18 N. Main St., Salado; (254) 947-0281; www.mudpiespottery.com. Open for over sixteen years, this maker of functional and decorative stoneware pottery is famous for its egg baker/egg poacher dishes, which are microwave and dishwasher safe. All items are handmade at either this location or two new studio outposts. Along with the ceramics, Mud Pies carries over fifty flavors of Sir Wigglesworth's Homemade Fudge. Mon through Sat, 11 a.m. to 5:30 p.m.

**Salado Wine Seller & Salado Winery.** 841 N. Main St., Salado; (254) 947-8011; www .saladowinery.com. Part tasting room, part winery, with a rotating art gallery thrown in, this lively spot has become something of a social hub for locals, thanks in large part to their fun events like wine-and-cheese nights and, on the first Saturday of each month, Jammin' on the Lawn live music days (bring your own lawn chair). A range of Texas wines are poured by the taste or glass, and sold by the bottle or case; the knowledgeable staff can guide you through the choices. On-site winemaking facilities are set to open in 2010. Sun through Wed, 12 to 6 p.m.; Thurs through Sat, noon to 7 p.m.

**Ya Gotta Have It.** 230 N Main St., Ste.101, Salado; (254) 947-5752. Stock up on Texas- and Tex-Mex-themed gourmet foods and gifts, from salsas, chips, and jams to hand-blown Mexican glass pieces. Pastas, drink mixers, and other edible goodies are thrown in for good measure. Mon through Sat, 10 a.m. to 6 p.m., Sun, 10 a.m. to 5 p.m.

# where to eat

**Adelea's on Main.** 302 N. Main St., Salado; (254) 947-0018; www.adeleas.com. Set in a restored 1925 home, this local favorite was opened in 2008 by sisters/trained chefs Jennifer Lohse Angell and Lea Anne Lohse Erwin, who named the place after their maternal grand-mother. (Lea Anne has since sold her half to Jennifer's husband, Kelly, who the sisters met in culinary school.) The menu pays homage to Grandma Adelea's classic recipes—chicken and dumplings, fresh quiches, tarragon chicken salad—while also offering gourmet twists, like homemade blue cheese kettle chips and chipotle shrimp wraps. The main restaurant serves lunch, dinner, and lovely afternoon tea, complete with finger sandwiches and platters of homemade desserts; a twenty-four-hour advance reservation is required for the teas. The adjacent Hemingway's Bar hosts Happy Hour Thu through Sat, from 3 to 6 p.m. (try the house sangria). Tues through Wed, 11 a.m. to 4 p.m., Thu through Sat, 11 a.m. to 9 p.m., closed Sun and Mon. $$–$$$.

**Ambrosia Tea Room.** 102 N. Main St., inside the Salado Haus Gift Shop, Salado; (254) 947-3733. A decor of vintage hats, shoes, and dresses—many for sale—adorn this charm-ing cottage overseen by proprietress Jane Voight, who also pays homage to Audrey Hep-burn throughout with black-and-white photos and quotes on the menus. Open for lunch and tea only, the restaurant serves staples like chicken salad, cucumber, and pimento cheese sandwiches, homemade soups, and decadent baked goods, all washed down with house-blend drinks like cranberry-lemon tea. They've got their own cookbook, too. Tues through Sat, 11 a.m. to 4 p.m. (lunch served until 3 p.m.), closed Sun and Mon. $–$$.

**The Range at the Barton House.** 101 N. Main St., Salado; (254) 947-3828; www .therangerestaurant.com. Chef Dave Hermann's Mediterranean-meets-country fine dining menu has earned accolades across the state, leading guests to drive to Salado especially for a meal at The Range. Dishes like crawfish-stuffed quail, three cheese tortellini, and grilled Tuscan Rib Eye are elegantly prepared and presented, along with a well-chosen wine list. Dinner served Tues through Sat, beginning at 5 p.m.; reservations required. $$$.

**Roy T's Old Salado Bakery.** 100 N. Church St., Salado; (254) 947-7181; www.oldsalado bakery.com. Locals load up on the sandwiches, salads, hand-tossed pizza, pies, and beignets served out of this converted Austin farmhouse. Goodies are available to go or for enjoying on the patio. Mon, 7 a.m. to noon, Tues through Thu, 7 a.m. to 3 p.m., Fri through Sat, 7 a.m. to 5 p.m., closed Sunday. $.

**Stagecoach Inn and Dining Room.** 401 S. Stagecoach Rd., Salado; (254) 947-5111 or (800) 732-8994; www.staystagecoach.com. As the longest continuously running inn in the state, the Stagecoach has seen a lot of history, much of which has traipsed in and out of its main dining room. Open for lunch and dinner, the restaurant serves a rotating menu of classics, from prime rib and rolls to chicken-fried steak prepared using a 150-year-old recipe. And just like the old days, the menu is recited verbally to each guest. The eighty-two accommodations feature one king or two full beds, and are spread out over grounds that include a swimming pool and conference center. Free Wi-Fi access. The on-site Stagecoach Club serves drinks every night except Sunday. $$.

# where to stay

In addition to Mill Creek Inn & Golf Club and the Stagecoach Inn (see above), these are some notable independently owned lodgings in town:

**Inn at Salado.** 307 N. Main St., Salado; (727) 894-1000; www.inn-at-salado.com. Salado's first B&B enjoys a prime location on Main Street, in the middle of the historic village center. Eleven guest rooms and one cottage are spread out in the 1872 former private residence, which has been listed with the National Register and boasts a Texas Historical Marker. Along with its antiques-laden accommodations and friendly staff, the inn is best known for its signature breakfast, which fills you up with biscuits, waffles, sausage gravy, and home-made quiche. $–$$.

**Inn on the Creek.** 602 Center Circle; (254) 947-5554; www.inncreek.com. A gourmet restaurant, elegant Alexander's Distillery bar and fourteen lovely guest rooms and suites— each with private, vintage-inspired baths— make up this romantic Victorian inn, where the landscaped grounds gently slope down toward Salado Creek. On Friday and Saturday, a four-course "dining experience"—complete with cocktails on the porch—is open to both hotel guests and outsiders (reservations are a must for both). The inn also manages a two-bedroom, two-bath cottage set one block away. $$.

**Old Salado Springs Retreat and Celebration Center.** 200 Royal St., Salado; (254) 947-5933; www.oldsaladosprings.com. The eight suites and cottages at this B&B are done up in themes like "Monet," "Zanzibar," and "Key West," with American and European antiques to match. Each comes with complimentary soda, water, and coffee, and a full breakfast with weekend bookings. The retreat hosted the rehearsal dinner and wedding day BBQ of former First Daughter Jenna Bush. $$.

# southwest

# day trip 01

southwest

>>> **the iconic small town:**
granbury

# granbury

When producers at CNN were planning their coverage of the Millennium New Year's festivities back in 1999, they were looking to include footage of one quintessential small town amid shots of the big international cities Their choice: Granbury, Texas, a growing lakeside community located about 30 miles southwest of Dallas/Fort Worth. So between images of the Washington Monument and Times Square, America was treated to scenes of fireworks around one of the most picturesque town squares in the country.

As the county seat of Hood County, with a strategic location along the Brazos River, Granbury started as a collection of log cabins around a square, but soon grew into a bustling Western town. Its Opera House, built in 1886, brought in crowds from miles around, while its prosperity (and saloons) attracted a number of notable, and notorious, residents; at one time or another, Davy Crockett, Jesse James, and Abraham Lincoln assassin John Wilkes Booth—who reportedly was hiding out under the name John St. Helen—are said to have lived in the area.

Thanks to the foresight of city leaders and prominent residents, Granbury began protecting and restoring its historic buildings in the 1970s—earlier than many small towns—and as a result, has been attracting tourists for decades. The Victorian-era Granbury Courthouse Square, consistently named one of the best in Texas, was the first in the state to be added in its entirety to the National Register of Historic Places, and went on to become the model

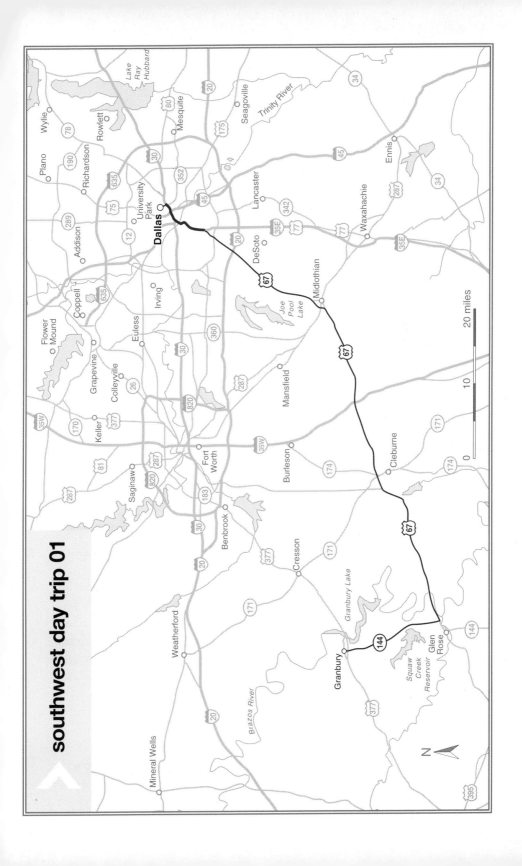

southwest day trip 01

for the National Trust's Main Street preservation program. With the damming of the Brazos River in 1969 and the creation of winding, snakelike Lake Granbury, the town also became a recreation hub for swimmers, boaters, and fisherman; in 2008, a wide beach was created along the lake's shores with sand imported from South Padre Island.

While tourism remains Granbury's primary industry (a fact reflected in the sophistication, and pricing, of many of the square-side shops and restaurants), it's also just a really nice place to live. Locals shop and dine along the square as much as the visitors, and there always seems to be some type of festival, market, or live music performance taking place around the courthouse. It's become a haven for artists and, as it continues to expand, a draw for retirees and those looking to escape the Metroplex rat race.

## getting there

To reach Granbury, take I-35E south to US 67 west, toward Glen Rose. Just before Glen Rose, connect to TX 144 north, directly into Granbury. Alternatively, take I-30 or I-20 west, passing through Fort Worth, then take the exit for TX 171 south (just outside of Weatherford) toward Cresson and Granbury. TX 171 connects to US 377, which leads into town. Along either way, keep your eyes open for a windmill or two—many functional ones still dot the countryside.

## where to go

**Granbury Live.** 110 N. Crockett St., Granbury; (817) 573-0303 or (800) 989-8240; www .granburylive.com. Nostalgia is the name of the game at this performance center, which puts on professional, family-friendly, Branson, Missouri–style musical revues.

**Granbury Opera House.** 133 E. Pearl St., Granbury; (817) 573-9191 or (800) 547-4697; www.granburyoperahouse.net. Since 1975, this restored nineteenth-century theater has hosted an annual calendar of musicals, plays, melodramas, and holiday specials, starring both out-of-town professional troupes and community theater players (including students from the Opera House Theater School). In 2009, a cable ghost-hunting show claimed to have found the spirit of John Wilkes Booth lurking in the building.

**Granbury State Historical Cemetery.** 801 N. Houston St., Granbury; (800) 950-2212. Visit the final resting places of town namesake/Civil War General Hiram Granbury, members of Alamo hero Davy Crockett's family, and (supposedly) outlaw Jesse James.

**Granbury Tourism Bureau.** 621 East Pearl St., Granbury; (682) 936-1205 or (800) 936-1201; www.granburytx.com. Stop by this visitors center, located just off the square, for brochures, suggestions, and maps on walking and driving tours of historical markers. Open Tues through Sat, 10 a.m. to 6 p.m., Sun, noon to 4 p.m.

**Hood County Jail and Museum.** 208 N. Crockett St., Granbury; (817) 573-5135. A block from the square, this classic Old Western stone jail was built in 1885, and still includes the original cell block and hanging tower—where locals swear you can often feel a ghostly chill or two. The adjacent museum gives you a glimpse into Granbury and Hood County history through artifacts and memorabilia. Sat through Sun, 1 to 4 p.m.

**Lake Granbury & Granbury City Beach.** There are numerous parks and recreational areas set along the lake, with most offering water access for swimming, fishing, water ski-ing, or boating; check with the visitors center for more details. Created in 2008 with sand

## local outlaws (and ghosts)

*Walking around pretty, cheery Granbury, it's easy to understand why so many city folks are choosing to move or retire to this community. Historically, though, the town has also attracted more than its fair share of notorious residents. Legend has it that Jesse James lived here to a ripe old age (despite reports that he had been killed in Missouri in 1882), and is buried in the Granbury Cemetery. William Bon-ney, better known as Billy the Kid, was also supposed to have come through town before settling in nearby Hico (though New Mexico claims he was killed in that state years earlier).*

*These days, the outlaw that gets the most attention in town is John Wilkes Booth, the actor who assassinated Abraham Lincoln. In the early 1870s, a man named John St. Helen moved to Granbury, where he lived for several years tend-ing bar at a saloon on the square and working as a teacher. (Murals supposedly painted by St. Helen can still be seen at Rinky Tink's soda shop.) A fan of Shake-speare, St. Helen also frequently participated in performances at the Granbury Opera House. People say that after a few drinks, St. Helen was known to start rambling about government conspiracies, and that eventually, on his deathbed, he confessed to being John Wilkes Booth, even leading officials to the gun used in the assassination—which they found wrapped in a newspaper from the day Lincoln died. But instead of dying that day, St. Helen skipped town; years later, in 1903, an Oklahoma man named David George confessed to being both Booth and St. Helen, before dying there. Was the mysterious man really the famous assassin? Stories of Booth living in this part of Texas (including towns like Glen Rose and Bandera) abound, and in recent times, shows like 20/20 and Unsolved Mysteries have dug up enough evidence to make the claim credible. Granbury locals also say the Opera House is haunted by a tall, stately ghost with a limp who likes to quote Shakespeare and indulge in a monologue now and then. Whether or not the legend is true, in 2009 a movie about Booth was filmed in town—connecting him once again to the place where he may or may not have lived.*

imported from South Padre Island, the City Beach is located a one-minute drive from the historic center, at 623 E. Pearl St.; (817) 573-5548. Extremely popular during the warmer months, the beach features a Tiki Hut, boardwalk, kids' water area, and concession stands.

# where to shop

The streets around the Courthouse Square are lined with more than forty upscale boutiques, antiques and home stores, and gourmet food purveyors, most located in beautiful nineteenth-century buildings crafted in the distinctive local limestone; HISTORICAL MARKER signs along the way tell stories of the buildings' origins. In general, stores are open Mon through Thurs, 10 a.m. to 5 p.m., Fri through Sat, 10 a.m. to 6 p.m., and Sun noon to 5 p.m., but several retailers will stay open on weekends as long as there are browsing customers, so call ahead to check. Some shops worth a look include:

**The Art of Chocolate Shoppe.** 115 E. Pearl St., Granbury; (817) 579-0075; www.theartof chocolateshoppe.com. Enjoy sweets (and a few wines) from around the world, most made using natural ingredients and limited preservatives. The store also stocks treats from Wiseman's Chocolates, made in nearby Hico. Closed Sun.

**Bisque House.** 100 N. Crockett St., Granbury; (817) 579-9595; www.thebisquehouse .com. Paint your own pottery, play with clay, or create a glass or mosaic piece at this store/ creative arts studio. Mon through Wed, 10 a.m. to 7 p.m., Thurs, 10 a.m. to 8 p.m., Fri through Sat, 10 a.m. to 9 p.m., Sun, noon to 5 p.m.

**Brazos Moon.** 124 N. Houston St., Granbury; (817) 579-8202; www.brazosmoon.com. More than a dozen different antiques and collectibles dealers are featured in this store, which is chock-a-block with vintage tableware, artwork, antique coins, furniture, and a large selection of Bond Arms derringers and vintage Winchester rifles.

**Dakota's Kabin.** 202 N. Houston St., Granbury; (817) 579-0275; www.tdakotaskabin .com. Catering to the upscale cowgirl, this temple to Western and rustic carries everything from dishes, bedding, boots, and belt buckles to clothing, accessories, furnishings, and even themed Christmas trees. If you need a Texas-shaped kitchen sink strainer or a cowboy-covered light switch plate, it's here. The owner also runs a small B&B upstairs.

**Silverado Custom Boot Company.** 106 N. Lambert St., Granbury; (817) 219-7209. Head a block off the main square for boots, chaps, belts, purses, and knives.

**The Texas Sampler.** 127 E. Pearl St., Granbury; (817) 573-3486; www.texassamplerfoods .com. Stocking everything from chili spices, BBQ marinades, and salsas galore to honey butters, Dr. Pepper, and even a few bath/body products, this is the place for all things sweet, spicy, and scented.

# where to eat

**Cafe Nutt.** 121 E. Bridge St., Granbury; (817) 579-6868; cafenutt.com. Located inside the historic Nutt House Hotel (see below), this restaurant updates American classics with an international touch. Artisan cheese boards, shrimp popovers, and Greek salads can be paired with creamy tomato bisque, pecan-accented chicken salad, or prime rib Philly cheese steaks. Wed through Thurs, 11 a.m. to 9 p.m., Fri through Sat, 11 a.m. to 10 p.m., Sun, 11 a.m. to 2 p.m. $–$$.

**The Coffee Grinder.** 129 W. Pearl St., Granbury; (817) 279-0977; www.koffeegrinder .com. Devotees come for miles to Granbury's alternative to Starbucks both for the coffee (there are five special blends a day and over fifty-five kinds of beans available to take home) and the yummy frozen granitas; the latter comes in the perennial favorite mocha latte flavor, as well as a rotating selection of over seventy-one other tastes. Everyone who comes in gets a free deluxe-size sample of the granita—guaranteed to get you hooked. Mon through Thurs, 7 a.m. to 7 p.m., Fri through Sat, 7:30 a.m. to 11 p.m., Sun, 9 a.m. to 7 p.m. $.

**Hank's on the Square.** 115 E. Pearl St., Granbury; (817) 579-1116. Set through the small portico of a pretty stone building, this fun, spacious eatery cooks up huge quesadillas, hamburger sliders, "rabbit food" (i.e., salads), and Dr. Pepper cake. Daily, 11 a.m. to midnight. $.

**The Merry Heart Tea Room.** 110 N. Houston St., Granbury; (817) 573-3800; www .granburyrestaurants.com. A knickknack-filled gift area gives way to a wood-paneled back tearoom, where a steady stream of ladies (and quite a few gents) lunch on soups, salads, quiches, and sandwiches. The popular afternoon tea service includes fresh-baked scones and clotted cream. Sun through Thurs, 11 a.m. to 3 p.m., Fri through Sat, 11 a.m. to 6 p.m.; Afternoon Tea daily from 3 to 5 p.m. by reservation only. $–$$.

**Nutshell Eatery & Bakery.** 137 E Pearl St., Granbury; (817) 279-8989. The sense of history is palpable at this old-school cafe, where a steady stream of locals stop in for thick sandwiches on homemade bread, daily hot specials, chicken-fried steak, and burgers like the Hinden Burger (with blue cheese and fried onions) and the John Wilkes Booth (topped with cheddar and chopped bacon)—all made using fresh ingredients. Most popular are the house-made pies, including coconut cream and buttermilk flavors; the latter is made using a thirty-year-old recipe. There's a lot of history in the building, too: Built in 1885, it was once a saloon (with a questionable upstairs "hotel"), then later the town's premier dry goods store. John Wilkes Booth tended bar here under his alias, John St. Helen, and like many places in town, it's supposedly haunted. Daily, 7 a.m. to 5 p.m. $.

**Pearl Street Station.** 120 W. Pearl St., Granbury; (817) 579-7233; www.pearlststation granbury.com. A lively converted gas station is the setting for Cajun and BBQ staples like gumbo, crawfish étouffée, blackened catfish, and jalapeño cheese buns. Open Mon through Sat at 11 a.m. (until whenever). $.

**Rinky Tink's Sandwich & Ice-Cream Shop.** 108 N.Houston St., Granbury; (817) 573-4323; www.rinkytinks.com. "Elvis eats here," proclaims the chalkboard at this long-standing eatery, and judging by the decor, the King would certainly feel right at home. 1950s memorabilia, a working juke box, and classic soda shop vinyl seats set the scene for a menu of sandwiches (Frankie's Reuben is a favorite), Frito Pie, homemade desserts, and dozens of Blue Bell ice-cream concoctions. Note the murals on the wall behind the soda fountain, which were reportedly painted by John Wilkes Booth. Sun through Thurs, 11 a.m. to 5 p.m., Fri through Sat, 11 a.m. to 9 p.m. $.

**Stringfellow's.** 101 E. Pearl St., Granbury; (817) 573-6262; www.granburyrestaurants .com. Sink into an oversized leather armchair while tucking into classic dishes like hand-cut Angus beef, chicken picata, grilled salmon, and tilapia tacos. Though it proclaims itself as "casual," the clubby restaurant is a local favorite for special occasions, too. Thurs through Sun, 11 a.m. to 9 p.m. $–$$.

## where to stay

**Inn on Lake Granbury.** 205 W. Doyle St., Granbury; (817) 573-0046; www.innonlake granbury.com. Within walking distance of the historic center, this lovely hotel boasts manicured gardens, a pool with waterfall, and sweeping lake views. Each room is individually furnished; some feature balconies, porches, or fireplaces, while all include fine linens, in-room Internet access, and private baths. Rates include breakfast and afternoon drinks and snacks. $$$.

**Nutt House Hotel.** 119 E. Bridge St., Granbury; (817) 279-1207; www.nutt-hotel.com. Built in 1893 out of hand-hewn local stone, this majestic building once held the mercantile store and guest house of brothers Jake and Jesse Nutt, two of Granbury's most prominent early citizens who also happened to both be blind since childhood. Still in the Nutt family, the site has been operating some type of hotel or restaurant ever since, and today, guests enjoy the sense of history found in the handful of antiques-filled suites. $$.

# day trip 02

## southwest

**where the wild things were:**
glen rose

# glen rose

About 82 miles from Dallas, and just down TX 144 from Granbury, sits the Dinosaur Capital of Texas. It's all about the prehistoric in Glen Rose, a picturesque, relaxed town where even the distinctive local rock and limestone buildings help add to the *Flintstones* vibe. Here, you can climb on giant natural rock formations, compare your footprint with that of a dino, and camp out alongside zebras. Meanwhile, in the historic town square, antiques stores, chummy eateries, and quaint inns help bring to life the town's more recent past.

Once the site of a bustling, mid-nineteenth-century trading post between the settlers and Native Americans, Glen Rose's setting in the southwestern part of North Texas's Plains and Lakes region puts it not too far from the borders of Hill Country and the Panhandle Plains. The Paluxy River meets the Brazos River near here, resulting in a hilly landscape lush with oak, juniper, sycamore, pecan, and walnut trees. The area is also rich in limestone, sandstone, and mudstone, which experts say were deposited some 113 million years ago along the shores of an ancient sea. Over time, the Paluxy River has worn a path through some of these layered rock formations, revealing an impressive collection of dinosaur prints along the riverbeds.

The verdant terrain makes Glen Rose an ideal place for nature activities like hiking, biking, canoeing, and tubing on the river. At the Fossil Rim Wildlife Center, visitors can drive through a 1,700-acre park that houses exotic—and often nearly extinct—animals,

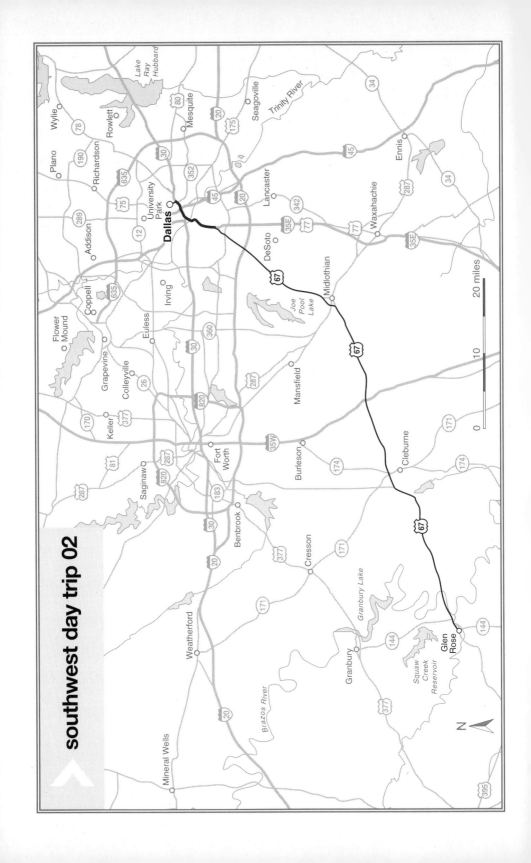

southwest day trip 02

from bongos, oryx, and kudu to giraffes, rhinos, and three types of zebras. (You can stay overnight there, too.) Meanwhile in town, antiques and home-baked goods can be spotted in their natural habitat.

## getting there

To reach Glen Rose from Dallas, take I-35E south toward Waco, merging onto I-35E/US 77 South. Take the US 67 South exit (423A) toward Cleburne; US 67 will lead into town. Take a left at Barnard Street to reach the historic center. From Granbury, TX 144 leads directly to Glen Rose.

## where to go

**Barnard's Mill & Art Museum.** 307 SW Barnard St., Glen Rose; (254) 897-7494 (weekends), (888) 346-6282 (weekdays); www.barnardsmill.org. Built in 1860 as a water-powered grist mill, Barnard's Mill churned out high-grade flour and cornmeal until it was turned into a cotton gin in 1895, then a health spa and hospital around World War II. In its latest incarnation, the restored mill and adjacent buildings house twelve rooms filled with over 200 original works of art, culled from the Fielder Foundation and previous owner Richard Moore's private collection. (The Mill now belongs to the Somervell History Foundation.) Open Sat, 10 a.m. to 5 p.m., Sun, 1 to 5 p.m.

**Big Rocks Park.** On Hwy.144/NE Barnard Street across from Oakdale park. Climb around on the—what else?—big boulders at this pretty park not far from the old town square.

**Camping and Water Sports.** Enjoy swimming, boating, canoeing, tubing, fishing, and more on Squaw Creek Lake (located four miles north of Glen Rose, off Hwy. 144) and along the Brazos and Paluxy Rivers. Companies like **Paluxy Outfitters** (www.paluxyoutfitters .com), **Low Water Bridge** (254-897-3666), and **Rhoades** (254-897-4212) rent canoes, tubes, and kayaks, and offer guides, lessons, overnight trips, and even round-trip transport to the river; hours are seasonal, so be sure to call ahead. **Tres Rios River Ranch** (254-221-0018) rents cabins and RV campsites.

**Dinosaur Valley State Park.** Park Road 59, 4 miles west of Glen Rose. Take US 67 to FM 205, then follow the signs to PR 59 and the park entrance. (254) 897-4588; www.tpwd .state.tx.us/park/dinosaur. Check out some of the best preserved dinosaur tracks in the world at this state park. The first tracks were found on this site in 1909, with later prints— including a double set of Sauropod tracks—discovered in the 1930s. Today, you can see footprints from three different types of dinosaurs, each a different shape and depth; the most unusual are the tracks made by a Pleurocoelus, which pair a four-toed clawprint with a horseshoe shape.

There are four main track sites in the park; pick up a free detailed map at the entrance. Most of the major tracks are located along the Paluxy River bed, so call ahead to check water level conditions, and avoid disappointment. The park also houses spots for picnicking and camping, and 12 miles of hiking and mountain biking trails. Daily, 8 a.m. to 10 p.m.; reservations recommended for camping. Admission $5.

**Dinosaur World.** 1058 PR 59, Glen Rose; (254) 898-1526; www.dinoworld.net. Over one hundred life-size, fiberglass dinosaur statues dot the nature paths of this kid-friendly attraction, located near Dinosaur Valley State Park. There's also a picnic area and a fossil dig, where you can search for authentic fossils—and take home what you find. Adults, $12.75, children, $9.75; Open daily at 9 a.m.

**Fossil Rim Wildlife Center.** 3022 (A) CR-2010, Glen Rose; Take US 67 through Glen Rose to CR 2010; (254) 897-2960; www.fossilrim.org. A true Texas hidden gem, this 1,700-acre wildlife conservation center is home to over 1,100 animals, most of whom roam freely in near-natural conditions. The goal here is education, research, and the conservation of species that are in danger of becoming extinct, so the focus is on keeping the environment as peaceful and unobtrusive to the creatures as possible. Visitors drive through the park along a beautiful 9-mile scenic drive, which goes through forests, up a hill, and along a lush "savannah"; an identification guide helps you spot the various inhabitants along the way, and you can get food pellets to feed to several of them (including the giraffes, the only ones who will eat out of your hand). There's also the Overlook Restaurant and a lodge and tented safari camp on the grounds (see the "Where to Stay" section for more on those). Admission from $15.95 for adults and $9.95 for kids in off-season to $16.95 to $22.95 in high-season. Hours vary by season, too, so call ahead.

**Glen Rose Visitors Bureau.** 1505 NE Big Bend Trail, Glen Rose; (254) 897-3081 or (888) DINO-CVB; www.glenrosetexas.net. Stop by this limestone building for free brochures, maps, and suggestions. US 67 turns into Big Bend Trail in town, so you'll pass the center on your way from Dallas to the historic downtown. Open Mon through Fri, 8 a.m. to 5 p.m. all year, and Sat, 10 a.m. to 3 p.m. in high season. If you call ahead, they can send out a visitors packet in the mail.

**Somervell County Museum.** 101 SW Vernon St.; (254) 898-0640. Learn about the history of the county through unique exhibits and antiques, including a Prohibition-era moonshiner's still. (Glen Rose was once known as the "Moonshine Capital of Texas," and many of the bootleggers were locked up in the Somervell County Jail at the corner of Vernon and Cedar Streets, which you can also visit). Admission is by donation. Open Mon through Sat, 10 a.m. to 5 p.m. from June until Labor Day, and Sat, 10 a.m. to 5 p.m., Sun, 1 to 5 p.m. the rest of the year.

# where to shop

Wander the streets around the courthouse in **Historic Downtown Glen Rose**—particularly Barnard, Elm, Vernon, and Walnut Streets—to find stores peddling antiques, gifts, books, artwork, and even native plants and flowers. Notable stops include the **Shop Around the Corner** (213 NE Barnard St.; 254-897-7007) for vintage linens, candles, and collectibles, and **The Junkyard Dog** (101 Elm St.; 254-989-2246), an eclectic selection of new and old, plus locally made jewelry and art, set in a former welding shop. The long-standing **Anderson's Antiques & Gifts** (102 Walnut St., 254-897-9421) specializes in stained glass and Victorian furniture, and is also a tearoom/restaurant serving comfort food and yummy deserts. As the shops around the square are often in flux, check out the Historic Downtown's Web site for more info; ww.historicdowntownglenrose.com.

# where to eat

**Hammond's BBQ.** 1106 N.E. Big Bend Trail, Glen Rose; (254) 897-3008; www.hammonds bbq.com. Located on US 67 (called Big Bend Trail in town), this classic joint is a convenient stop on the way into or out of town. A wall of colorful license plates and Texas-themed memorabilia watches over the large, barnlike space, where diners settle in for classic plates with your choice of sliced of chopped brisket, turkey, pork ribs, or sausage, plus sides. There are also mixed baskets, sandwiches, and Blue Bell ice-cream–topped cobbler. Note that on Tuesday, it's buffet-style service only. Sun through Tue, 11 a.m. to 3 p.m., Wed, closed, Thurs through Sat, 11 a.m. to 8 p.m. $–$$.

**Inn on the River.** 205 SW Barnard St., Glen Rose; (800) 575-2101 or (254) 897-2929. www.innontheriver.com (See also "Where to Stay.") For special occasions and romantic dates, this elegant dining room is a local favorite. The four- and five-course gourmet dinner menu changes every month, but might include items like grilled beef tenderloin with roasted poblanos and blue cheese, chicken breast stuffed with walnuts and brie, or Cajun shrimp on baked grits—all accompanied by homemade bread and finished with a decadent dessert. Note that the inn is BYOB, and that dinner is served on Friday and Saturday only; reservations recommended. $$–$$$.

**Pie Peddlers.** 104 SW Barnard St., Glen Rose; (254) 897-9228; www.piepeddlers.com. Founded by two school teachers, this cute, country kitchen–style bakery pushes all manner of pies, from cream-filled and seasonal (like pumpkin), to pecan and strawberry-rhubarb. Pies are sold whole or by the slice, and a few tables and chairs are available for when you just can't wait to dig in. The holidays are the busiest times here, when seemingly the entire county is coming by to pick up their dessert orders. Because the pie makers are still working teachers, the shop is only open on Fri, 4 to 6 p.m. and Sat, 10 a.m. to 6 p.m. during the school year, and Fri and Sat, 10 a.m. to 6 p.m. during the summer holidays. $.

**Riverhouse Grill.** 210 S.W. Barnard St., Glen Rose; (254) 898-8514; www.theriverhouse grill.net. Right off the square, in a renovated plantation-style house, you'll enjoy a diverse lunch, dinner, and Sunday brunch menu of favorites like tortilla soup, sesame-crusted catfish nuggets, shrimp "voodoo" pasta, and salads and sandwiches; top it off with beignets with honey butter or chocolate heavenly cake. Tues through Thurs, 11:30 a.m. to 2 p.m. and 5:30 to 9 p.m., Fri through Sat, 11:30 a.m. to 2 p.m. and 5:30 to 10 p.m., Sun, 10:30 a.m. to 2 p.m. $$.

**Rough Creek Lodge.** 5165 CR 2013, Glen Rose; (888) 670-1223; www.roughcreek.com. (See also "Where to Stay.") Seemingly every foodie and travel magazine has showered praise on this five-star hotel and fine dining restaurant, located about 10 miles outside of Glen Rose. Chef Gerard Thompson serves a modern interpretation of rustic American favorites using seasonal ingredients; menus change daily, but think handmade pheasant ravioli, Stilton blue cheese quesadillas, tea-smoked duck breast, and pan-roasted Tasmanian salmon. (Save room for brown butter plum tarts and Varlhona chocolate angel food cake.) Reservations recommended for all meals. Daily from 8 to 10 a.m. (breakfast), noon to 2 p.m. (lunch), and 6 to 9 p.m. (dinner). $$$.

**Storiebook Cafe.** 502 NE Barnard St., Glen Rose; (254) 897-2665; www.storiebookcafe .com. Owner Storie Bonner Sharp (yup, that's her real first name) turned an old garage into this cheery bookstore/cafe/local hangout, complete with an outdoor space for book clubs, art shows, tea parties, live music, and girl's night out events (the latter take place the third Saturday of every month). Both new and used tomes are sold, there's Wi-Fi access and kids' story time hours, and every table is topped with a notebook in which patrons can write down a parting thought. The menu offers a satisfying selection of homemade soups, sandwiches, salads, and wraps, plus a full coffee bar. Mon through Fri, 11 a.m. to 6 p.m., Sat, 11 a.m. to 11 p.m. (depending on live music schedule), and every other Sun, noon to 3 p.m. $–$$.

# where to stay

**Cedars on the Brazos.** 2920 CR 413, Glen Rose; (254) 898-1000; www.cedarsonthe brazos.com. White-tailed deer, rabbits, and great horned owls are just some the neighbors at this three-suite B&B, located on a 110-acre cedar and oak forest right along the river. Enjoy river activities, strolling the grounds, or just lazing about the two-story log cabin–style house. Multicourse candle-lit diners and picnic baskets can be arranged in advance. $$.

**Inn on the River.** 205 SW Barnard St., Glen Rose; (800) 575-2101 or (254) 897-2929. www.innontheriver.com. (See also "Where to Eat.") Located just blocks from the courthouse square, this twenty-two-room inn complex was, in the early 1900s, the health spa of a self-proclaimed "magnetic healer." These days, guests are able to relax courtesy of garden views, feather beds, and attentive service. $$.

**The Lodge at Fossil Rim & The Foothills Safari Camp.** 3022 (A) CR 2010, Glen Rose; Take US 67 through Glen Rose to CR 2010; (254) 897-2960; www.fossilrim.org. Enjoy the closest thing Texas has to an African safari experience at this wildlife conservation center, where you can stay overnight in two different locations. The upscale, hilltop lodge boasts antiques-filled rooms—some with Jacuzzis, fireplaces, and private entrances—and sweeping views over the grounds, while the Foothills Camp's seven tented cabins (each with private bath and twin beds) are set close to one of the main animal watering holes. Guests spending the night in the center get the added bonus of daily morning game drives, while dinner is served in the Safari Camp pavilion on Friday and Saturday (with advance reservations). $$–$$$.

**Rough Creek Lodge.** 5165 CR 2013, Glen Rose; (888) 670-1223; www.roughcreek.com. (See also "Where to Eat.") Consistently named one of the best places for a romantic getaway or wedding in the state, this luxury resort offers a few different overnight options: the main lodge houses fifty-one rooms and suites, each with balcony and handcrafted rocking chairs; four "rustic" cabins boast whirlpools and screened porches; and two spacious guest houses—one with a private lake—are ideal for families and groups. $$$.

# day trip 03

## southwest

### for the sweet tooth:
dublin, hico

**Traveling further southwest** from Granbury and Glen Rose leads you into Erath and Hamilton Counties, where scenic prairies and farmlands gently give way to Texas Hill Country. Here, set about 20 miles apart along TX 6, are two towns united in sugar: Dublin, legendary for its historic Dr. Pepper bottling facility, and Hico, whose handcrafted Wiseman House Chocolates are shipped around the world. Visitor's flock to both places on the reputation of these sweet spots and, once there, discover charming small towns big on history and character.

Most North Texas towns built in the late 1800s seem to follow either the central courthouse square layout or the more Old West–looking setup of a brick-lined main street with brick-fronted facades; both Dublin and Hico favor the latter, and at first glance, a few rolling tumbleweeds wouldn't seem out of place at either. But outside of their downtowns, both also boast stellar examples of the Victorian mansions (and in Dublin's case, Craftsman bungalows) of the wealthy merchants, ranchers, and railroad men of the late nineteenth century. Each village also has its share of notable residents—from Dublin's golfer Ben Hogan (his museum will open in 2010) to outlaw Billy the Kid in Hico, though the latter's story is steeped in controversy (learn more about that at the Hico Billy the Kid Museum). And of course, there are the eats: gourmet chocolates and giant pies in Hico, and old-fashioned soda shops and fresh Dr. Pepper—famously made with real cane sugar, not corn syrup—in Dublin.

Dublin is about 120 miles southwest of Dallas; Hico about 105 miles. We suggest hitting Dublin first, then heading east to Hico, from where it's a straight shot back to Dallas.

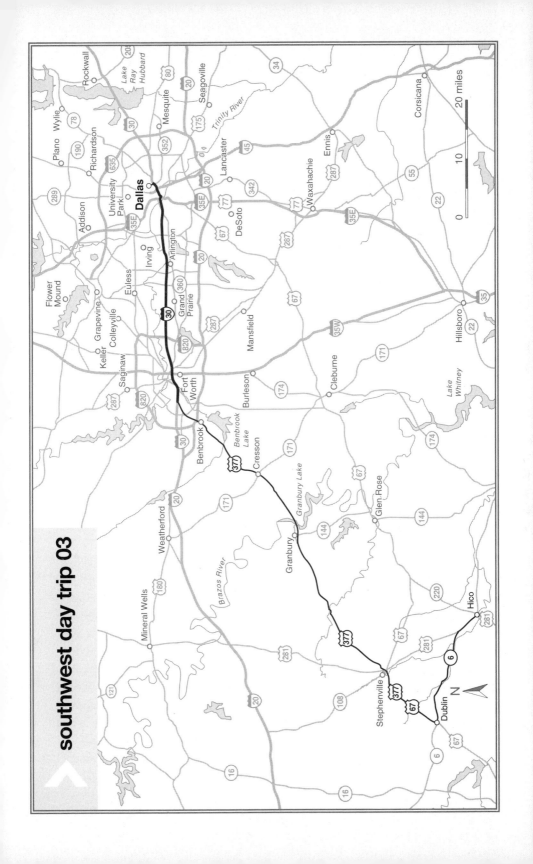

southwest day trip 03

# dublin

It's not unusual for the folks at the Dublin Dr. Pepper Bottling Company to get a phone call from the local private plane airport outside of town, asking if they could drive out a few cold cases for a thirsty fly-in customer. So hooked are fans of the Texas soda that they come from far and wide, by plane, car, and tour bus, to visit the first, and oldest, Dr. Pepper bottler in the world—and the only one still using the original formula. During the plant's week-long birthday celebration every June, Dublin is officially known as Dr. Pepper, Texas, with even the city limits signs changing for the occasion.

Though soda and nostalgia is what draws crowds to Dublin now, the town has had many other claims to fame throughout the years. The settlement was founded in 1854 and named in 1860—not, as you might expect, for the city in Ireland. The debate still rages on about the exact origins of the name, but the general consensus is that it was either for the settlers' warning cry during Native American attacks (the residents would circle their wagons and shout, "Double in!"), or for the "double end" shape of the old stagecoach stop. In any case, residents eventually ran with the Irish theme in the 1930s, naming streets "Patrick" and "Blackjack," and today the town uses shamrocks as a symbol and has even been named the Irish Capital of Texas.

The location of a stagecoach and, later, railroad stop brought prosperity to the town, while its dairy and cattle ranches brought it fame. (The county is still one of the state's leading milk providers.) In the 1940s and 1950s, much of the top quality rodeo stock was raised in the area, and would be transported by railcar directly from Dublin to Madison Square Garden in New York City, site of the largest rodeo. Naturally, the rodeo cowgirls and cowboys wanted to get a sneak peak—and test out—the animals before hitting the big show, so country singing star Gene Autrey eventually started the Dublin Rodeo, which attracted all the top riders of the circuit.

You can learn about the town's history in its two museums, and get a feel for its present by just wandering its streets and chatting with the very friendly locals. With a population of under 4,000, Dublin enjoys that everybody-knows-everybody feel, while still remaining welcoming to outsiders and embracing of the offbeat. You'll find artisan saddlemakers and jewelers (both women), chatty shop owners and, of course, all the Dr. Pepper you could want.

## getting there

To reach Dublin, take I-30W to exit 21A (I-820S), then take the exit for I-20W, direction Abilene. Take exit 429A to merge onto US 377S, which will take you through Granbury right into Dublin. Note that in Dublin, US 377 is called Patrick Street, and that US 377, US 67, and TX 6 all intersect in town.

# where to go

**Dublin Chamber of Commerce and Visitors Center.** 111 S. Patrick St., Dublin; (254) 445-3422; www.dublintxchamber.com. Stop in for brochures, driving and walking maps of the historic buildings, Victorian mansions, and Craftsman bungalows, and a chat; Chamber Executive Director Karen Wright wrote the book, literally, on Dublin's Dr. Pepper history (it's called *The Road to Dr. Pepper, Texas*), and is happy to share her knowledge. The visitors center is only open during the week, but if you might be coming by on the weekend, call ahead, and they'd be glad to "figure something out."

**Dublin Dr. Pepper Museum and Bottling Plant.** 105 E. Elm St., Dublin; (888) 398-1024; www.olddocs.com. Since 1891, this bottling plant has been whipping up fresh, cold cases of Dr. Pepper soda, earning it the distinction of being the first and oldest bottler of the drink in the world. Though the soda itself was invented in Waco, this center is the only maker still using the original formula (for more on the drink's history, see the sidebar in this chapter). You can find Dublin Dr. Pepper proudly sold at shops within a 44-mile radius (this franchise's long-standing territory), but this is the place to learn about its past, see the bottling line and—on one Wednesday every month—watch it being made on the original equipment. (The "newest" machine on-site is from 1965.) There's also a soda fountain, small museum, and shop stocking all manner of retro memorabilia. Of course, you can also buy cases of the fizzy stuff (three case limit per customer) in newer 8-ounce bottles and 12-ounce cans, or vintage 6.5-ounce and 12-ounce bottles, which customers are encouraged to recycle and trade in. Tours are offered every forty-five minutes, from 10:15 a.m. to 4:15 p.m.; adults, $2.50, seniors and kids 6 to 12, $2; kids under 6 are free. Open every day in the summer and Tues through Sun from Labor Day to Memorial Day; call ahead to confirm.

**Dublin Historical Museum.** 116 W. Blackjack St., Dublin; (254) 445-4550. Separated by topics like home, school, church, and military, this small, packed museum brings local history to life through exhibits that are lively and accessible (few things are behind glass). There's clothing, furniture, memorabilia, and a section on local boy/golf legend Ben Hogan, who will get his own museum in 2010. Free; open daily 1 to 5 p.m.

**Dublin Rodeo Heritage Museum.** 118 Blackjack St., Dublin; (254) 445-0200; www .dublinrodeo.org. From 1937–1959, the World Championship Rodeo Company was head-quartered in Dublin, and this fun museum celebrates that era. Check out antique saddles, costumes, exhibits on prominent riders, and a wall detailing the different branding symbols. Free; call ahead for hours.

**Veldhuizen Family Farm.** 425 PR 1169, Dublin; (254) 968-3098; www.veldhuizencheese .com. Watch cheese being made at this family-run farm, which has been churning out tasty cheddars, goudas, and specialty varieties (like jalapeño, caraway, and Bosque Blue) for years. Farms tours are also available by appointment; $3 for adults, $2 for kids. From

Dublin, takc US 377E about 5 miles to CR 299; lurn right and travel about 2 miles to PR 1169, the farm's drive. Mon through Fri, 10 a.m. to 5:30 p.m., Sat, 10 a.m. to 4 p.m., closed Sun.

## the story of the doc

*Two towns in North Texas (and this book) claim a connection to Dr. Pepper, and both are legit. The drink was created at the Old Corner Drug Store in Waco in 1885, by pharmacist Charles Alderton, who based the soda on a combination of all the fruity scents that lingered in the drugstore. Originally, the drink was just called a "Waco"—"Gimme a shot of Waco," customers would cry—but the store's owner, Wade Morrison, eventually named it Dr. Pepper (some say in honor of the father of a girl he loved back in Virginia). For a few years, you could only get Dr. Pepper at Waco soda fountains, but when businessman Sam Houston Prim had a taste, he thought it might be nice to bottle the drink. In 1891, he established the first Dr. Pepper bottling plant in Dublin and took on a franchise to only sell the drink within a 44-mile radius of town (a restriction that still holds true today). That same year, the Artesian Manufacturing & Bottling Company was formed by Morrison in Waco, and the soda began to take off all across the state. In 1904, Dr. Pepper was introduced to the rest of the country at the St. Louis World's Fair—the same fair where hamburgers, hot dogs, and ice-cream cones made their debut.*

*While the Artesian company moved to Dallas in 1923, the Dublin plant has been in the same place since 1891, and was owned by the same family for one hundred years. (Mr. Prim left the plant to his daughter, Grace Prim Lyon, and when she passed away—on the morning of the plant's centennial celebration—it was willed to the longtime plant manager, Bill Kloster, Today, Bill's son and grandsons run the plant.) Of course, Dublin is also the only place that still makes the drink using pure cane sugar instead of high fructose corn syrup—a fact that explains all the passionate Dublin DP fans.*

*Aside from the formula, travelers often wonder what the difference is between the Waco and Dublin Dr. Pepper Museums, both of which boast memorabilia, gift shops, and soda fountains. In truth, they're both worth a visit: In Waco you'll learn about the history of the drink and soda in general, with lots of videos and exhibits, while in Dublin you'll see a more personal and local connection to the drink, and view a vast array of unique items collected by Mr. Kloster himself.*

# where to shop

**Deep in the Art Studio and Shop.** 110 S. Patrick St. (254) 968–7839; www.deepinthe heart.com. Artist Sandy Parker makes all types of jewelry and creative craft pieces out of this cheery studio, but her main calling card are Phenominoes, stylish, fun pendants painted on real dominoes. Come check out her wares here, or learn how to make your own jewelry and craft items using a variety of techniques. Call ahead for store hours and class schedules, or to reserve a private lesson.

**Three Sisters.** 101 S. Patrick St., Dublin; (254) 445-2212; www.threesistersofdublin.com. Sisters Mary Haley, Brenda Horn, and Lisa Leatherwood—two retired teachers, one a current bank employee—opened this large shop in 2008, and it's become something of a favorite with local ladies. Browse an ever-changing stock of gift items, knickknacks, home décor, and Dublin-centric goods, and don't miss the Dublin history/claim to fame wall along one side. Tues through Fri, 9:30 a.m. to 5:30 p.m.; Sat, 9:30 a.m. to 4:30 p.m.

**Wendy Allen Saddlery.** 201 N. Patrick St., Dublin; (254) 445-4766; www.wendyallen saddlery.com. Serious riders appreciate the quality, comfort, and craftsmanship of a saddle by Wendy Allen, a renowned artisan and four-time nominee into Fort Worth's Cowgirl Hall of Fame. All saddles are custom made to suit both rider and horse; hours vary, so call ahead.

# where to eat

**Granny Clarks.** 213 N. Patrick St., Dublin; (254) 445-3444. You may be hard pressed to find a parking space at this buffet-style, home-cooking favorite, named for the chef-owner's maternal grandmother. Customers come in from both Dublin and the surrounding farms for real Texas country kitchen staples like chicken-fried steak, chicken and dumplings, green beans, and rotating lunch specials like meat loaf and pork chops—all topped off by fresh fruit cobbler, of course. Thursday night is Burger Night, with $1.25 homemade quarter-pounders, while Friday night is all-you-can-eat fried catfish and popcorn shrimp, and Saturday night is all the steak and butterfly shrimp you can handle. There are breakfast items, too—also just like Granny used to make. Mon through Wed, 6 a.m. to 2:30 p.m., Thurs through Sat, 6 a.m. to 9 p.m. $.

**Old Doc's Soda Shop.** 105 E. Elm St., Dublin; (888) 398-1024; www.olddocs.com. Located in the Dr. Pepper bottling plant, this casual snack shop has been operating since the 1950s—and some of the prices are downright historic, too. Enjoy PB&J sandwiches for $1.50, other varieties for $3, and Dr. Pepper Frosties—a creamy blend of Blue Bell ice cream and Dr. Pepper syrup—for $3.75. See the museum listing above for hours. $.

**Patrick Street Pharmacy Soda Fountain.** 925 N. Patrick St., Dublin; (254) 445-3679. Though it looks like it's been here for a hundred years, this pharmacy/soda shop only moved to this location in April 2009. (The pharmacy had been in business in another spot since the 1990s.) Care was taken to make the place feel rustic and well worn: The original hardwood floors were unearthed, mainly salvaged wood was used for the interiors, and the bead board came from an 1800s church in a nearby town. On one side there's a working pharmacy, on the other a lunch spot serving daily specials, sandwiches, wraps, and an array of salads; a popular choice is the salad boat, which includes your choice of three varieties (most people go for the homemade chicken salad and pimento cheese). Dessert is old-school, too, with Blue Bell ice-cream floats and milkshakes, and "Chill Pills"—thick, Blizzard-like concoctions with your choice of candy mixed in. Both sections are open Mon through Fri, 8 a.m. to 5 p.m., but only the pharmacy is open Sat. 8:30 a.m. to noon. (The soda shop opens on Saturday during festivals and events, like Dr. Pepper Day.) $.

## worth more time

If time permits before you head to Hico or back to Dallas, take a detour west on TX 6 to De Leon, located about 13 miles from Dublin. This peanut, peach, and cattle town is home to the **Terrill Antique Car Museum** (500 N. Texas St., De Leon; 254-893-3773; www.deleon texas.com), the collection of Feltz Terrill, a local peanut farmer who has long dabbled in restoring old cars. Terrill originally purchased this building to serve as a warehouse for his car parts, but today, there are nearly a dozen unique autos here, from a 1909 Buck Model 10 Toy Tonneau, 1909 one-cylinder Brush, and a 1901 Coffin steam carriage to a 1925 Ford Model T Touring and a red 1941 Packard Deluxe convertible coupe. The museum is free, and open Tues through Sat, 10 a.m. to noon and 1 to 5 p.m., and Sun, 1 to 4 p.m.

# hico

First things first: It's pronounced "HIGH-ko"—say it correctly and you're as good as local. Southeast of Dublin, at the crossroads of TX 6, TX 220, and US 281, sits this once-thriving Old West town of under 1,500 residents, which is currently enjoying a re-invention as a charming gateway to Hill Country. (Media types have even labeled it "the next Fredricks-burg," though it's still got some way to go to reach those tourist numbers). Its main street boasts beautiful examples of Western architecture—think brick facades, wrap-around wooden balconies, and big old mercantile stores—that are slowly reopening as boutiques and eateries. (In a telling example of past-meets-present, the old drug store is relaunching as a cappuccino bar and soda fountain, and the whole downtown enjoys free Wi-Fi.)

Historically, the town was a focal point for Hamilton County, but it's name hit the national stage in the 1950s, after local resident Ollie "Brushy Bill" Roberts was revealed to be infamous outlaw Billy the Kid. (This claim is still up for debate, and the controversy is covered in the Hico museum.) These days, the name Hico, Texas, is familiar to lovers of chocolate and pie, as two famous makers of both are located right in town.

## getting there

To reach Hico from Dublin, take TX 6S east, which will merge with US 281S and lead into town. At the main town traffic light (Wiseman House Chocolates will be on your left), TX 6 and US 281 separate, so to reach the visitors center and main historic street, stay on TX 6 for a couple of blocks to Pecan Street. (Turning on US 281S will lead you to a small residential area, then out of town faster than you can blink.)

## where to go

**Billy the Kid Museum and Hico Chamber of Commerce.** 114 N. Pecan St., Hico; (254) 796-2523 or (800) 361-HICO; www.hico-tx.com and www.billythekidmuseum.com. At the front of this main street storefront you'll find info on Hico attractions, plus a smattering of gift items and art work for sale. In the back, it's all about Billy the Kid, the notorious nineteenth-century outlaw who reportedly was discovered in 1948, in Hico, living under the name "Brushy Bill" Roberts—a startling revelation, since Billy the Kid was supposedly killed in New Mexico decades earlier. While the debate rages on between Texas and New Mexico, this small exhibit details the controversy, and features items on The Kid's history and local connection. There's also an antique jail cell and other Hico memorabilia. Mon through Sat, 10 a.m. to 4 p.m., Sun, 1 to 4 p.m., closed Tues.

**Wiseman House Chocolates.** 406 W. Grubbs St., Hico; (254) 796-2565; www.wiseman housechocolates. The sweet smell of cocoa wafts out of this Queen Anne Victorian house at the corner of TX 6 and W. Grubbs St., home base to the famous Wiseman House gourmet chocolate company. Founders Kevin and LaDonne Wenzel (he's the chocolatier) used to live in the historic house, which was originally built for local artist Rufus Wiseman, but now use it as the showcase for their truffles, bars, barks, caramels, and other candy-related items. (The goodies themselves are made a couple blocks away, behind the Bliss boutique on South Pecan Street.) Signature truffles include the Wild Woman (a mix of two dark Belgian chocolates), Snooky (coffee-flavored dark chocolate rolled in cinnamon and sugar), and Southern Hospitality (milk chocolate with Jack Daniel's whiskey). Everything is made with high-grade Belgian and Venezuelan chocolate and natural ingredients like Madagascar vanilla, fresh cream, crushed coffee beans, and real fruit. Mon through Sat, 10 a.m. to 6 p.m., Sun, 1 to 5 p.m.

## where to shop

**Bliss Living.** 106 S. Pecan St., Hico; (254) 796-2499; www.bliss-living.com. Founded by LaDonne Wenzel, the wife of Wiseman's chocolate master, this high-end store carries a lovely selection of clothing, home items, accessories, and jewelry, all curated by the owner (who was educated at New York's Fashion Institute of Technology). The pricing is more Dallas than Hico, but it's worth a look; plus, you can watch Wiseman's chocolate being made in the back. Mon through Sat, 10 a.m. to 5 p.m., Sun, 1 to 5 p.m.

**Blue Star Trading.** 112 S. Pecan St., Hico; (254) 796-2828; www.bluestartrading.com. This massive space—part of which was once the 1895 Perry Brothers Mercantile—includes three separate sections: Ranch Outfitters for upscale menswear and equine supplies, Blur Star Home for furnishings, and Blur Star Trading, for women's wear, jewelry, accessories, and gifts. A Western theme runs throughout, but the aesthetic is definitely more stylish and discerning than kitschy. Don't miss the event space upstairs, where there's a great photo retrospective detailing the early days of the town. Mon through Sat, 9:30 a.m. to 6 p.m., Sun, 1 to 5 p.m.

**It's a Texas Thang.** 115 S. Pecan St., Hico; (254) 796-9806. Actually, it's an *every* thang: owner Melody Harbour packs her multiroom space with antiques, flea market finds, tea pots, Western memorabilia, gourmet foods, and more. There are even a collection of antique spurs, vintage vending machines, and unique, decorative cow skulls hand-painted by an artist who's in prison. Even if you don't find anything, it's worth stopping in for a chat with the vivacious Harbour. Mon through Sat, 10 a.m. to 5:30 p.m., Sun, 1 to 5 p.m.

**Sugar Moon Antiques & Art Gallery.** 101 S. Pecan St., Hico; (254) 796-4155; www.sugar moonantiques.com. A variety of vendors sell out of this two-floor space, so you'll find a rotating stock of antiques, collectibles, home decor, artwork, and new items, like flax-based women's clothing. Mon through Sat,10 a.m. to 5:30 p.m., Sun, 1 to 5 p.m.

## where to eat

**Jersey Lilly's.** 128 N. Pecan St., Hico; (254) 796-0999. Quality Tex-Mex favorites like faji-tas, enchiladas, and combo platters are served out of this great historic space—though, this being Texas, you'll also find burgers, steaks, and fried pickles on the menu. $–$$.

**Koffee Kup.** 300 W. 2nd St., off TX 6 (across from Wiseman House Chocolates), Hico; (254) 796-4839; www.koffeekupfamilyrestaurant. Hardly a Best of Texas list comes out that doesn't mention this legendary family-owned place, which has been satisfying locals and travelers from this current location since 1968. Along with the eight signature burgers (all served on homemade buns) and Texas staples like chicken-fried steak, you won't want to pass up the giant hand-cut onion rings, hand-battered fried pickles, and breaded shrimp. Most famous of all are the baked goods, made here daily starting at 5 a.m.: donuts the size of two fists, and dozens of flavors of mile-high pies, from peanut butter meringue to lemon chess, key lime, and "Doctor's Office" (cream cheese and vanilla custard with a graham cracker crust and coconut-pecan topping). A smooth wooden table near the front is emblazoned with the names of regu-lars who have since headed to the big cafe in the sky. Open daily, 6 a.m. to 9:30 p.m. $–$$.

**Texas Trails.** 204 W. 2nd St., Hico; (254) 796-0916. Located along TX 6, in a cool gray tin building with red trim and a big front porch, Texas Trails is owned by Tracy and Bill Travis, who put the focus on solid home cooking with Texas and Tex-Mex flavors. Fans stream in for the rib eye steaks, chicken salad sandwiches, and homemade cornbread, pinto beans, and pecan pie. Wed through Sat, 10:30 a.m. to 9 p.m., Sun, 10:30 a.m. to 3 p.m. $–$$.

west

# day trip 01

>>> **culture and cowboys:**
fort worth

# fort worth

About 35 miles west along I-30 sits the other bookend to the Dallas/Fort Worth Metroplex. While Dallas and Fort Worth share an airport and metropolitan area, the cities are actually different in many ways, from size (Dallas is close to 1.5 million, Fort Worth around 700,000) to history and atmosphere. Dallasites may make occasional trips westward to see the stockyards or the museums, but it's worth spending a day or two here to get a taste of all that this friendly, accessible city—officially the number one tourist destination in Texas—has to offer.

Rich in culture, cuisine, and nightlife activities, Fort Worth's popularity with tourists both domestic and foreign is likely due in large part to its cowboy past—and decidedly Western present. This is where you can still glimpse the iconic Texas that visitors are looking to see, where cowboy hats and boots are a common sight and where most restaurants—regardless of type of cuisine—have some kind of steak or Tex-Mex flavors on the menu. The relaxed charm and "yes, ma'm" drawl long-gone from the cosmopolitan sprawl of Dallas is alive and well in Fort Worth, the city that's been described as "where the West begins."

Fort Worth's roots go back to early 1849, when decorated Mexican-American War veteran General William Jenkins Worth—who personally planted the first American flag on the Rio Grande—suggested building ten forts to mark the area where the Texas frontier began, near the intersection of two branches of the Trinity River. Though the general passed away

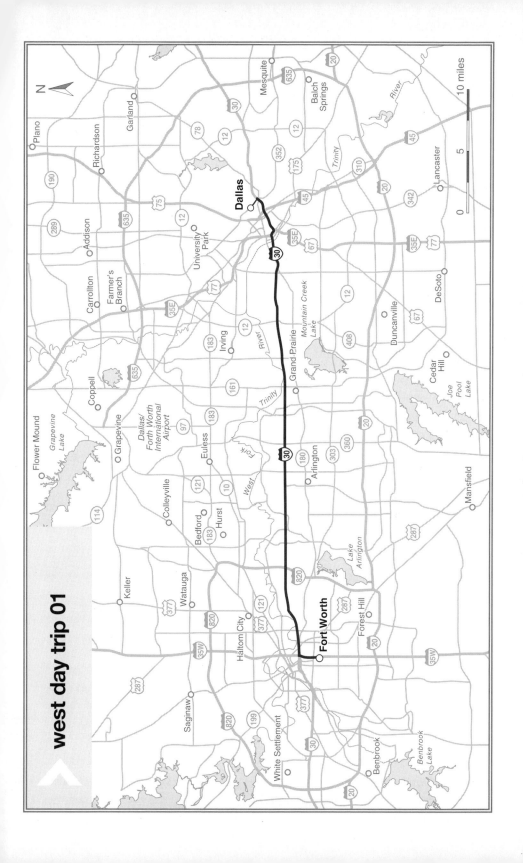

west day trip 01

just a few months later, the initial camps were built on bluffs overlooking the mouth of the Trinity, and in November, the name Fort Worth was officially granted to the site. Though technically manned by the military, the fort began to attract settlers, so when the army left just four years later, the pioneers took over the complex.

Despite the threat of Native American attacks, the town grew steadily over the next few years—until the Civil War and Reconstruction nearly wiped it out, cutting its population by more than half. In 1866, though, things started to turn around when Fort Worth became a stop on the Chisholm Trail. For the thousands of ragged cowboys driving cattle up though Texas, past the Red River and on to Kansas, Fort Worth was considered the last "civilized" point between the prairies and the Great Plains—an image helped, no doubt, by all the shops, saloons, gambling halls, and brothels that were opened to cater to them. By the 1870s, the south side of downtown had so many bars, dance halls, and places of ill repute that it became known as "Hell's Half Acre." Rife with violence and crime, the area attracted such notorious patrons as the Wild Bunch and Butch Cassidy and the Sundance Kid—and became off-limits to the more respectable residents.

When a financial crisis prompted the railroad to stop laying tracks 24 miles short of town in 1876, the pioneer spirit once again took hold and the citizens banded together to lay the track themselves. With the cattle industry, railroad, and commercial sectors all boom-ing, Cowtown was born. After the trail ended in the 1880s, the cattle business took a little dip, until the Fort Worth Stockyards were established by a group of local and out-of-town businessmen. Home to major meatpacking plants and one of the country's most important cattle markets, The Stockyards were a major part of the city's income until closing in the 1960s—and live on as a historical and entertainment district today.

In the twentieth century, oil joined cattle and the railroad as an important part of the local economy. Airplanes, too, were soon added to the mix: Fort Worth was where Texas Air Transport—now called American Airlines—was founded in 1929, and during World War II, Bell Helicopter and General Dynamics built over 3,000 aircrafts in the area. These days, corporations like Lockheed Martin, Pier 1 Imports, and Radio Shack call Fort Worth home and, along with tourism, help Cowtown continue to thrive.

## getting there

Drive west on I-30 for about 35 miles to reach the city center. Alternatively, take the Trinity Railway Express (TRE) commuter train from downtown Dallas to downtown Fort Worth; see www.trinityrailwayexpress.org for schedules and fares. TRE tickets are also good for twenty-four-hours free transport on the Fort Worth bus system, so hold on to your stub. Note that because this is a commuter train, it can be quite crowded during peak hours.

## where to go

**Bureau of Engraving and Printing—Western Currency Center.** 9000 Blue Mound Rd., Fort Worth; (817) 231-4000; www.moneyfactory.gov. Take a look at any U.S. currency bill in your wallet and you might see a small "FW" for Fort Worth printed to the right of the portrait. That's because all bills in the country are printed either at this western bureau of the BEP or at the federal facility in Washington, D.C. During the forty-five-minute tour, you'll stroll along an elevated glass walkway as billions of dollars get printed underneath; you can see how they are transformed from blank sheets into cold, hard cash. (The BEP doesn't mint any coins.) In the visitors center, enjoy a short movie and two floors of exhibits on the history of currency and the details of the printing process. Note that this is a secured facility, so many items—including cell phones, cameras, and backpacks—are not allowed; add on thirty minutes to your visit for clearing security. The visitors center and exhibits are open Mon through Fri, 8:30 a.m. to 3:30 p.m. (5:30 p.m. in June and July), closed Sat, Sun, Federal holidays, and the week between Christmas and New Year's; tours are offered every thirty minutes between 9 a.m. and 2 p.m. (4 p.m. in June and July). Free.

**Fort Worth Cultural District.** www.fortworth.com. Five museums are all within walking distance of each other in this west side district, making it easy to hit a couple—or all—at the same time. Visitors may park at one and explore the others; parking is free, as are two out of five of the museums (see pricing detail below).

**Amon Carter Museum.** 3501 Camp Bowie Blvd., Fort Worth; (817) 738-1933; www .cartermuseum.org. Browse American art work from the 1830s up to today, from such noted artists as Georgia O'Keefe, Winslow Homer, and John Singer Sargent. The Amon Carter is particularly known for its photography collection, which includes pieces by shutterbugs like Alfred Stieglitz. Free; Tues, Wed, Fri, Sat, 10 a.m. to 5 p.m., Thurs, 10 a.m. to 8 p.m., Sun, noon to 5 p.m.

**Forth Worth Museum of Science and History.** 1600 Gendy St., Fort Worth; (817) 255-9300 and (888) 255-9300; www.fwmuseum.org. Reopened in this new space next to the Cowgirl Museum in fall 2009 (after it outgrew its previous home of fifty years), this education-focused facility uses interactive exhibits to make science and history come alive for kids. There are section on dino digs and how energy works, plus a planetarium and IMAX theater on-site. Adults, $14; kids, $10; Daily, 10 a.m. to 5 p.m.

**Kimbell Art Museum.** 3333 Camp Bowie Blvd., Fort Worth; (817) 332-8451; www .kimbellart.org. Designed by noted architect Louis Kahn, the Kimbell is considered the best small museum in the country, and is certainly one of Fort Worth's star attractions. Along with works by masters like Cezanne, Matisse, Rembrandt, and El Greco, the museum is now home to a piece by Michelangelo—believed to be his earliest painting, this is the only work by the artist to be on display in the United States. The museum also has a popular cafe for lunch; the buffet price is by the plate size, so you get the size you want—small or large—and load up as much fresh salad, quiche, fruit, and sweets as will fit. Entry to the permanent collection galleries is free; special exhibits are

$14 for adults, $12 for students and seniors. Tues through Thurs and Sat, 10 a.m. to 5 p.m., Fri, noon to 8 p.m., Sun, noon to 5 p.m.

**Modern Art Museum of Fort Worth.** 3200 Darnell St., Fort Worth; (817) 738-9215. Across the street from the Kimbell, this stunning structure designed by Japanese architect Tadao Ando features walls of windows, an 1.5-acre reflecting pond, and a clean, streamlined interior to showcase the diverse works. The focus is on American and European pieces from 1945 until today, so the roster includes Cindy Sherman, Ellsworth Kelley, Anselm Kiefer, Roy Lichtenstein, Henry Moore, and countless other art world stars. Considered one of the premiere modern art museums in America, this one really is worth a look. The on-site Cafe Modern has also received praise, with *Gourmet* magazine calling it one of the best. Adults, $10; students and seniors, $4; children under 12, free; Tues through Sat, 10 a.m. to 5 p.m., Sat, 11 a.m. to 5 p.m., closed Mon and major holidays. There are extended hours on the first Friday of each month, and on Tuesday from Feb through Apr and Sept through Nov; see the Web site for specifics.

**National Cowgirl Museum and Hall of Fame.** 1720 Gendy St., Fort Worth; (817) 336-4475; www.cowgirl.net. Fun and inspiring for girls and women of all ages, this two-floor rotunda honors the female trailblazers of the American West, from the mid-1800s to the present. In one section, learn about the various Hall of Fame inductees, who range from ranchers, horsewomen, and rodeo performers to artists and writers. The rest of the exhibits detail various aspects of the cowgirl experience using vintage movie clips, memorabilia, clothing, and even a mechanical bull. The sections on female rodeo riders past are illuminating, as you learn about what it was like to be a woman in that world—and in those times. Adults, $8, kids, $7; Daily 10 a.m. to 5 p.m., closed major holidays.

**Fort Worth Visitor Information Centers.** (817) 336-8791 or (800) 433-5747; www .fortworth.com. In addition to offering event calendars and coupons on their Web site, Fort Worth has three Fort Worth info centers to pick up brochures, maps, dining and accommodation details, and trip planning advice. The city's convention and visitors bureau also offers foreign-language guides (in eight languages) and walking tours in certain areas; call for more info. The three centers are located at:

**Fort Worth Cultural District.** 3401 West Lancaster Ave., Fort Worth; (817) 882-8588. Mon through Sat, 10 a.m. to 5 p.m., closed Sunday.

**iFort Worth—Downtown Sundance Square.** 508 Main St., Fort Worth; (817) 698-3300; Mon through Fri, 10 a.m. to 6 p.m., Sat, 10 a.m. to 6 p.m.

**Stockyards National Historic District.** 130 East Exchange Ave., Fort Worth; (817) 624-4741; Mon through Fri, 9 a.m. to 6 p.m., Sun, noon to 5 p.m.

**Fort Worth Zoo.** 11989 Colonial Pkwy., Fort Worth; (817) 759-7555; www.fortworthzoo .com. Considered one of the Metroplex's top attractions (particularly for families), this zoo is technically the oldest in Texas—it was founded in 1909 to house two bear cubs, an alligator, a coyote, one lion, and a peacock. A century later, the extensive grounds are filled with every creature you could imagine, separated by species or native habitat. Over a dozen exhibits have opened since 1992 alone, including the Asian rhino ridge, the penguins section, the Australian Outback, and the World of Primates. In the eight-acre Texas Wild! section, find species native to this region, plus a re-created Old West town complete with "general store" and sweet shop, and the Texas Hall of Wonders, with exhibits covering the state's weather, topography, and natural resources. The "Yellow Rose Express" toy train runs on a regular daily loop from Texas Wild! to the main entrance. Adults, $12; children 3 to 12, $9; under 3, free. Open daily from 10 a.m. to 5 p.m. from mid-Feb to mid-Oct, and 10 a.m. to 4 p.m. from mid-Oct to mid-Feb. There are also extended weekend summer hours and special holiday times, so check the Web site for details.

**Sid Richardson Museum.** 309 Main St., in Sundance Square, Fort Worth; (888) 332-6554; www.sidrichardsonmuseum.org. Experience the majesty of the American West through the works of premier early-twentieth-century Western artists Frederic Remington and Charles M. Russell who, each in his own style, depicted the lives of the cowboys and Native Americans and captured a frontier that was quickly disappearing. Open since 1982, the collection—one of the finest to focus on Western art in the country—was the work of late oilman and philanthropist Sid Richardson, who was dedicated to preserving this part of the nation's history. Free; Mon through Thurs, 9 a.m. to 5 p.m., Fri through Sat, 9 a.m. to 8 p.m., Sun, noon to 5 p.m., closed major holidays.

**Stockyards National Historic District.** 130 E. Exchange Ave., Fort Worth; (817) 624-4741; www.fortworthstockyards.org and www.stockyardsstation.com. Fort Worth's Cow-town past comes alive in this 125-acre National Historic District, founded in 1893 and once home to the city's thriving livestock market, meatpacking plants, and cattle-related businesses. Most of the main attractions, shops, and restaurants line Exchange Avenue, between Packer and Main Streets. Visit the **Stockyards Museum** (131 E. Exchange Ave., #110, Fort Worth; 817-625-5082) to view photos, clothing, and other memorabilia that tells the area's story. Twice a day, at 11:30 a.m. and 4 p.m., a group of twelve "drovers" in authentic costume lead a mini-cattle drive of majestic longhorns down the brick avenue, a nod to the neighborhood's past; gather around the cattle pen for the best views. The **Cow-town Cattlepen Maze** (145 E. Exchange Ave., 817-624-6666) is another fun activity for all ages, in which visitors try to make their way around a 5,400 square-foot labyrinth designed to resemble the cattle pens of the Old West (the activity even stumped the contestants on a season of *The Amazing Race*). If time permits, ride the **Grapevine Vintage Railroad**'s steam and diesel engine trains between here and Grapevine, or take a **Historic Walking Tour** of the area; visit www.stockyardsstation.com for details on both.

> ## panther city

*Fort Worth has had many nicknames over the years, from "Queen City of the Prairies" and "The Paris of the Plains" to the more enduring "Cowtown." One of the most unusual, though, is "Panther City"—a name still proudly used by local businesses and residents. The origins of this moniker go back to 1875, when the once-bustling town was in the throes of a deep decline after the end of the Chisholm Trail and the Civil War, and the failure of the railroad to reach city limits. (During that time, the population had dropped as low as 175 people.) In an article in the Dallas Herald newspaper, a former Fort Worth lawyer said that the town had been so badly affected, and become so sleepy, that he saw a panther asleep by the courthouse. At the time, the insult hurt, but when the town recovered economically soon after, the name "Panther City" was embraced by the residents as a symbol of their survival. Even today, the Fort Worth police badges feature the figure of a panther, and many businesses use the word in their names. "Panther City" continues to be a testament to the city's past—and their friendly rivalry with neighboring Dallas.*

On Friday and Saturday nights, there's always a lively show at **Cowtown Coliseum** (121 E. Exchange Ave., 817-625-1025), the world's first indoor rodeo arena (the box office is only open on show days; check www.cowtowncoliseum.com for a schedule). And don't miss the chance to show your two-steppin' moves (or learn some) at the famous **Billy Bob's Texas** (2520 Rodeo Plaza, just behind the Coliseum, 817-624-7117, www.billybobs texas.com), the world's largest honky-tonk. Along with dance floors, bars, video game arcades, and a restaurant, the three-acre place has its own indoor arena for professional bull riding shows.

## where to shop

At **Roy Earl's Metal Art** (2501 Rodeo Plaza; 817-626-0066), unique jewelry and home decor items are handmade using copper, iron, stones, and even horseshoe nails, while **Texas Hot Stuff** (140 E. Exchange Ave. Ste. 105; 817-625-1221) is the place for spicy sauces and zesty marinades. A complete list of the stockyard shops can be found on their Web site.

**Camp Bowie Boulevard.** The low-rises along this historic street house an array of shops, both name-brand and independent; find clothing, home goods, jewelry, and more. The highest concentration of stores lay west of downtown and the Cultural District, generally between University Drive and I-30. One notable spot is **Chicks off the Bricks** (4911 Camp Bowie Blvd.; 817-735-9989), a consortium of local designer fashions set in the brick-lined section of the boulevard.

**Stockyards Station.** Along Exchange Avenue and Main Street, Fort Worth. www.fortworth stockyards.org. Dozens of stores line the preserved streets of Cowtown, many focusing on Western-themed fashions, gifts, jewelry, and souvenirs, while a number of artisan shops create custom pieces using time-honed techniques. The legendary **M. L. Leddy's** (2455 Main St.; 817-625-2725) produces completely handmade boots, belts, and saddles, tailored to each customer and taking up to two years to complete (for the boots, they measure your feet and have you try on different leather forms, to find the perfect fit); everyone from Elvis to Prince Charles has ordered from Leddy's. (They also carry upscale clothing for men and women.) **The Sean Ryon Western Store & Saddle Shop** (2707 N. Main St.; 817-626-5390) also has a long history in the stockyards, with this current generation of owners—the sixth—creating handmade boots and hand-creased hats. More Western wear can be found at **Luskey's** (2601 N. Main St.; 817-625-2391), which has been serving the area for close to ninety years.

**Sundance Square.** Around Main and 4th Streets, Downtown Forth Worth, www.sundance square.com. The city's main shopping and entertainment district is spread over 20 blocks in historic downtown. Many of the shops are outposts of familiar chains, but some of the local gems include **Leddy's Ranch at Sundance Square** (410 Houston St.; 817-336-0800; www.leddys.com), for modern ranch-chic clothing and lifestyle pieces; and **Retro Cowboy** (406 Houston St.; 817-338-1194), the place for Texas souvenirs, funky accessories, and vintage pearl-snap Western shirts.

Note that the square offers great parking deals for its customers: Park in any designated "Sundance Square" garage, the Chisholm Trail Parking lot (3rd Street between Houston and Main Streets) or the Saucer Parking Lot (3rd Street between Main and Commerce Streets), and you will enjoy free parking after 5 p.m. during the week and all day on the weekend. Numerous retailers will also validate tickets for 2.5 hours of free parking on weekdays (again, only for the above lots and garages); see the Web site for a list of participating stores.

# where to eat

**Grace.** 777 Main St., Fort Worth; (817) 877-3388; www.gracefortworth.com. This relatively new addition to the downtown/Sundance Square area serves contemporary American fare made using seasonal (and some organic) ingredients and award-winning Chef Blaine Staniford's creative recipes. Choices are separated into categories like beef, fish, starches, sauces, vegetables, and toppings, so you can mix and match your prime strip with an espresso horseradish and cheesy spatzle, for example. There are also starters, salads, and an extensive wine and cocktail list perfect for enjoying out on the terrace. The seasonal "Wine Me, Dine Me" prix-fixe menu pairs four courses with a complementary wine. Dining room open for dinner only, Mon through Thurs, 5:30 to 9:30 p.m., Fri through Sat, 5:30 to 10:30 p.m. $$–$$$.

**Hunter Brother's H3 Ranch.** 105 E. Exchange Ave., Fort Worth; (817) 624-1246; www .h3ranch.com. As befits an eatery in the heart of the Stockyards District, this beloved steakhouse serves mouth-watering ribs, perfectly juicy wood-fired steaks, and other proteins like rainbow trout and hickory grilled shrimp. Don't miss signature starters like the deep-fried, spicy-sweet chicken thighs, made-at-your-table, guacamole, and "Nine Miles of Dirt Road" dip, with six tasty layers. Mon through Thurs, 11 a.m. to 10 p.m., Fri, 11 a.m. to 11 p.m., Sat, 9 a.m. to 11 p.m., Sun, 9 a.m. to 10 p.m. $$–$$$.

**Joe T. Garcia's.** 2201 N. Commerce St., Fort Worth; (817) 626-4356; www.joets.com. What started in 1935 as a sixteen-seat eatery serving mainly enchiladas has stretched to an almost city-block-long Fort Worth tradition for homemade Tex-Mex. The dinner menu is still pretty simple, with beef or chicken fajitas, a small selection of appetizers, and the best-selling family-style dinner, a one-to-two-person combo of a small order of cheese nachos, two cheese enchiladas, two beef tacos, and guacamole. The breakfast menu offers classics like chiliquiles and huevos rancheros, while lunch is more extensive with tamales, mini-chimichangas, chicken flautas, and chili rellenos. Everything comes with chips and the famous house salsa, which is also available by the jar to take home. On the weekends, you'll most likely have to circle the restaurant a few times looking for parking, but once inside, the service is quick and friendly and the atmosphere lively, both in the main dining room and out on the patio, overlooking the fountain. The family also runs **Esperanza's Mexican Cafe & Bakery** around the corner (2122 N. Main St.; 817-626-5770), where you'll find solid breakfast and lunch items and tons of take-home goodies (like tamales) in a casual atmosphere. Mon through Thurs, 11 a.m. to 2:30 p.m. and 5 to 10 p.m., Fri through Sat, 11 a.m. to 11 p.m., Sun, 11 a.m. to 10 p.m. $–$$.

**Kincaid's Grocery & Market.** 4901 Camp Bowie Blvd., Fort Worth; (817) 732-2881; www .kincaidshamburgers. A few years ago, a national panel of food critics and magazine editors voted Kincaid's the best burger in the nation, after sampling over 400 choices—and the next day, the eatery cooked up over 3,300 patties. Though not as large, the crowd is still steady for this mainstay, which has been grilling burgers since 1947. (It started as a grocery store and meat market, but once the burgers became so popular, the produce fell by the wayside.) Only choice beef, ground fresh daily and free from hormones or preservatives, are used in the patties, which come topped with fixins and cheese, bacon, or chili. Junior sizes are also available. Mon through Sat, 11 a.m. to 8 p.m. $.

**Lonesome Dove Western Bistro.** 2406 N. Main St., Fort Worth; (817) 740-8810; www .lonesomedovebistro.com. Featured on such shows as *Iron Chef* (where he beat the reigning champion), chef-owner Tim Love's modern, gourmet take on favored Western dishes have earned his upscale restaurant praise from such publications as *Food & Wine, Esquire,* and *The New York Times*. The menu is full of tasty twists: Quesadillas are filled with grilled quail, hush puppies are created with blue corn and lobster, sliders are made with elk, and featured meats include rabbit-rattlesnake sausage, kangaroo, and buffalo. Desserts like fresh Mexican doughnuts and homemade ice-cream sandwiches are less exotic, but just as delicious. Tues through Sat, 11:30 a.m. to 2:30 p.m. and 5 to 10 p.m. (Fri through Sat, until 11 p.m.) $$–$$$.

Chef Love also oversees the eats at **Love Shack** (110 E. Exchange Ave.; 817-740-8812), located around the corner. One of Fort Worth's best-loved burger joints, the casual Shack boasts indoor and outdoor seating, and a menu of sides like chili-parmesan chips, "Crazy Good" onion rings, hot dogs, and thick shakes. The medium-well burgers are made with a mix of prime tenderloin and brisket, and smothered in the house-special Love Sauce; most popular is the Dirty Love Burger, which comes topped with cheese and a fried quail egg. Sun through Wed, 11 a.m. to 7 p.m., Thurs, 11 a.m. to 8 p.m., Fri through Sat, 11 a.m. to midnight. $.

**Nonna Tata.** 1400 W. Magnolia Ave., Fort Worth; (817) 332-0250. The subtle, home-cooked flavors of Northern Italy draw fans to this foodie favorite, where former fashion industry exec Donatella Trotti presides over a familial atmosphere and much-praised menu. Choices change daily, but expect fresh pastas, frittatas, and herb-seasoned meats. One downside: the popular place only seats about thirty guests, inside and out, so a wait is inevitable. Cash only and BYOB. Tues through Thurs, 11 a.m. to 3 p.m. and 5:30 to 8:30 p.m., Fri, 11 a.m. to 3 p.m. and 5:30 to 9:30 p.m. $$–$$$.

**Rahr & Sons Brewery.** 701 Galveston Ave., Fort Worth; (817) 810-9266; www.rahr brewery.com. Following in the footsteps of his great-great-grandfather, who established a successful German lager house in Wisconsin back in 1847, Fritz Rahr Jr. produces around 5,000 barrels of ale and lager a year at this South Main Street–area brewery—all made using time-tested family recipes. Sample a glass of Stormcloud pale ale, "Ugly Pug" black lager, or the signature "Buffalo Butt." Brewery tours are offered every Saturday from 1 to 3 p.m., along with live music and barbecue; tour admission is $5. $.

**Spiral Diner.** 1314 W. Magnolia, Fort Worth; (817) 332-8834; www.spiraldiner.com. Who would have thought that a tried-and-true, steak-and-burger, cattle-based town like Fort Worth would have one of the top vegetarian restaurants in the country? This busy, retro-chic eatery has made fans of carnivores, vegans, and everyone in-between with its extensive menu of tasty dishes, all scratch-made using 100 percent vegan (and organic when possible) ingredients. From Mexican quinoa, hearty salads and dozens of wraps and sandwiches (served hot or cold) to hot plates like "Sketti & Meatballs" and red coconut curry noodles, the choices are interesting and flavorful, and fun; desserts include "Deathstar Sundaes" and "Chocolate Mountain Mudslides," and there's a menu of microbrews, too. Tues through Sat, 11 a.m. to 10 p.m., Sun, 11 a.m. to 5 p.m. $.

## where to stay

**The Ashton.** 610 Main St., Fort Worth; (866) 327-4866; www.theashtonhotel.com. In the heart of downtown, and just blocks from Sundance Square, this lovely hotel boasts a casually elegant atmosphere, top-notch service, and thirty-nine large rooms and suites, each well appointed with plush linens, flatscreen TVs, iPod docks, and free Wi-Fi. (Not to mention chewy chocolate chip cookies at turndown.) Two historic buildings were joined to create the hotel, and architectural touches like wrought iron balconies and decorative brick work can still be spotted throughout. $$–$$$.

**Stockyards Hotel.** 109 E. Exchange Ave., Fort Worth; (800) 423-8471; www.stockyards hotel.com. There's been a hotel on this site since 1907, when the nearby stockyards were thriving, and in the years since then, everyone from Garth Brooks, Willie Nelson, and Tanya Tucker to Bonnie and Clyde have spent the night. (The latter holed up in room 305, where a suite now bears their names.) These days, guests enjoy fifty-two spacious rooms and suites done up in Victorian, Native American, Mountain, or Western themes, as well as amenities like DISH Network Wi-Fi. Best of all is the location right in the thick of the Stockyards Historic District and all its shops, restaurants, and nightlife. $$.

# day trip 02

## west

**peach city:**
weatherford

# weatherford

Every July, close to 35,000 visitors head 20 miles west of Fort Worth in pursuit of the big-gest, sweetest, juiciest peaches around. Designated the "Peach Capital of Texas," Weath-erford, along with much of surrounding Parker County, is home to numerous working peach farms, as well as plenty of trees bearing pecans and other natural bounty. (It's even home to the official National Champion Pecan Tree, a 90-foot-tall beauty that's around 1,000 years old.) Though only a few of the farms are open to the public, the peach is very much a sym-bol of the town, and in season it can be found overflowing roadside stalls and sweetening the jams, pies, and juleps found at the long-running Weatherford Farmers' Market. The fruit played a significant part in the area's history and growth, too: Records show that in 1910, there were almost 90,000 acres of cotton here, and well over 144,000 fruit trees.

The area's native sandy loam soil—which provides good cushioning—had proved ideal for horses as well as agriculture. Today, Weatherford also bears the title "Cutting Horse Capital of the World" for its wealth of professional "cutter" training and breeding facilities, and in the late 1800s, it was part of the Goodnight-Loving Trails, which led cattle up from south Texas over the Brazos, and onward north. Oliver Loving of the Goodnight-Loving Trail was from Parker County, and the story of his dying wish to be buried here—and his friend Charles Goodnight's 600-mile wagon journey to bring his body home—was the inspiration for the novel *Lonesome Dove,* by Texan author Larry McMurtry.

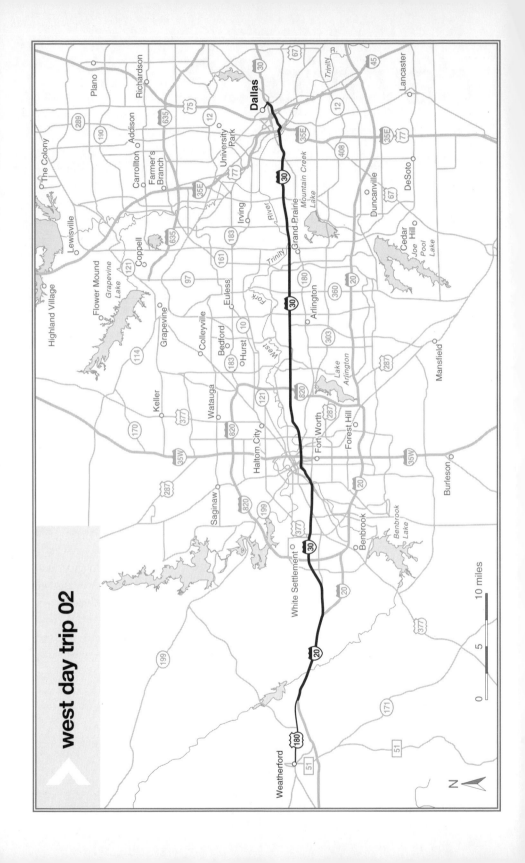

west day trip 02

Later, it was the railroad that helped grow the town, which was once part of Kiowa and Comanche Native American territory before the arrival of the first settlers. After being designated the country seat in 1855—and becoming home to the beautiful Second Empire–style Parker County Courthouse—Weatherford benefited from being a terminus along the Northwestern Railroad in the 1880s. (The Chamber of Commerce and Visitors Center now occupy the historic Santa Fe train depot building.) The discovery of oil and the building of the interstate helped sustain the town in the twentieth century, and today, more than acting as just a bedroom community for nearby Fort Worth, Weatherford is an active, picturesque town with a surprising amount—and caliber—of culture and cuisine in its own right.

## getting there

To reach Weatherford from Dallas, take I-30W toward Fort Worth, then merge onto I-20W. Take the exit for US 180, which leads into town. Note that within Weatherford, US 180 is called Fort Worth Street and Fort Worth Highway east of the courthouse, and Palo Pinto Street west of the building. Hwy. 51 is called Main Street in town.

## where to go

**Chandor Gardens.** 711 W. Lee Ave., Weatherford; (817) 613-1700; www.chandorgardens .com. For sheer romance, the story can't be beat: English artist Douglas Chandor, who painted portraits for luminaries like Winston Churchill, Queen Elizabeth, and Franklin and Eleanor Roosevelt, meets and falls in love with Ina Kuteman Hill, a girl from Weatherford, Texas. Soon after getting married in 1935, the couple moves to the small town, where Chandor proceeds to channel his artistic talents into creating this magical house and garden for his bride. After years of dedicated work, four acres of what was once cow pastures and rock-hard terrain were tuned into a whimsical green space complete with grottos, waterfalls, rambling walks, and lush Chinese and English gardens. The gardens remained open to the public until both the Chandors passed away (he in 1953, she in the 1970s), after which it sat tangled and unattended for nearly twenty years. A local couple bought and restored the property in the 1990s, before the City of Weatherford obtained it in 2002, and opened it to the public once again. (Needless to say, it's a popular spot for weddings.)

The house and grounds are open for self-guided tours Sat, 9 a.m. to 3 p.m. and Sun, 1 to 5 p.m.; admission $5, kids 12 and under free. Guided garden tours are offered Apr through Nov; check the site for details.

**Disc Golf Course.** 115 E. Lake Dr., Weatherford; www.weatherfordparks.com. Since about 2004, the Weatherford City Parks Department has done wonders with the green spaces around the area; there are now nine parks in town, boasting everything from lakes with boat docks (Cartwright Park) to skate ramps (McGratton Park). Most unique of all is this free, 18-hole course for disc golf, in which players throw flying discs into regulation baskets.

**Doss Heritage & Cultural Center.** 1400 Texas Dr., Weatherford; (817) 599-6168; www .dosscenter.org. Made using local materials like fieldstone and mesquite hardwood floors, this large center is dedicated to preserving the artistic and cultural heritage of the county. Browse through three sections: The Heritage Gallery houses permanent displays about the origins of the area, including kid-friendly interactive components; the E. B. & Grace Cartwright Gallery features rotating exhibits throughout the year; and the Mary Martin & Larry Hagman Gallery honors Weatherford-raised Broadway and singing star, Mary Martin (the original Peter Pan), as well as her son, actor Larry Hagman, best known as J.R. from the TV show *Dallas*. Tues through Sat, 10 a.m. to 5 p.m., Sun, 1 to 5 p.m.

**Museum of the Americas.** 216 Fort Worth Hwy., Weatherford; (817) 341-8668; www .museumoftheamericas.com. Harold and Elizabeth Lawrence—he a retired professor from Weatherford College—have enjoyed a long-standing relationship with Mexico, Central, and Latin America, traveling there frequently over the years and amassing a vast collection of related art, folk art, and artifacts along the way. In 2001, they opened this free museum in a converted car dealership to display their items, which offer a unique insight into these rich cultures. The packed rooms are separated by destination, and feature everything from Native American ceramics (some of it centuries old), Guatemalan masks and Peruvian textiles to Mexican miniatures, religious pieces, and a whole section on the Day of the Dead. The museum is open Tues through Sat, 10 a.m. to 5 p.m., and is closed for part of January and all of August, so the owners can continue to travel—and pick up more things.

**Weatherford Chamber of Commerce & Visitors Center.** 401 Fort Worth Hwy., Weatherford; (817) 596-3801; www.visitweatherford.com. Visit the old Santa Fe depot building to pick up brochures and city maps, including the very well-done *Historic Downtown Walking Tour and Historic Residential Driving Tour* guides, and a map of cutting-horse ranches.

**Weatherford City Greenwood Cemetery.** At N. Mill St. and Front St., Weatherford; www .weatherfordparks.com. Known simply as "the burial ground" when it was founded over 150 years ago, this cemetery houses the final resting places for several notable locals, including Oliver Loving of the Goodnight-Loving Trail; Samuel Redgate, one of the "Original Three Hundred" settlers who came to Texas with Stephen F. Austin; artist Douglas Chandor; and Broadway star Mary Martin. The oldest recorded headstone still on the site is from 1859.

## where to shop

**Historic Downtown.** www.visitweatherford.com. The streets around the towering Parker County Courthouse—particularly College, Church, York, Main, and Trinity—are home to dozens of locally owned shops. Check out **Something Special** (126 B York; 817-599-0294), for custom-painted clothing and accessories (Larry Hagman is a fan); **Country Pine Furniture** (133 York; 817-341-7463; www.countrypinetexas.com), for beautiful furnishings handmade using local hardwoods and reclaimed lumber; **Cowgirl Junkie** (115 N. Main St; 817-599-5176), boasting unique accessories and home decor items with a funky-Western style; and **Horse Creek Trading Post** (127 York; 817-599-5600), for furnishings, antiques, and Dublin Dr. Pepper. There are also numerous antiques stores, stocking everything from Victorian collectibles and Depression glass to furniture and artwork.

Free parking is available on the square (though it can get busy), as well as on the side streets. There are two church parking lots between Main Street and College Avenue north of Oak Street that are also free.

**Weatherford Farmers' Market.** Fort Worth Highway (US 180) and Santa Fe Drive, across the street from the old train depot housing the visitors center; www.visitweatherford.com. Find seasonal produce as well as locally made preserves, salsas, and more, at Weatherford's long-running farmers' market. Open daily 8 a.m. to 6 p.m.

# where to eat

**Back Street Bakery.** 120 College Ave., Weatherford; (817) 594-1880. Head a block south of the square for tasty sandwiches on homemade bread and foccacia (some of which include fruit in the fillings), plus desserts and other light fare. Call for hours. $.

**Chicken Scratch Bistro & Coffee.** 105 College Ave., Weatherford; (817) 594-6226. The sandwiches are all named after the owners' grandchildren at this spacious eatery on the square (they added a new one in fall 2009). In addition to homey lunchtime favorites, there's an extensive (and popular) Sunday brunch, a full coffee bar, sushi night dinner on Thursday, and live music with dinner on Friday. Lunch: Tues through Sat, 11 a.m. to 4 p.m., Sun, 11 a.m. to 2 p.m.; Dinner: Thurs through Fri, 5 to 9 p.m. $–$$.

**Downtown Cafe.** 101 W. Church St., Weatherford; (817) 594-8717. It might seem strange to be famous for your toast, but the thick, homemade slices are one of the main draws at this very local, family-friendly place on the square, which is typically packed during breakfast. Three-egg omelets, huevos rancheros, grits, fluffy buttermilk biscuits, and chicken-fried steak are some of the other classics. Mon through Sat, 7 a.m. to 2 p.m., Sun, 8 a.m. to 2 p.m. $.

**Fire Oak Grill.** 114 Austin Ave., Weatherford; (817) 598-0400. Bringing a touch of gourmet to the square, the menu here offers pepper-crusted ahi tuna, beef tenderloin tacos, Kobe burgers, braised buffalo short ribs, and butternut squash lasagna—plus sweet endings like chili-chocolate brownies and bananas foster for two. $$–$$$.

**Jeri's Back Home Bakery.** 131 York Ave., Weatherford; (817) 594-6700; www.jerisback homebakery.com. An array of whimsical, elaborately decorated baked confections line the windows and racks of this adorable bakery, staffed by ladies who know their way around a mixer. Their main trade is in special-order layered cakes—available in four sizes and in flavors like chocolate-cinnamon, peanut butter cup, and coconut cream—but there are also snickerdoodles, sand tarts, walnut-maple-pecan shortbread, and iced lemon cookies. The popular cupcakes come in most all of the cake flavors (one's even designed to look like a wedding cake), and the "little ugly pies" are smaller versions of meringue and fruit creations. But it's the cinnamon rolls that have the most fanatical following: Only a limited number are made each day, and on the weekends, they often sell out before they come out of the oven. Mon through Fri, 9 a.m. to 5 p.m., Sat, 10 a.m. to 4 p.m. $–$$.

**The Malt Shop.** 2028 Fort Worth Highway, Weatherford; (817) 594-2524. For over fifty years, locals have been heading out to this brightly colored shack just outside of downtown for burgers, shakes, and taters made the old-fashioned way (and at old-school prices). Diners park around the shack, order at the window, and eat either in their cars or at the few available picnic tables. The homemade ice cream is a must, too, particularly when peaches are in season. Call for hours. $.

**Skinny's Hamburgers.** 504 Palo Pinto, Weatherford; (817) 594-3101; www.skinnys hamburgers.com. Juicy, ½-pound burgers made from fresh ground beef are the signature of this friendly spot just a few blocks from the main square. There are also catfish baskets, beer-battered onion rings, signature fries topped with jalapeños and onions, and lots more fried goodness. $.

**Yesterdays Sandwich & Ice Cream.** 1280B York Ave., Weatherford; (817) 599-3903. Consistently voted the best place for lunch by readers of the local paper, this cozy, casual spot creates sublime sandwiches on homemade sourdough or wheat bread, as well as loaded baked potatoes, salads, soups, milkshakes, and fresh-baked desserts. The Brown Bag Special includes a sandwich, chips, and dessert (a bag of cookies, a brownie, or a scoop of ice cream) for $6. Daily 11 a.m. to 4 p.m. $.

# day trip 03

west

>>> **next stop, "crazy" town:**
mineral wells

# mineral wells

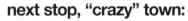

Another 20 or so miles along US 180 from Weatherford brings you to a "crazy" town—so nicknamed for the famous Crazy Water that's been bottled locally for over one hundred years. Here, you'll find plenty of natural goodness, from parks, lakes, trailways, and the Brazos River to one of the region's top botanical gardens and a fascinating herb farm. Though the town of about 17,000 is not much like what it was in its early-twentieth-century heyday—when movie stars and moguls regularly flew in to "take the waters"—it boasts a unique place in North Texas history, and has some notable sites that bring those stories to life.

Mineral Wells is part of Palo Pinto County, a green belt of hills and valleys along the western part of the Prairies and Lakes region. The story goes that when the Spanish came though the area in the nineteenth century, they named the creek here Palo Pinto—or "painted stick"—because of the colorful markings the local Native Americans would make on the tree trunks. In 1877, James Alvis Lynch was leading his family of eleven (plus fifty head of livestock) west from Denison, in search of a drier climate that would be easier on the rheumatism he and his wife suffered from. When news came of Comanche attacks further along their route, they decided to settle in Palo Pinto County. Water, however, was a bit of a problem—the Lynches lived 4 miles from the Brazos River, the only source—so in 1880, they traded some oxen to have a well drilled on their property. The water that bubbled up

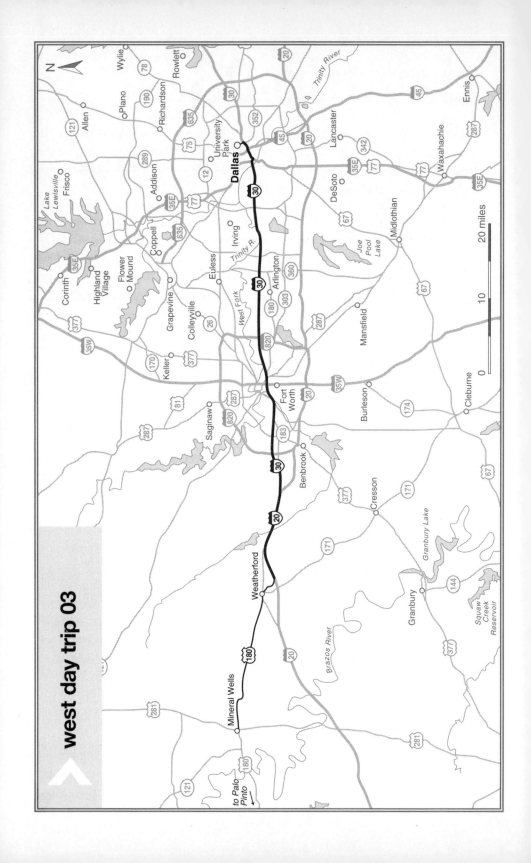

smelled and tasted a little strange, but after testing it on their animals, the Lynches began drinking the liquid—and soon after, their ailments were cured. News quickly spread of the "magical" water—which we now know to be rich in dozens of minerals—and within months, thousands of people were showing up to get a taste. The Lynch's well only produced one hundread gallons a day, so in 1881, the town of Mineral Wells was created—with Mr. Lynch as the first mayor—and numerous new wells were drilled.

Over the first few decades of the twentieth century, the town continued to grow, with spas, bathhouses, and drinking pavilions drawing crowds from far and wide. In 1904, the Famous Mineral Water Company was founded, and was soon sending railcar-loads of their Crazy Water all over the country (for more on them, see the "Where to Go" section). In 1929, the majestic 450-room Baker Hotel, complete with a mineral spa, was built in the center of town, and went on to attract a celebrity clientele for decades. Along with its liquid claim to fame, Mineral Wells was also the home of Fort Walters, which served as everything from a German prisoner of war camp during World War II to the nation's primary helicopter training ground for the Vietnam War. Because of this connection, today the town boasts the National Vietnam War Museum, complete with educational exhibits and a replica of the memorial wall in Washington, D.C.

## getting there

Mineral Wells is located along US 180, west of Fort Worth and Weatherford. From Dallas, take I-30W toward Fort Worth, then merge onto I-20W. Take the exit for US 180, which leads through Weatherford and into Mineral Wells. Note that in town, US 180 is called Hubbard Street going west, and 1st Street heading east (both are one-way streets). For more on the town, visit www.mineralwellstx.com.

## where to go

**Boudreau Herb Farm.** 5546 US 281 North, 6 miles north of downtown Mineral Wells; (940) 325-8674. There are native perennials, antique roses, and herbs galore on the grounds of this seventy-seven-acre farm, but the main attraction is owner JoAnne Boudreau, an herbal expert who writes regular newspaper columns and hosts a radio show. "My grandmother was the local healer," she says, explaining her facility with natural remedies, and these days Boudreau herself unofficially serves in that role, advising customers on gardening and herbal cures and supplements, and whipping up her own effective products. The farm store is packed with house-brand teas, plants, bath and body products, organic gardening supplies, and more, plus tons of information. Open Wed through Sat, 10 a.m. to 5 p.m.

**Clark Gardens Botanical Park.** 567 Maddux Rd., Weatherford; (940) 682-4856; www .clarkgardens.org Though its address is technically in Weatherford, this thirty-five-acre oasis is actually closer to central Mineral Wells, off Hwy 180 and near the National Vietnam

Museum. Begun as a small, private garden in 1972, the park has grown to include over fifty different gardens highlighting flora and fauna native to Texas, or that's Texas-adaptable. There are also waterfalls, ponds, meandering pathways, and shaded gazebos at which to rest while exploring. Mon through Sat, 7:30 a.m. to 6 p.m., Sun, 10 a.m. to 5 p.m.

**The Famous Mineral Water Company.** 209 N.W. 6th St., Mineral Wells; (940) 325-8870; www.famouswater.com. Among some of the first wells to be dug in newly created Mineral Wells was one by "Uncle" Billy Wiggins in 1881. As the story goes, an eccentric (and possibly mentally ill) townswoman would hang out by the well, drinking the water all day long. Locals felt that the healing water had a positive effect on her "craziness," and dubbed the spot "Crazy Lady Well"—later shortened to "Crazy Well." The Crazy Water Company was started at the site at the turn of the twentieth century, offering a couple drinking pavilions and, later, bottles of water. Today, it's the only Mineral Wells water company left standing.

At this store, you can taste the company's four waters—which range from low- to high-mineral content—and pick up cases or individual bottles; a steady stream of locals come in daily to stock-up on $H_2O$, and the company delivers in the area, as well. There are also soaps and skin care products made with the healing waters, T-shirts and memorabilia, and a small soda fountain/ice-cream counter.

**Lake Mineral Wells State Park and Trailway.** 100 PR 71, 3 miles east of downtown Mineral Wells on US 180; (940) 328-1171 or (512) 389-8900; www.tpwd.state.tx.us. A 646-acre lake serves as the center of this exemplary park, where the list of offered activities is long and varied. There are swimming beaches, fishing areas, and places for paddleboats and canoes, plus over one hundred picnic sites and an amphitheater hosting events like cowboy poetry and stargazing. At Penitentiary Hollow, a trail takes you through a labyrinth of giant boulders and narrow canyons, while rock walls are the site of the only rappelling courses in the area.

The park also serves as the entrance to the 20-mile Lake Mineral Wells State Trailway, which runs from downtown Mineral Wells to just north of Weatherford along old railroad runs. There are paths there for walking, biking, and horseback riding. Entrance to the park and trailway is $5 for adults, free for kids 12 and under; nominal extra charges apply for rock climbing/rappelling and overnight camping. Hours vary depending on the time of year, so call ahead for details.

**National Vietnam War Museum Complex.** 12685 Mineral Wells Highway (US 180), Mineral Wells; (940) 664-3918; www.nationalvnwarmuseum.org. During the Vietnam War, Fort Walters in Mineral Wells served as the primary training facility for all the helicopter pilots headed into battle. To honor that connection, and educate on all aspects of that controversial war, this center offers educational exhibits on a range of topics, from military training and political tactics to the home front and the Vietnamese people. There's also a reflection pool and a garden, plus a replica of the memorial wall in Washington, D.C. Call for hours.

**Old Jail Museum Complex.** At the corner of 5th and Elm Streets, Palo Pinto. Take US 180 (called W. Hubbard in downtown Mineral Wells) heading west about 23 miles into Palo Pinto (where the highway is called Cedar Street); make a left at the old town square and head 3 blocks to Elm Street; (940) 659-2555. Enjoy a taste of what Palo Pinto County once was at this well-done complex of historic buildings, located a short drive from Mineral Wells in the next town over. Begin at the small museum in the reception building, which includes local memorabilia like clothing, furnishings, and the touching artwork painted by a teenage German prisoner of war held in the area during World War II. The rest of the grounds house an original "dog trot" ranch cabin furnished with chamber pots, dolls, and a foot-powered

## the fabulous baker

*Drive into Mineral Wells and it's one of the first things you see in downtown: a majestic, fourteen-floor building with a distinctive curved façade and arches lining the ground floor. Unfortunately, you might also see a big FOR-SALE sign out front. Once the town's crowning glory, and the favorite of senators and Hollywood stars, the Baker Hotel has been standing empty for decades just waiting for its second act.*

*Built by hotelier T. B. Baker, who also owned properties in Dallas and San Antonio, the 450-room place cost a then-astronomical sum of $1.2 million when it opened on November 22, 1929—just two weeks after the devastating stock market crash that kicked off the Great Depression. Nevertheless, the place operated successfully for a number of years, offering luxurious services, top-notch entertainment, and access to the famous healing waters to a high-end clientele; stars like Judy Garland, Clark Gable, Marlene Dietrich, Helen Keller, Jean Harlow, and even The Three Stooges were frequent guests. This was the first hotel in Texas to have a swimming pool, the first skyscraper outside a metropolitan area, and one of the few places to boast touches like air conditioning and key-controlled lights and fans.*

*In 1932, T. B. transferred the hotel over to his nephew, Earl Baker, a married man whose mistress, Virginia, lived on the seventh floor of the hotel. (People say poor Virginia's ghost still roams that floor, leaving a waft of perfume in her wake.) Though the popularity of the mineral springs had gone down by the 1940s, the hotel continued to operate for the next couple of decades, hosting Republican and Democratic state conventions in the 1950s. Baker had long said that he would close the hotel on his seventieth birthday, and true to his word, he shut the doors on April 30, 1963. Though it reopened briefly under new management a few years later, The Baker Hotel was permanently closed in 1972, and now watches over the town of which it was once the social center.*

sewing machine; an early-pioneer cabin complete with handcrafted sleigh bed; a black-smith shop; a fort; a one-room log cabin; and a carriage house holding the beautifully restored Crossland Buggy. The centerpiece of the museum is the Palo Pinto Country Jail, constructed in 1880 and used until 1941. There, find tons of items related to the area, from branding irons and arrowheads to telegraph machines, doctor's equipment, and a railroad display. Don't miss the hangman's noose and trapdoor on the second floor—added in 1906, but never used. Wed through Sun, 10 a.m. to 3 p.m.

## where to eat

**The Black Horse.** 113 N. Oak St., Mineral Wells; (940) 325-8787. Chef-owner Joe Folley makes pretty much everything—from the dressings, sauces, and best-selling chicken salad to the coconut and Derby pies—at this casual cafe. There are also daily specials, like pastas and soup-sandwich combos. Order at the counter then settle in at one of the big wooden tables. $.

**The Hash Knife.** At the intersection of US 281 N. and TX 254, north of downtown, Mineral Wells; (940) 325-5150. It's worth the 6 mile drive north of town for the Hash Knife's much-loved barbecue, and the casual spot's fun vibe. *Texas Monthly* magazine has singled out the pork ribs and steaks, but regulars are always up for the chopped brisket, "buckin' beans," and fresh-ground ½-lb burgers, as well. Desserts include homemade cobbler and the Oilfield Pudding—vanilla pudding topped with Cool Whip, cookies, and "a little drip gas." There are tables for shuffleboard and horseshoe games, ice-cold longnecks, and gentle reminders to "clean up after yourself." Tues through Thurs, 11 a.m. to 8 p.m., Fri through Sat, 11a.m. to 9 p.m. $–$$.

# northwest

# day trip 01

northwest

**for the wine lover:**
grapevine

# grapevine

If your image of Grapevine is just of the giant mall you pass on the way to the Dallas/Fort Worth Airport, think again: This growing community—which has earned the title of "Christmas Capital of Texas"—is home to a number of interesting activities, over 180 restaurants and, of course, lots of wine. (Its annual fall GrapeFest attracts over 400,000 visitors over the course of four days.) While most of the bustle around the brick-lined main street is centered on the tasting rooms, wineries, and eateries, teetotalers and families will find plenty to enjoy at Lake Grapevine, and at entertainment centers like the Opry. There are also artisan studios, festivals galore, historical museums, and on the weekends and certain holidays, vintage steam train rides in Victorian-style coaches. (Particularly popular are the "North Pole Express"–themed rides before Christmas.) Thanks to its proximity to Dallas and Forth Worth, Grapevine is able to cater to the sophisticated tastes of urban visitors without sacrificing its picturesque, small-town charm.

Nestled between Dallas and Fort Worth, Grapevine has a significant claim to fame over its larger neighbors: It's the oldest settlement in Tarrant County, founded under the Lone Star flag in 1844—a year before Texas officially became part of the United States. The story goes that in 1843, General Sam Houston and fellow commissioners of the Republic visited the area, then known as both Tah-Wah-Karro Creek and Grape Vine Springs, to meet with leaders of ten Native American nations. The resulting peace treaty—called the Treaty of

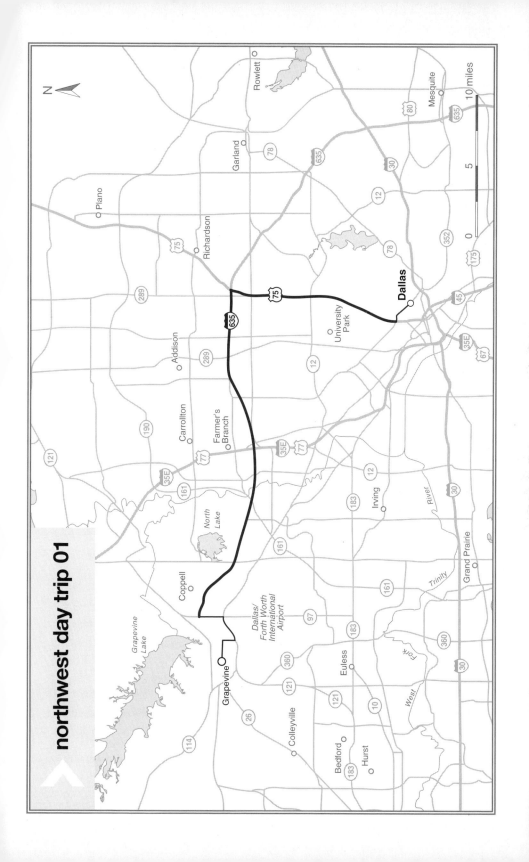

northwest day trip 01

Birds Fort—opened up the region to homesteaders, many of whom came from the Ohio Valley. The new residents named their settlement Grapevine because of its proximity to Grape Vine Springs—which itself was named for the wild Mustang grapes found along the prairie. (Hence the name of the current high school sports teams, the Mustangs.) Over the next several decades, Grapevine boomed along with the cotton and railroad industries, and even earned some notoriety as the scene of a Bonnie and Clyde heist/murder in 1934.

Today, over 50,000 people live in the town, which—taking a cue from its name—has reinvented itself as a North Texas wine hub. It's also become somewhat of a festival favorite, hosting everything from celebrations of chocolate and fireworks to the annual GrapeFest, the largest wine festival in the southwest. Check www.grapevinetexasusa.com for a calendar of scheduled events.

## getting there

Grapevine is located north of D/FW Airport, about 21 miles northwest of Dallas, and 19 miles northeast of Fort Worth. To get there, take I-635 (LBJ) toward the airport, then follow the signs for TX 121/TX 114. Once on TX 112/TX 114, take the exit for Main Street; head north a few blocks to reach the historic center.

## where to go

**Art Walk.** 705 South Main St., Grapevine; (817) 410-8136; www.grapevinetexasusa.com. The Historic Downtown celebrates art through galleries and artisan studios, as well as a series of public artworks that line Main Street. A complete walking tour map detailing the outdoor sculptures is available at the visitors center, but some of the highlights include *The Sidewalk Judge,* honoring an older generation that liked to sit on park benches and dispense advice (usually unsolicited!) to passerby; *Walking to Texas,* an homage to the pioneer settlers; and *The Grapevine Nightwatchman,* an 8-foot-tall, 640-pound tribute to the patrolmen who guarded the town in the early 1900s.

To watch contemporary artists at work, head across the parking lot from the visitors center (in the same Cotton Belt Depot complex) to **Vetro** (701 S. Main St., Studio 103; 817-251-1668; www.vertroartglass.com), a glassblowing studio and gallery showcasing live demos most Wednesdays through Saturdays (the shop and gallery are open every day except Mon). You can help design your own glass tree ornaments, flowers, and trinkets during special events throughout the year, and classes are also offered; call or visit the Web site for more info. Next door to Vetro is the studio of internationally renowned bronze sculptor Archie St. Clair (see sidebar for more on Archie); it's not officially open to the public, but if you pop your head in and he's available, he's happy to explain what he's working on.

**Grapevine Opry.** 300 South Main St., Grapevine; (817) 481-8733; www.grapevinetexas usa.com. Started in 1975 and considered one of the best weekly country music shows in the southwest, the Opry takes place in Grapevine's historic Palace Arts Theater, which was built in 1939. Under the direction of musician Rocky Gribble, the showcase features both new and established artists in genres as diverse as bluegrass, gospel, Big Band, '50s doo-wop and rock-and-roll, and Western swing. (Plus, they've got a legendary house band.) Alumni include singers LeAnn Rimes and Boxcar Willie. Visit the Web site for a schedule of upcoming shows.

**Grapevine Vintage Railroad.** 707 South Main St., Grapevine; (817) 410-3123; www.gvrr .com. When driving down Main Street from the highway, you can't miss the magnificent "iron horse" steam trains lined up alongside the visitors center in the old Cotton Belt Depot complex (unless they happen to be out on a run, of course). The Vintage Railroad runs trips along the historic Cotton Belt route between Grapevine and the Fort Worth Stockyards, pulled by two engines: "Puffy," an 1896 locomotive that's the oldest continuously operating steam engine in the South; and a 1953 diesel version. (Travelers ride in 1920s- and 1930s-era Victorian-style coaches.) Along with several themed trips throughout the year, including

# the man behind the art

*Walk down Grapevine's main street and you'll notice some distinctive bronze sculptures hanging around on the corners, including one of the city's third mayor, B. R. Wall, and one depicting three generations of Sunday Skaters. Several of these works were created by Grapevine's artist-in-residence, Archie St. Clair, whose workshop sits across from the visitors center. How did an Australian Outback–born former helicopter pilot come to be the go-to artist of a Texas town? St. Clair's story is made for the big screen: Born in the very center of Australia, in a cattle ranching town called Alice Springs, St. Clair earned his pilot's license at twenty-two—a skill he used to gather cattle, horses, and wild camels by air, as well as fly rescue and firefighting operations. In 1994, tragedy stuck when his copter went down and St. Clair was stranded for seventeen hours in subzero temperatures. Once rescued, the pilot was told he would never walk again—but after spending three-and-a-half years in a wheelchair, he proved doctors wrong.*

*It was during that rehabilitation time that St. Clair first picked up some clay and explored the world of sculpting, and once his recovery was underway, he went on to learn more detailed techniques like mold-making and casting. Eventually, he moved to the United States to work at foundries in Arizona, honing his craft and establishing himself as a professional sculptor. Though today his pieces can be found all over the world, his first two commissioned monuments reside in Australia. One depicting a pioneer is the largest monument of a horse and rider Down Under—a fitting distinction for a man whose talent and determination are both larger than life.*

Murder Mysteries and the kid-friendly North Pole Express, the trains run to the stockyards and back most Fridays, Saturdays, and Sundays; regular service is typically suspended in the winter, so call ahead for a schedule.

**Grapevine Visitors Information Center and Historical Museum.** 705 South Main St., Grapevine; (817) 410-8136; www.grapevinetexasusa.com. Set right off the railroad tracks on Main Street, in the mustard-colored former cotton belt depot, the visitors center will load you up with info on local restaurants, winery trails, art walks, and nature activities. The adjacent museum holds a range of memorabilia from the city's history, from antique clothing, furniture, and photographs to farming equipment and World War II items. Admission is free; open Mon through Sat, 9 a.m. to 5 p.m., Sun noon to 5 p.m.

**Lake Grapevine.** www.grapevinetexasusa.com. Located just north of downtown (take Main Street to Dove Loop Road and follow the signs), this 8,000-acre recreation area boasts 9 miles of hiking trails, 146 miles of shoreline, and plenty of spots for boating, camping, fishing, and picnicking. There are two marinas (Scott's Landing at Oak Grove Park and Silver Lake on the north east side of the lake), and numerous boat ramps (fee is $5 per launch) and swimming areas at the various parks. Entry to Katie's Woods Park is free, while others, like Meadowmere Park and Rockledge Park, cost $5 per car, but includes access to a designated swimming beach, picnic tables, and sand volleyball courts. The Vineyards Campground (1501 N. Dooley St.; 888-329-8993; www.vinyardscampground.com) is outfitted with boat ramps, fishing piers, trails, and even free Wi-Fi.

# where to shop

Browse the independent shops along **Main Street,** between College and Wall Streets, for unique gifts, clothing, and home items. Antiques can be scored at **Red Shed Antiques** (317 Church St.; 817-310-6006) and **Antique Revival** (418 S. Main St.; 817-329-7882), while **Revolving Closet** (120 S. Main St.; 817-416-1579) stocks designer resale fashions. Pick up wine and wine-related accessories at **Off the Vine** (324 S. Main St.; 817-421-1091)—the only retail liquor shop amid all the tasting rooms. At the corner of Main and W. Worth Streets, stop into the **Bermuda Gold** jewelry shop (412 Main St.; 817-481-5115), which once housed a bank that was held up by Bonnie and Clyde.

**Grapevine Mills Mall.** 3000 Grapevine Mills Parkway, Grapevine; (972) 724-4900; www .grapevinemills.com. This mega-mall may not be in the heart of the historic town, but for serious shoppers, skipping it would be like heading to Egypt and not seeing the pyramids. One of the largest malls in the southwest, Grapevine Mills encompasses 1.6 million square feet of stores, restaurants, and entertainment, from retail standards like Abercrombie & Fitch and Build-A-Bear Workshop to factory/discount outlets for Lane Bryant, Ann Taylor, BCBG, Nike, Hanes, and—the Holy Grail—a Neiman Marcus Last Call. Located 2 miles north of Dallas/Fort Worth, off Hwy. 121; open Mon through Sat, 10 a.m. to 9:30 p.m., Sun, 11 a.m. to 7 p.m.

# where to eat

**Back Porch Tavern.** 210 N. Main St., Grapevine; (817) 251-8434; www.backporchtavern .com. In a town that's all about wine, this friendly throw-back is the place for straight-up beer food: buffalo wings, stuffed jalapeños, fried pickles, loaded spuds, catfish po' boys, and brisket smoked on-site. There's live entertainment—from Texas Hold'em, open mic and karaoke to country bands—on most nights, and happy hour every day from 3 to 7 p.m. Open Mon through Thurs, 11 a.m. to midnight, Fri through Sat, 11 a.m. to 2 a.m., Sun, noon to 10 p.m. $.

**Cero's Heros.** 104 Jenkins St., Grapevine; (817) 488-8800. A lunch favorite since 1970, this shacklike indie eatery set at the intersection of Main Street and Northwest Highway serves fresh sub sandwiches to a line of drooling locals. Choices include meatball, Italian (salami and provolone), Mexican (turkey and jalapeño), and German (sausage and Swiss); all are available regular, with standard fixins, or spicy, with green and crushed red peppers. The half is 8-inches and the whole 16-inches, so chances are you'll take some to go (and there's no indoor seating, anyway). Mon through Sat, 11 a.m. to 3 p.m. $.

**Esparza's Mexican Restaurant.** 124 E. Worth St., Grapevine; (817) 481-4668; www .esparzastexas.com. The patio is the place to be at this local favorite, which has been serving up tasty Tex-Mex and "notorious" margaritas since 1985. Located in a renovated nineteenth-century house just a couple of blocks off Main Street (which, legend has it, was once a funeral parlor), the hangout can get pretty packed (and loud), so don't be surprised if you have to circle the back lot a bit for parking, or look for a spot on the surrounding streets. Fans swear the enchiladas, seafood tostadas, and fried stuffed jalapeño "ratones" are worth braving the crowds. Mon through Thurs, 11 a.m. to 10 p.m., Fri through Sat, 11 a.m. to 11 p.m., Sun, 11 a.m. to 9:30 p.m. $$.

**Farina's Winery & Cafe.** 420 S. Main St., Grapevine; (817) 442-9095; www.farinaswinery .com. Despite the name, this popular spot is more a restaurant than winery, offering a full lunch and dinner menu of Italian standards, and an extensive international wine list. The elegant space, which occupies two storefronts overlooking Main Street, is outfitted with a European bar from the 1800s, and a smattering of for-sale antiques in the second room. Mon through Tues, 11 a.m. to 6 p.m., Wed through Thurs, 11 a.m. to 10 p.m., Fri through Sat, 11 a.m. to 11 p.m., closed Sun. $$–$$$.

**Into the Glass Wine Bar and Texas Cafe.** 322 S. Main St., Grapevine; (817) 442-1969; www.intotheglass.com. "Don't over think it . . . just drink it," goes the motto at this dimly lit spot, where a cadre of regulars are sure to be propping up the bar at any given time. (The place has such a loyal following, one regular even wrote a novel centered on the bar and its patrons.) After earning his restaurant-industry stripes in cities like Los Angeles, San Francisco, and New Orleans, owner Wayne Turner opened Into the Glass in 2004 to focus on boutique vintages and wine-friendly eats. Changing every couple of weeks, the wine list is separated into quirky categories like "Primordial," "Virile," and "Ecumenical," while the refined food menu tempts with duck confit gorditas, beef tenderloin tacos, chicken and waffles, and a slew of homemade desserts (don't miss the lavender blackberry pound cake). Mon through Tues, 11 a.m. to 10 p.m., Wed through Thurs, 11 a.m. to 11 p.m., Fri through Sat, 11 a.m. to midnight, closed Sun. $$–$$$.

**Main Street Bread Baking Company.** 316 S. Main St., Grapevine; (817) 424-4333; www .themainbakery.com. The smell of fresh baked treats wafts out from this casual bistro, sister to outposts in Plano and Richardson. The cases are full of French-style pastries and breads, while the menu offers breakfast (waffles, eggs, crepes), lunch (quiches, salads, brioche sandwiches), and dinner (pastas, beef tenderloin). Mon through Wed, 6:30 a.m. to 3:30 p.m., Thurs through Sat, 6:30 a.m. to 6:30 p.m., Sun, 6:30 a.m. to 5 p.m. $–$$.

**Wineries.** www.grapevinetexasusa.com. Grapevine is home to several wineries and a couple of vineyards, most located in the downtown area off of Main Street, between College and Wall Streets; maps of the wine trail are available at the visitors center. The majority of the places have their wines produced off-site or feature vintages from other Texas vinters, though a couple—like **D'Vine Wine** (409 S. Main St.; 817-329-1011; www.dvinewineusa .com) and **Su Vino Winery** (120 S. Main St.; 817-424-0123; www.suvinowinery.com)— offer customers the chance to create their own private label blends. Founded by one of Texas's original grape growers, **Inwood Estates Winery's** tasting room (603 Main St., Ste. 303; 817-488-3761; www.inwoodwines.com) pours Lone Star–made Tempranillos, Cabernets, and Chardonnays. For more of the Napa Valley vibe, head a few blocks off Main Street to **La Buena Vida Vineyards** (416 E. College St.; 817-481-9463; www.labuenavida .com), where you can taste the house vintages amid lush gardens, Spanish tiled fountains, and live music. Also a short drive from downtown is **Cross Timbers Winery** (805 Main St., 817-488-6789), set in one of the oldest farmsteads in the area. Along with lovely special event facilities, the winery serves glasses of their award-winning Merlots, Chardonnay, and Cabernet Sauvignon, as well as wines from Grapevine's sister cities, Parras de Fuente, Mexico, and Krems, Austria.

## where to stay

**Garden Manor.** 205 East College St., Grapevine; (817) 424-9177; www.gardenmanor bandb.com. There are plenty of deluxe chain hotels and lakeside resorts in the area, but this B&B has a big advantage: Its location is just half a block from the wineries along Main Street, making it the best choice for when driving home isn't an option. Innkeepers Judy and Gunther Dusek host guests in four uniquely furnished rooms, each boasting a different garden theme, private bath with whirlpool or claw-foot tub, and nightly turn-down with fresh chocolate truffles. $$.

# day trip 02

northwest

**the grasslands:**
decatur, caddo-lbj national
grasslands

**Heading further northwest,** almost to where the Prairies and Lakes region gives way to the Panhandle Plains, affords travelers the chance to bond with history and commune with nature. Stop in Decatur, the seat of Wise County, for a look at some well-preserved nineteenth- and twentieth-century buildings, from the iconic, Romanesque courthouse to a sixteen-room mansion and a petrified rock–covered 1920s "tourist camp." Fuel up at one of the unique independent restaurants (the choice ranges from fresh-from-the garden organic to cheese fries topped with bacon and served in a skillet), then head up to the protected Grasslands for fishing, biking, or lazing in the sun.

# decatur

Among the first settlers to arrive in this part of North Central Texas was a colonel named Absalom Bishop, who dropped stakes in 1854. The colonel quickly became a leader in the organization of the new area—labeled Wise County—and decided he wanted the county seat to be on top of a "bald" hill overlooking the West Fork of the Trinity River and the West Cross Timbers land. In addition to being the highest point in the county, the hilltop was large enough to hold a town square, but a good portion of the settlers had other ideas and wanted the seat to be in another area. A bitter election followed, but the colonel and his crew won, with the colonel raising the Stars and Stripes over the hill in victory. For his leadership in turning that hilltop into a town, Colonel Bishop is considered the Father of Decatur.

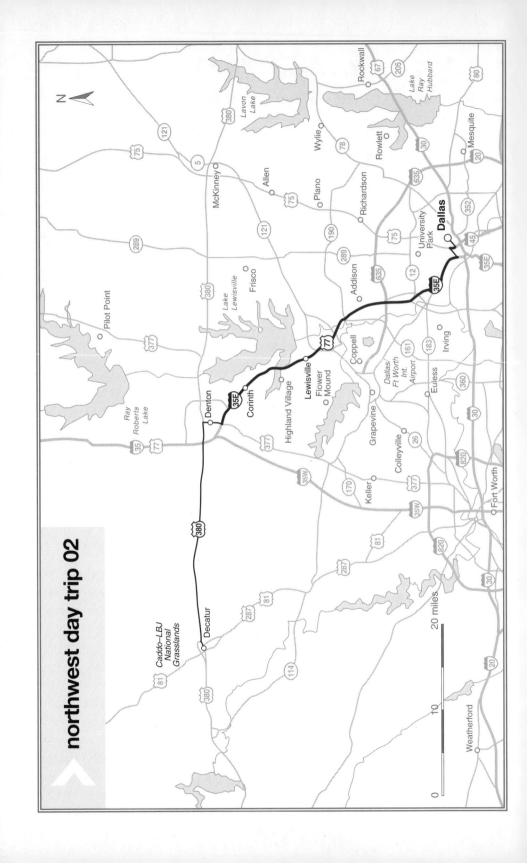

northwest day trip 02

Originally called Taylorsville for President Taylor—then later changed when Bishop soured on the president—Decatur was named for naval hero, Stephen Decatur. The town grew through the 1850s and 1860s and was a stop on both the Butterfield Mail stage route and the Chisholm Trail; the latter connection is still celebrated during the annual Chisholm Days festival. These days, the city has a population of just under 6,000, though with its proximity to both Dallas and Fort Worth, it is steadily expanding with commuters looking for a quieter, more affordable place in which to settle. Presided over by the pink granite fairy-tale courthouse, the town square and downtown are currently undergoing a regeneration, with the hope that more stores and businesses will move into the beautiful historic buildings. While the town builds its future, it's still, for now, one of the best small towns in which to get a glimpse of the past.

## getting there

To reach Decatur, take I-35E north to just past Denton, then take the exit for US 380. Head west on US 380, which leads directly into town. Decatur is at the intersection of US 380 and US 287, about 30 miles north of Dallas/Fort Worth.

## where to go

**Decatur Visitors Center.** 106 South Trinity, Decatur; (940) 627-6158; www.decaturtx.org and www.decaturmainstreet.com. Located in the historic post office (which was built as part of Franklin Delano Roosevelt's "New Deal" Works Project during the Great Depression), this visitors center can load you up with brochures, suggestions, and maps, including the detailed *Main Street Walking Tour* brochure. The office is typically staffed Mon through Fri, 11 a.m. to 6 p.m., Sat, 10 a.m. to 2 p.m., and Sun, 1 to 4 p.m., but there's also a twenty-four-hour info kiosk out back, stocked with all the literature.

**Main Street and Wise County Courthouse.** Between Walnut, State, Main, and Trinity Streets, Decatur; www.decaturmainstreet.com. Pick up the detailed *Historic Downtown Decatur Walking Tour* brochure from the visitors center (or have one mailed to you in advance). The quick-and-easy walk takes you around the majestic courthouse, providing details about the buildings—many made with locally quarried limestone—and their former occupants. You'll see the site of the square's first native limestone building, erected in 1863, which went on to become the 1940s Plaza Theater (and now law offices). At 100 W. Walnut St., spot the original 1880 double doors, 7-foot-tall windows and stove pipes on the Ingram-Hancock building, while at 102 N. Trinity, stop in to the longest continuously operated business on the square—a barber shop that's been here since 1926.

In the middle of the square sits the distinctive Wise County Courthouse, a Romanesque Revival confection of turrets, archways, and an extra-tall clock tower. Built in 1896 for a cost of $110,000, and now listed on the National Register of Historic Places, the courthouse is made mainly of pink Texas granite—a fire-safety decision made by architect James Riley

Gordon after three previous courthouses had burned down. Visitors are welcome to come inside to view the original woodwork, iron staircases, and Vermont marble accents. Open Mon through Fri. during regular courthouse hours; tours may be arranged through the county judge's office on the first floor.

**Texas Tourist Camp/Petrified Wood Gas Station.** 900–904 South Business 81-287, at the corner of Hale Street. In the early part of the twentieth century, this area was the site of a campground just outside of town. In 1927, site owner E. F. Boydston saw potential for attracting the growing leisure travel market, so he constructed a gas station on the land; a couple years later he added the Texas Lunchroom, and in the early 1930s, a few cabins with garages. In 1935, Boydston's brother got the idea to cover the building in petrified wood gathered from the surrounding area—and the distinctive look made the tourist camp a destination in its own right. The place became a hangout for travelers and college kids—trains would even stop for engineers and passengers to jump off and get a bite—and it's rumored that Bonnie and Clyde holed up in one of the cabins for a few nights. With the construction of the interstate highway, the camp's popularity began to decline; the lunchroom closed in 1964, the cabins in the 1970s, and the gas station in 1989.

In the 1990s, the site underwent a revival. Thanks to the unique architectural style, the buildings were awarded a Historical Marker in 1995, and were also added to the National Historic Registry. New owners reopened the lunchroom as the Whistle Stop Cafe (see "Where to Eat" below), and though the other buildings are still in private use, it's worth a visit to see this unique landmark—one of the few still-intact examples of the tourist camps that dotted the southwest in the last century.

**The Waggoner Mansion.** At the east end of Main Street (the street dead-ends at the house), Decatur. This private residence is not open to visitors, but it's worth a drive-by to check out the legendary structure. Often referred to as "El Castille," the Victorian limestone mansion was built in 1883 for the prominent Waggoner ranching (and later, oil) family, and still retains about 90 percent of its original materials and craftsmanship, including details like wrought-iron railing and roof-top grills. Inside, there are sixteen bedrooms, six and a half baths, 18-foot ceilings (some with frescos by a French artist), stained glass windows, and a Texas Lone Star motif on all the hinges and doorknobs, all topped by an ornate cupola; the rest of the grounds includes a smokehouse and a few original bunkhouses. Fans of the movie *Giant* might recognize the main house's façade—the filmmakers recreated the exterior for one of the movie sets—but that's as close as one can get these days; the Luker family has lived here since 1942, and continue to maintain this as a private residence.

**Wise County Heritage Museum.** 1603 South Trinity, Decatur; (940) 627-5586; www.decaturtx.org. What was once the Decatur Baptist College (the world's first junior college, founded in 1892), now houses an extensive collection of local artifacts and memorabilia. There are old medical equipment, a full-sized stagecoach, antique pharmacy and shop furnishings, clothing, housewares, children's playthings, and more, spread out over two floors.

## let 'em roll

*Gambling or craps fans are probably familiar with the cry, "Eighter from Decatur, County Seat of Wise!," which is used by dice rollers when they're looking for a hard eight (a four on each die). The phrase does originate in Decatur, Texas, (not the one in Georgia or anywhere else), but of course, no one can totally confirm how it came about. After much research, the city was able to determine two things: that the phrase was originally "Ada from Decatur," and that it was always related to rolling dice. One of the most credible stories they found came from one Dr. Ira Nash, who grew up in Decatur in the late 1800s. As Dr. Nash remembered, there was a guy named Will Cooper in town back then who did odd jobs, liked to play dice, and was in love with a local servant girl named Ada. Whenever he would gamble, Will would shout, "Ada from Decatur, County Seat of Wise!" as a good luck mantra. The phrase became popular in town with those who knew Will. In 1900, a group of Decatur Home Guards and Army regulars traveled to Virginia by train to participate in a reenactment of the Civil War Battle of Manassas, and Will was on board as their cook. As the travelers played dice on the long train ride, Will's good luck chant spread to a larger group of Texas troops. Once they reached the tent city in Manassas that housed all the reenactors, the phrase spread like wildfire, and went from being a general good luck chant to a call for a hard eight. When all the reenactors went back to their various corners of the country, the phrase went with them—and is still uttered by people who have no idea where Decatur even is.*

The museum also operates an extensive genealogical archive spanning several states. Adults, $1; kids 50 cents; open Mon through Fri, 10 a.m. to 3 p.m.

## where to eat

**Main Street Home & Gardens.** 603 W. Main St., Decatur; (940) 627-0235. Set a few blocks from the main square, this stellar spot is part store, part garden center, part organic cafe—and completely memorable. Owners Beth and Cary Hardin operated a garden center in Fort Worth for over ten years, commuting, for part of that time, from this lovely 1929 home. After faithfully restoring the house, backyard, and a few adjacent lots, the couple moved their operations here, creating a store in the main house and a garden center out back; the indoor/outdoor cafe came shortly after. The focus here is on natural, healthy, and organic, from the bamboo shawls, cute recyclable bags, organic teas, and gift items stocked in the store to the eco-conscious garden supplies held in a 135-year-old barn. (You can also pick up seeds, herbs, plants, and flowers, and consult the owners on garden-planning matters;

they also run landscape design classes—from which you'll leave with a fully implementable plan—a few times a year. Call for more info.)

The meandering back gardens, blooming with native flowers and organic fruits and veggies, are the setting for the cafe, which also focuses on organic and tasty items. Best-sellers include the tarragon chicken salad, sandwiches using fresh ingredients (like tomatoes and basil) from the gardens, a decadent grilled cheese, daily hot specials, and yummy desserts. (Thursday is "Meatless Day"—a concept that Decatur has slowly warmed up to.) The setup is very casual: Drinks and tableware are self-serve, tables are strewn around the house and gardens, and the vibe is peaceful and relaxed. This has become the place people escape to with a book or to catch up with friends—a hidden hideaway just off Main Street. Open Tues through Sat, 10 a.m. to 5 p.m. (store and garden center) and 11 a.m. to 2 p.m. (cafe). $–$$.

**Sweetie Pie's Ribeyes.** 201 W. Main St., Decatur; (940) 626-4555. Set in a historic stone and red cedar building on the main square, Decatur's go-to place for burgers and steaks is run by the folks behind the legendary Babe's Chicken Dinner House (which has several locations around North Texas) and Bubba's near SMU in Dallas. You'll find chicken-fried steaks and rib eyes, green chili burgers, and pot pies for lunch, and juicy, slightly caramelized steaks served with homemade yeast rolls, salad with hot bacon dressing, and fluffy "Rosin" baked potatoes for dinner. Mon through Fri, 11 a.m. to 2 p.m. and 5 to 9 p.m., Sat through Sun, 11 a.m. to 9 p.m. $–$$.

**Whistle Stop Cafe.** 904 S. Hwy. 81, at Hale St., Decatur; (940) 627-7785. The historic Texas Cafe (see the Texas Tourist Camp blurb above) is once again a local hangout. Sometimes referred to as the "Rock Cafe" or the "Tourist Camp," the cozy, twelve-table country kitchen—complete with old-fashioned checkerboard floor—serves burgers, roasts, "breakfast-on-a-bun," and scratch-made pies that have earned it a place as one of the Top 50 "home cooking" restaurants in Texas. Mon through Fri, 6 a.m. to 2 p.m. $.

**Yesterdays.** 100 S. Hwy. 287, Decatur; (940) 627-5866; www.yesterdaystexas.com. Oodles of 1950s and 1960s memorabilia line the walls, ceilings, and countertops of this family-operated retro eatery, a lively local hangout. Posters of Marilyn Monroe and James Dean will watch over you as you settle into a vinyl booth or at the classic dinner-style counter for "Ba-Ba Loo" cheddar fries (loaded with bacon, chives, and jalapeños), taco salads made with homemade chili, "Jayne Mansfield" char-grilled chicken breast (wink, wink), and grilled-to-order *Gunsmoke* rib-eye steaks. There's also a Tex-Mex menu, seafood, and half-, one-, and even two-pound burgers made with fresh ground chuck (finish the latter and get a prize). You can't leave without dessert: s'mores, peanut butter cup shakes, and the legendary apple pie—served sizzling in a skillet and topped with Blue Bell ice cream and brandy-butter sauce. On Friday and Saturday night the staff dress up as their favorite 1950s and 1960s icons, and guests who roll up anytime in a classic car or hot rod (pre-1972) enjoy free fountain drinks for up to four patrons. The highway location makes it a convenient stop before or after visiting The Grasslands. Mon through Thurs, 11 a.m. to 8:30 p.m., Fri through Sat, 11 a.m. to 9 p.m., Sun, 11 a.m. to 2 p.m. $–$$.

## where to stay

**Abbercromby Penthouse Suites.** 103 W. Main St., Decatur; (940) 321-3673; www .4romanticweddings.com/penthousesuites.html. Bob and Margaret Atkinson watch over three well-appointed suites set overlooking the town square. Each has a theme: the "City Slicker" takes you back to the Old West with period artifacts, a cedar bed, and a soaking tub; the "Cattle Baron" evokes the grandeur of an oil tycoon's manor with elegant furnishings; and the "Summmbersby" is a romantic pale pink-and-green chamber with Jacuzzi tub for two. $$.

# caddo–lbj national grasslands

The Caddo-LBJ National Grasslands is one of five areas in Texas supervised by the U.S. Forest Service. Officially, this preserve is called the Caddo–Lyndon B. Johnson National Grasslands, and is separated into two sections: the LBJ Grasslands are closer to Decatur and part of this itinerary, while the Caddo section is northeast of Dallas, toward Honey Grove and Paris. Both offer areas for recreational activities, camping, and fishing, while hunting is mainly limited to the Caddo.

For maps and details on hours, activities, and hunting and fishing regulations, contact the Caddo–LBJ District Office at 1400 N. Hwy 81/287, P.O. Box 507, Decatur, Texas 76234; (940) 627-5475; www.fs.fed.us/r8/texas. Note that a Texas Hunting or Fishing License is required on both Grasslands, and an additional Texas Public Hunting Permit is needed if you venture east to the Caddo.

## getting there

Continuing north on US 81/287 from Decatur brings you to the Caddo–LBJ National Grasslands.

## where to go

**LBJ Grasslands.** The protected lands of the Caddo–LBJ serve multiple purposes: Cattle graze here; white-tailed deer, bobcats, and red fox live on the grounds; catfish, bass, perch and crappie swim its lakes; and humans come by for hiking, fishing, camping, mountain biking, and scores of other nature-bonding activities. The LBJ is made up of over 20,250 acres, which are separated into several recreational areas and lakes. The main ones include:

**Black Creek Lake.** Here you'll find fourteen campsites, a fishing bridge, restrooms, and a boat ramp leading into the thirty-five-acre lake. Note that there is no hunting or horses allowed at this site; admission is $2 a day.

To reach Black Creek Lake, take US 287 north from Decatur for 4.5 miles, then turn right onto CR 2175. Cross the railroad tracks and continue on for 1 mile, then turn left on Old Decatur Road. Proceed for another 4 miles, then turn right on CR 2372 and, 2 miles later, left on CR 2461. A half a mile down that road, take the first left onto FS 902 to the campground.

**Clear Lake.** This fourteen-acre lake allows fly fishing only (no motorized boats or floats). To reach this lake, take US 287 north through Alvord, then continue north for 4 miles. Turn left on CR 1596, right on CR 1591, and right again onto FS 969.

**Cottonwood Lake.** This is a forty-acre lake with fishing, boat ramp, and a trailhead for hiking to Black Creek Lake. To reach Cottonwood, take FM 730 north 10 miles, turn left onto CR 2461 then, at the fork, go right onto CR 2560 for 3 miles. Turn left on FS 900 for the park.

# day trip 03

# northwest

## on the chisholm trail:
bowie, nocona

**When heading northwest** on US 81 from Decatur, or traveling due west on US 82 from Gainesville, you'll just need to look out the window to know you're deep into Texas's Prairies and Lakes region. Both routes will take you past the expansive, gently rolling farms and ranches of Red River country, most dotted with cows, horses, and shimmering ponds and creeks. A few larger industrial structures or windmill farms can be seen on the horizon, but for the most part, this drive offers a peaceful trek though a fertile countryside relatively free of billboards or other man-made distractions (or gas stations, so be sure to fill up before leaving the Interstate).

The towns along these quiet roads are a little different, too—small, traditionally Western in layout, and minus the typical strip-malls or mega-stores along their outskirts. Most of this area belongs to Montague County—pronounced "mon-tayg" with a hard "g," like in "gun"—which was officially designated in 1857. With rich soil perfect for agriculture and livestock, the area was coveted by both settlers and Native Americans, so was the site of regular battles and attacks throughout the 1850s and 1860s, giving it the reputation as the rough-and-tumble "wild west." Once the area became more secure, the towns started booming, and the railroad lines brought in droves of new residents toward the end of the nineteenth century—as did the discovery of oil in 1923.

Most of these towns owe their early growth to cattle and horses, and two in particular—Bowie (pronounced "boo-ee") and Nocona (that's "know-kona")—still play up that connection. Both are in locations that were once along the historic Chisholm Trail, one of the main longhorn driving routes of the late 1800s that took stock up from south Texas to Kansas, where the cows would then board trains bound for the north. Named for Jesse Chisholm, a

191

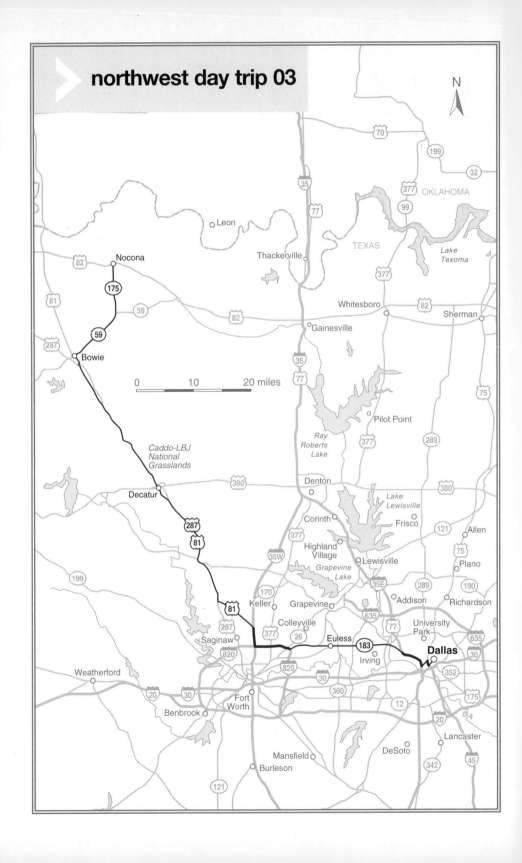

Native American trader who first blazed the trail from the Red River up past Indian Territory (present-day Oklahoma) and into Kansas, the Chisholm Trail helped ferry 700,000 cattle in 1871 alone. While it wasn't the only driving route of the day (the Shawnee and Goodnight-Loving Trails were other major lines through North Texas), the Chisholm was one that was frequently immortalized in stories and songs—which in turn helped spread the myth of the "Western cowboy" across the rest of the country.

Cattle ranching is still a big part of the region (though Angus beef has replaced long-horns), as is leather; Nocona was home to one of the most prominent boot makers in the state and is still the only place in the United States to factory-produce leather baseball gloves (you can even tour the facility). For day-trippers, both towns also offer good restaurants, a sense of history, and a hearty dose of cowboy charm.

# bowie

"Few stories are too bloody, few tales too bawdy for the Bowie of the 1800s," reads the official Bowie Chamber of Commerce history, and sure enough, this Old West town was the scene of many a shootout and mob brawl. Today, brick-paved Smythe Street in downtown is lined with antiques shops, but back then it was called "Smokey Row," on account of all the saloons, pool halls, and houses of ill repute that occupied its buildings.

Incorporated in 1883, Bowie was thriving with close to 19,000 residents by 1890 (by contrast, the population today is around 6,000). The town was in all likelihood named for Alamo hero, Jim Bowie, though it's possible that a popular railroad workman named Buie was also being honored, to recognize the pioneer spirit that helped build the town. Railroad and agriculture were Bowie's early main trades, with farms and cotton gins covering its environs. As a point along the Chisholm Trail, Bowie was big on cattle, too, and modern-day visitors can visit a small park commemorating this connection. These days, the downtown is still in the process of re-generating—with gorgeous nineteenth-century brick buildings just waiting for the right tenants—and the city doesn't offer much in the way of museums or regular attractions. But it does keep its history alive through great antiques stores, nostalgic eateries, and a bevy of annual festivals, including the Bowie Trail Ride in May, Jim Bowie Days in June (with storytellers and chuck wagon food), and the Chicken & Bread Days Heritage Festival in October.

## getting there

From Decatur, take US 81 north into Bowie; the town sits at the crossroads of US 287, US 81, and TX 59.

## where to go

**2nd Monday Trade Days.** Located at the edge of town, on Business Hwy.-81/287; see their site for more details; www.secondmonday.com. Crafts, antiques, farm tools, and live animals from over 280 vendors pack this twenty-acre market, which takes place the week-end before the second Monday of each month. Started in 1893, this is one of the oldest trade day markets in North Texas.

**Bowie Chamber of Commerce Office.** 309 N. Smythe St., Bowie; (940) 872-1173; www.bowietxchamber.org. Load up on brochures, maps, and tips from the local chamber. They are only open Mon through Fri, 9 a.m. to 5 p.m., but if you're planning to come on a weekend, call ahead and they would be happy to leave you a packet on the outside racks.

**Chisholm Trail Memorial Park.** www.bowietxchamber.org. At the junction of US 81 (West Wise Street) and TX 174. From the corner of N. Mason Street and W. Wise Street in downtown, head west on W. Wise for about 7 blocks, until you see a fork in the road; the park sits right in front of you. The small greenspace is more of a lawn than a park, but it boasts an official historic marker designating a point along the Chisholm Trail, as well as several life-sized cutouts of cows and cowboys. Stop by for a quick photo op.

## where to shop & eat

**The Antique Gallery of Bowie.** 222 N. Mason St., Bowie; (940) 872-8700. Find antiques and collectibles from five different vendors under one roof. There are also a few new items, including chunky stone and semi-precious jewelry from local designer Nelda Coffman, whose line is called Early Attic. Tues through Sat, 10 a.m. to 5 p.m.

**Martha's Attic.** 206 N. Smythe St., Bowie; (940) 872-4705. Who needs trade day mar-kets where there's Martha's Attic, a consignment store made up of several rambling, jam-packed rooms. You would need hours to sift through even one corner of the place, as every surface is covered with glassware, furniture, books, figurines, costume jewelry, old tins, artwork—pretty much whatever people bring in to sell, or that's culled from estate sales. The back room is the "garage sale" area, where stock that's been around for a while gets majorly marked down. Tues through Sat, 10 a.m. to 5 p.m.

**Nostalgia Antiques & Soda Fountain.** 200 N. Mason St., Bowie; (940) 872-6272; www .nostalgiainbowietexas.com. Part antiques store, part lunch cafe and soda shop, this fun stop is housed in a two-floor building from 1894, set right on Bowie's main street. The cafe tables and chairs are located all around the space, tucked into nooks and crannies and sur-rounded by all the eclectic wares, so you're guaranteed to have something to look at as you munch on cornbread, chicken salad, bread pudding, and old-fashioned shakes and malts. Open Tues through Sat, 10 a.m. to 5 p.m., with lunch served from 11 a.m. to 2 p.m. (soda fountain treats are always available). Nostalgia's owner is also a pastor, so sometimes the shop shuts early on Wednesday, for church night. $.

**Sharing the Love of Dolls.** 114 W. Tarrant St., Bowie; (940) 872-1211. You don't see many shops solely devoted to dolls anymore, so this boutique is worth a stop for its large stock of girly playthings. Mon through Fri, 10 a.m. to 4 p.m.

## where to stay

**John H. Matthews B&B.** 306 E. Tarrant St., Bowie; (940) 872-6272; www.nostalgiain bowietexas.com/guesthouse.htm. The owners of Nostalgia Antiques & Soda Fountain also operate this quaint six-room guest house, set in a stunning Victorian mansion that was once home to Bowie's first mayor. Located 2 blocks from the downtown shops. $.

# nocona

That old "where everybody knows your name" song could have been written for Nocona, a small, friendly town along the historic Chisholm Trail route where you'll still see a lot of cowboy hats, where folks catch up at the second-generation, family-owned Dairy Queen, and where the mayor runs the most popular barbecue joint around. There's only one grocery store and no Wal-Marts, chain restaurants, or movie theaters (residents head to Wichita Falls for that), so instead you'll find lots of locals ready to chat, and a town in the midst of an interesting regeneration.

For many in the southwest, Nocona is synonymous with fine leather goods—for over one hundred years it was home to the Nocona Boot Shop (a forerunner of Justin Boots), and is still the site of Nokona Athletic Goods, the last major leather baseball glove maker in the United States. (Visitors can watch the gloves being made and pick up discounted items at the factory.) Cattle and thoroughbred ranching, oil, and farming are still the main livelihoods, and you can feel that cowboy influence throughout, from the dress of the people to the menus and decor of the restaurants. (There's also some of the best Tex-Mex for miles.) Though the old main street became something of a ghost town in the 1970s and 1980s, big things are now afoot: many of the old buildings have been bought and renovated by residents and have become (or will become) stores and restaurants. (One's even a cool recording studio.) A Montague County Museum—honoring the area's Native American, Chisholm Trail, pioneer, and industrial heritage—is set to open in 2010, as is the new Veranda hotel and RV park. Stay in touch with the chamber of commerce for updates.

## getting there

From Bowie, take TX 59 north to the town of Montague, then TX 175 north to Nocona. The town is also along US 82, which runs into Gainesville and connects to I-35. Note that locals often refer to Clay Street as "Main Street."

## where to go

**Nocona Chamber of Commerce Office/Texas Trails Art Gallery.** 100 E. US 82, Nocona; (940) 825-3526; www.nocona.org. Browse a small gallery highlighting local artists, and some interesting memorabilia from the town's Old West past, including a stagecoach and items from the famous 1939 Pony Express riding contest, which ran from Bowie to

San Francisco. There are also brochures and maps to get you out exploring. Mon through Fri, 10 a.m. to 4 p.m.

**Nokona Athletic Goods.** 901 E. US 82 (entrance on Clay Street), Nocona; (940) 825-3326; www.nokona.com. Though it's spelled with a "k" instead of a "c" (thanks to laws about copyrighting a city name), Nokona Athletics has become synonymous with the town it began nearly one hundred years ago. A maker of fine leather billfolds and purses in the 1920s, the company switched to baseball gloves in the 1930s, and is now the only major

## nocona names

*I hadn't been in Nocona more than an hour when a resident told me that there were two words even those just visiting needed to know how to pronounce. One was Montague, for the county—pronounced here as "MON-tayg" (not like in Romeo and Juliet). The other, she said, was "Fenoglio" (pronounced "Fin-o-lio")—one of the most common last names in town. And she was right, because even just wandering around town for a bit, that name comes up a lot. Robert Fenoglio is the mayor and the owner of a popular barbecue place, Rusty Fenolgio and his wife own the pharmacy on Main Street (located in a restored historic building), and there's even a Fenoglio Street in the county. The clan's roots in the area go way back, with forefathers who owned the town grocery and one who was a state senator. (You can see "Reelect Fenoglio" memorabilia at Robert's restaurant.) "There are probably about 300 of us in the county," one of the Fenoglio ladies told me, and I believe it—in the phone book, they take up half a page.*

*One Fenoglio who's getting a bit of attention these days is Dan, a construction business owner who, a few years back, started buying and restoring some of the abandoned historic buildings downtown. His first project was "Daddy Sam's," a beautiful brick building he restored to its 1920s heritage and filled with his private collection of Nocona photographs, antiques, and memorabilia. Next came the building next door—which once housed his grandfather Sam's grocery—which was also restored and named "Gertie's Dancehall." The buildings are privately used by the family but are available for parties and special events. These projects—which earned Dan a Texas Downtown Association's Recognition/Heritage Award—sort of kick-started the town's regeneration, and now other locals are buying the old buildings and working to bring them back to life. (Dan himself has bought another five.) It's a cool thing to see people who grew up here—Fenoglio or not—make a mark on the town's future.*

leather ball glove manufacturer left in the United States. Here, you can see a few display cases detailing the brand's past, then tour the factory to watch how the gloves are hand-crafted using about fifty-two different processes. Tours are free, and are given Mon through Thurs at 9 a.m., 10 a.m., 11 a.m., 1 p.m., 2 p.m., and 3 p.m.; no reservations are required, but if you call ahead, they can make sure there's a glove at every step of the process for you to see. The factory store stocks discounted seconds and logo merchandise; open Mon through Fri, 8 a.m. to 4:30 p.m.

**Nocona Nights Music Series.** (940) 825-3526; www.nocona.org. Celebrating its eighth season in 2010, this monthly dinner concert series showcases an array of Texas music, from country and bluegrass to Tejano. Contact the chamber for a current schedule. Concerts are held at Daddy Sam's/Gertie's Dance Hall, two interconnected spaces set in the beautifully restored historic grocery on Clay Street.

## where to shop

**Dolly's Gifts.** 310 E. US 82, Nocona; (940) 825-3030. A diverse selection of gift items, accessories, home décor, and holiday pieces are packed into this brick house. Mon through Sat, 9:30 a.m. to 5:30 p.m.

**Legacy Beauty Salon.** 208 Clay St., Nocona; (940) 872-3411. Pop in to this full-service salon for a cut, blow-dry, or just to see the great space, which has housed a barbershop or beauty parlor since the early 1900s. Check out the restored antique glass-panel advertisements set along one wall.

**Montage Boot Company.** 105 Clay St., Nocona; (940) 825-4108. www.montagueboot .com. Though it's not the original Nocona Boot Company that made the town famous (that one has since moved), this manufacturer carries on the tradition through its stock of hand-crafted cowboy boots made of ostrich, alligator, and other exotic leathers. Call for hours.

**Two Blondes Antique Mall.** 917 E. US 82., Nocona; (940) 825-4266. Lots of different vendors ply their treasures at this large space, set behind the Western Store on US 82. Mon through Sat, 10 a.m. to 5 p.m., Sun, 1 to 5 p.m.

## where to eat

**Dairy Queen.** 301 E. US 82, Nocona; (940) 825-3301. A fast-food chain might not typically appear on a "recommended restaurants" list, but this place is something of a town legend. Family-owned for two generations, the DQ was for a long time one of the only restaurants in town (it's got plenty of seating), and it still remains a daily must-stop for many. Plus, you can't beat a Blizzard on a hot day. $.

**Fenoglio's BBQ & Station.** 510 W. US 82, Nocona; (940) 825-3843. Since 1972, this former service station and garage has been the place for authentic barbecue; what started

## miss enid

*While the famous Nocona Boot Company is no longer here, the town was greatly influenced by its presence—and that of its inspiring leader, Miss Enid Justin. The boot business actually started with Miss Enid's father, "Daddy Joe" Justin, who came to West Texas from Indiana in 1879. With just 25 cents and some boot making tools, he set up shop making custom leather boots for the cowboys passing through on the Chisholm Trail. (They'd order them on the way up, and pick them up when coming back down.) As word of his artisan skill spread, and the railroad brought more customers to town, the shop took off, so from the age of twelve on, Miss Enid worked in the store alongside her father. When "Daddy Joe" died in 1918, some members of the family—including her brothers—wanted to move the company to Fort Worth, but Miss Enid firmly believed that her dad would want the company to stay in Nocona. So her brothers took the equipment and headed to Fort Worth—and she stayed. Borrowing $5,000, and armed with just seven employees, she opened the Nocona Boot Company.*

*At first, times were slim: Miss Enid had to work as a clerk, stenographer, and credit manager, and turn her home into a boarding house, to keep the company afloat. Plus, some men had an issue coming to a lady boot maker, but they soon found her quality to be on par with her late father's. Taking it upon herself to make sales trips to small towns—courageous for a woman in those days—she built the company up until it achieved a national name, and gave Nocona the reputation as a leather goods capital. In 1981, the Nocona Boot Company merged with Justin Industries—the Fort Worth branch started by her brothers—and Miss Enid passed away in 1990, at the age of ninety-six. You can still see her influence around town, though, like in the children's park she helped found—a still active memorial to the hardworking lady who wouldn't leave Nocona.*

as a pick-up only space has been expanded twice over the years. Owned by the affable Robert Fenoglio, who's also been Nocona's mayor since 2005, this is the place old-timers come in to get their "morning information" over breakfast burritos, and where a steady lunch crowd heads for barbecue sandwiches and hamburgers (made from fresh daily ground beef), cobbler, and the signature "Bowl of Crap"—chopped beef or sausage topped with beans, grilled jalapeños, and more, for $4. Mon through Fri, 6 a.m. to 2:30 p.m., closed Sat and Sun. $.

**Times Forgotten Steakhouse.** 204 Clay St., Nocona; (940) 825-6100. After retiring from the school district (he was the former superintendant), Harold and Sandra Reynolds—both

Nocona natives—bought and restored this historic former bank on the town's main street, turning it into a steakhouse and homage to Montague Country. The bi-level space boasts signature area themes like leather and Native American art, along with the building's original wrought-iron balcony and exquisite pressed-tin ceiling. Nothing like this existed in town before, so the restaurant has become a popular gathering place, both for its warm, community atmosphere (a framed copy of the local paper gets displayed every week) and its extensive menu of favorites like hand-cut rib eyes, chicken-fried steak, PB&J with fresh strawberry slices and peanuts, and "home style" Sunday lunches, like pot roast; the Friday night fish fry—all you can eat, plus a drink, for $7.99—is particularly packed. This is also the only place in town, outside of a liquor store, to serve alcohol (you have to become a "member" to drink, but membership is free, and instantaneous). Wed through Sat, 11 a.m. to 2 p.m. and 5 to 9 p.m., Sun, 11 a.m. to 2 p.m. $–$$.

**Tres Niños.** 604 E. US 82, Nocona; (940) 825-3313. There's been a Mexican restaurant at this address for as long as most people can remember, but this latest incarnation—opened for a few years—is mixing things up with atypical dishes like spinach-and-cheese enchiladas, brisket tacos with spicy sauce, Tex-Mex stir fry, and a popular spinach salad. Of course, you will also find tons of staples, from tomatillo-topped enchiladas to quesadillas, fajitas, and guacamole—all made fresh, and super-delicious. All Tex-Mex combo platters come with rice, beans, and "Daddy Ben's" onion rings—giant, spicy versions made using a family recipe. This is a real local favorite, where the excellent waitstaff know all the regulars—and exactly what they're going to order. $–$$.

# festivals and celebrations

One of the best ways to experience some of North Texas's smaller towns is to visit during a festival. From summer ice-cream "crankoffs" and holiday tree-lighting parties to events honoring local history, people, and traditions (and foods!), this is a chance to see the residents in their element and enjoy insight into what makes each community so unique. Note that most towns also host summer and/or fall farmers' markets, holiday tree-lighting celebrations, annual historic home tours, and, in many cases, a monthly trade day or flea market. Check www.visitdallas-fortworth.com for updated event calendars.

## january

**Southwestern Exposition and Live Stock Show and Rodeo,** Fort Worth. Established in 1896, the nation's oldest livestock show attracts over one million visitors to the Will Rogers Memorial Center for nearly three weeks of livestock markets, rodeo shows, classes, competitions, and more. Typically from the end of January to the beginning of February. (817) 877-2400; www.fwssr.com.

## february

**Antique Tractor & Machinery Club Winter Show,** Glen Rose. Vintage tractor and farm machinery fans gather for exhibits and competitions. www.glenrosetractorclub.com.

**Ennis Czech Music Festival,** Ennis. A day of live music, polka jams, costumes, traditional food, and more. www.ennisczechmusicfestival.com.

## march

**Annual Chocolate Festival,** Grapevine. Two days of art, entertainment, live music, wine, food, and lots of delicious homemade gourmet chocolate. www.grapevinetexasusa.com.

**Annual Texas Storytelling Festival,** Denton. Storytellers from all over the country celebrate the oral tradition with a variety of events, including cowboy poetry, live music, children's events, and stories honoring different ethnic heritages. www.dentonlive.com.

**Cowtown Goes Green,** Fort Worth. The historic Stockyards District's annual St. Patrick's Day celebration. www.stockyardsstation.com.

**General Granbury's Birthday Party,** Granbury. Honor the town founder at this annual festival on the square, complete with shopping deals, activities, live entertainment, and the Bean, Ribs, and Brisket Cook-Off. www.granburytx.com.

**Tyler Azalea Trail,** Tyler. Celebrating the bloom of azaleas, tulips, wisteria, and dogwood with historic home and residential garden tours, arts and crafts fairs, flower shows, quilt fairs, and more, since 1959. www.tylerazaleatrail.com.

# april

**Denton Arts & Jazz Festival,** Denton. Enjoy over 2,000 performers—including many known names—on six stages, plus kids' art activities, craft fairs, fine arts displays, games, and much more. www.dentonjazzfest.com.

**Denton Redbud Festival and Romp,** Denton. This annual Arbor Day event includes a home and garden show, a kids' zone, and over sixty booths showcasing landscaping, gardening, and home improvement products. www.kdb.org/redbud_festival.shtml.

**Derrick Days,** Corsicana. For over three decades, this festival has celebrated the town's oil history with food, music, contests, arts and crafts, and entertainment for the entire family—plus a mini-marathon and "Cow Patty Bingo." www.derrickdays.com.

**Ennis Bluebonnet Trails and Festival,** Ennis. Enjoy over 40 miles of mapped driving trails, plus a weekend of events, food, and fun, all in celebration of the "Official Bluebonnet City" of Texas. www.visitennis.org.

**Fort Worth Prairie Fest,** Fort Worth. Enjoy music, art, dance, wildflower tours, silent auctions, and hundreds of arts and crafts stalls, all celebrating the area's connection to the natural world. www.tandyhills.org.

**Main St. Fort Worth Arts Festival,** Fort Worth. Ranked as the number three arts fest in the country, this free four-day celebration of arts, entertainment, and culture includes juried arts and crafts competitions, street performers, and performance artists, concerts, and food stalls. www.mainstreetartsfest.org.

**Scarborough Renaissance Festival,** Waxahachie. Step back in time—about 400-plus years—with six weeks of unique activities. Shop over 200 artisan and craft stalls, enjoy entertainment on twenty-one stages, feast like a king, and check out swordplay demos, live music, and more. www.scarboroughrenfest.com.

**Spring into Nash Farm Event,** Grapevine. Learn about life on the farm—and have some old-fashioned, family-friendly fun—with pony rides, sack races, farm tours, cooking demos, a petting zoo, and more. Watch bees make honey and artisans make quilts. www.grape vinetexasusa.com.

# may

**Dog Days of Denton,** Denton. Since 1993, this two-day fest honors our four-legged friends with a pet parade, canine contests, animal performances, live entertainment, and food for both pets and their owners. www.dogdaysdenton.com.

**Downtown Blooms,** Greenville. A day of fun with sidewalk sales, prize drawings, and lots of great live music, capped by the signature Threadgill Concert. www.greenvillechamber.com.

**Main Street Days,** Grapevine. Kick off summer with dozens of outdoor activities, from trampoline and BMX bike shows, rock climbing walls, carnivals, kayak tanks, and more, plus winery tours. www.grapevinetexasusa.com.

**Mayfest,** Fort Worth. Family-friendly arts, crafts, live performances, and food stalls along the banks of the Trinity River. www.mayfest.org.

**National Polka Festival,** Ennis. Celebrate the town's Czech heritage at this annual Memorial Day weekend event, full of food, games, arts and crafts, parade, dance contests, and over a dozen live polka bands. www.nationalpolkafestival.com.

**Old Fiddlers Contest & Reunion,** Athens. Bring your own lawn chair and settle in around the downtown square for a day of top-notch fiddling and traditional music from performers young and old, followed by street dancing to a swing band. (903) 677-0775, (888) 294-2847 or www.athenstx.org.

**Paris Art Festival,** Paris. See springtime in Paris while enjoying works from artists from four states, plus food and craft booths and kid's activities. www.paristexas.com.

**Twilight Tunes Concert Series,** Denton. Local musicians perform for free every Thursday evening on the lawn of the historic Courthouse-on-the-Square typically from early May until the end of June. www.dentonmainstreet.org.

# june

**Audie Murphy Days,** Greenville. Greenville's favorite son—World War II hero and Hollywood star Audie Murphy—is honored with live music performances, movie screenings, and lots of fun activities. www.cottonmuseum.com.

**Chisholm Trail Days,** Decatur. Western heritage is celebrated with stagecoach runs, theme activities, and lots of live music. www.decaturmainstreet.com.

**Chisholm Trail Rodeo Round-Up and Parade,** Nocona. Honoring the area's cattle-drive past with livestock shows, rodeos, a parade, and more, since 1951. http://noconachamber.netfirms.com.

**Gingerbread Trail Historic Home Tour and Arts & Craft Fair,** Waxahachie. At this annual event, get a look at historically recognized structures like the iconic Ellis County Courthouse, as well as numerous Victorian, Gingerbread, Gothic Revival, and Queen Anne homes. At the same time, arts and crafts events and kids activities take place in Getzendaner Park. www.waxahachiechamber.com.

**Hopkins County Dairy Festival & State Champion Ice Cream Freeze Off,** Sulphur Springs. The dairy capital's annual event includes homemade ice cream "crank-off" contests, plus a carnival, parade, dancing, and a hot air balloon festival. www.sulphurspringstx .org.

**Independence Festival,** Sulphur Spring. The two-day fest features a farmer's market, fun activities, and live music, from guitar performances to classical concerts. www.sulphur springstx.org.

**Jim Bowie Days Festival and Rodeo,** Bowie. Taking place the last weekend in June, the town's biggest celebration includes a Blue Grass Round-Up, Chuck Wagon Cook-Off, parades, pioneer-style games, Indian Artifact Show, nightly rodeo, contests, and lots of music and food. www.jimbowiedays.org.

# july

**Crape Myrtle Festival,** Waxahachie. Parades, fireworks, tailgate parties, live music, and more, in celebration of the bright, beautiful blooms. www.waxahachiechamber.com.

**Fireworks Extravaganza,** Grapevine. Since 1982, this brilliant display has lit up the sky over the 8,000-acre Lake Grapevine. www.GrapevineTexasUSA.com.

**Fourth of July Celebration,** Granbury. Four days of live music, performing arts shows, arts and crafts, and food vendors, old-fashioned family games, and even a fun run. www .granburytx.com.

**National Day of the Cowboy,** Fort Worth. Celebrate the lives of cowboys and cowgirls past with a day of family fun, from riding demos and gun fighting shows to lively contests like Best Mustache, Most Worn-Out Boots, and Best Seed–Spitting. www.fortworthstock yards.org.

**Paris Rodeo and Horse Club Street Dance and Rodeo,** Paris. Get a taste of Texas history at this lively event, featuring rodeo events with over 300 contestants. www.paristexas .com.

**Parker County Peach Festival,** Weatherford. Fill up on peach ice cream, pie, and other treats, shop over 200 arts and crafts stalls, and enjoy three stages of live entertainment in the Peach Capital of Texas. www.weatherford-chamber.com.

**Red White & Boom,** McKinney. Enjoy live entertainment from name performers, an antique car show, parade, kids' activities, and more, all topped off by a spectacular fireworks display. www.visitmckinney.com.

**Tour de Paris,** Paris. Around 800 riders participate in this annual rally, which offers a variety of course lengths to suit all ages and stamina levels. There's also a pancake breakfast, hamburger after-party, and watching event for the real Tour de France. (903) 784-2501; www.tourdeparis.com or www.paristexas.com.

**Wise County Old Settlers Reunion,** Decatur. Happening since 1864, this week-long, family-friendly event celebrates the pioneer spirit with games and activities for all ages, lively concerts, and plenty of designated campsites. www.decaturtx.org.

# august

**North Texas State Fair & Rodeo,** Denton. A week of music, rides, games, fiddling contests, barbecue cook-offs, and championship rodeos. www.ntfair.com.

# september

**Arts, Antiques, and Autos,** Denton. Classic, custom and hot rod cars line the square, while juried art shows, antiques appraisals, and live entertainment round out the activities. www.dentonmainstreet.com.

**Blues Fest,** Denton. Presented by the Denton Black Chamber of Commerce, this free fest brings top blues entertainment—plus kids' activities, food booths, and more—to this music-friendly town. www.dentonbluesfestival.org.

**Grapefest,** Grapevine. Drawing foodies and oenophiles from around the country, the largest wine festival in the southwest includes four days of music, food and wine tastings, and even a carnival for the kids. www.grapevinetexasusa.com.

**Heritage Festival and Uncle Fletch Hamburger Cook-Off,** Athens. Enjoy activities, reenactments and good eats in the town square in celebration of Henderson County heritage, plus the famous hamburger cook-off honoring Athens' own Uncle Fletch, creator of the burger. www.athenstx.org.

**Hopkins County Fall Festival and World Champion Stew Contest,** Sulphur Springs. Along with the tasty stew-making contest, enjoy a week of parades, gospel concerts, carnivals, quilt shows, under-the-stars live music, and more. www.hopkinscountyfallfestival.com.

**Oktoberfest,** McKinney. Over 20,000 people descend on the town square to celebrate the German tradition with live music, food, shopping, activities, kids arts and crafts, games like keg barrel races, and the official first tapping of the keg. www.downtownmckinney.com.

**Pioneer Days,** Fort Worth. Celebrate the frontier past with fiddling contests, parades, foot-races, and a fajita cook-off. www.fortworth.com.

**Rally 'Round Greenville,** Greenville. There's something for everyone at this two-day town celebration, from cook-offs, arts and crafts stalls, and art exhibits to animal rides for the kids and two stages of live music. www.greenvillechamber.com.

**Red River Valley Fair & Exposition,** Paris. A tradition since 1911, this five-day event fea-tures live entertainment, carnivals, livestock shows, and general family fun. (903) 785-7971; www.paristexas.com.

**Texas Motorplex NHRA Fall Nationals,** Ennis. Held every September in Ennis, this large drag racing event draws thousands of fans from all over the country. www.texasmotoplex .com.

**Wild Beast Feast,** Denton. Adventurous eaters head to this annual fest to sample buffalo, elk, prairie chicken, rabbit, and other wild game, while live music and auctions provide the entertainment. www.dentonlive.com.

# october

**Autumn Days in Ennis Fall Festival,** Ennis. Celebrate the changing of the seasons with a day of food, arts and crafts, live music, and free children's activities. Held annually on the third Saturday of October. www.visitennis.org.

**Boo at the Zoo,** Fort Worth. Come in costume to mingle with live animals and a variety of spooks and goblins at this annual party, when the zoo is filled with pumpkin patches, themed trails, and lots of treats. www.fortworth.com.

**Butterfly Flutterby,** Grapevine. This family-oriented event celebrates the annual migration of the Monarch butterfly with a kids' (and pets') costume parade and a live butterfly release. www.grapevinetexasusa.com.

**Chicken & Bread Days Heritage Festival,** Bowie. Fiddle contests, classic car shows, food and craft vendors, live entertainment, and lots of good eats at an annual celebration of local history. www.bowietxchamber.org.

**Depot Day,** Gainesville. Held annually on the second Saturday in October in and around the downtown courthouse square, this even celebrates the importance of railroad history to Gainesville with a day of live music and entertainment, antique and classic car shows, food and craft vendors, a kids zone, a Depot Dash 5K Fun Run, and the Depot After Dark BBQ party. www.depotdaygainesville.com.

**Fall Festival at the East Texas Arboretum,** Athens. Art shows, kids train rides, pumpkin decorating, and the always popular Black-Eyed Pea Cook-Off, which in years past has yielded such favorites as the "Peatini" and "Cowpea Cheesecake." www.athenstx.org.

**Harvest Moon Festival,** Granbury. Celebrate the season with a carnival, pumpkin decorating contests, Pooch Parade, kids' costume contests, cooking demos, hot dog and pie eating contests, antique tractor shows, and arts and crafts from over one hundred vendors. www.granburysquare.com and www.granburytx.com.

**Indian Summer Festival and Dutch Oven Cook-Off,** Sulphur Springs. Celebrate regional history with Native American dancers, Civil War reenactments, quilt shows, and craft demos like candle, soap, and quilt making, butter churning, and blacksmithing. www .sulphurspringstx.org.

**Paluxy Pedal Bike Ride,** Glen Rose. Ranging in length from 29 to 80 miles, the annual bike ride winds through the back roads of northern Hill Country. www.paluxypedal.com.

**Red Steagall Cowboy Gathering & Western Swing Fest,** Fort Worth. Honoring cowboy traditions with wagon rides, chuck wagon parades, and cook-offs, tons of live music, Western swing dancing, rodeos, cowboy poetry, children's activities, and more. www.red steagallcowboygathering.com.

**Screams,** Waxahachie. Taking place all month long, the world's largest Halloween theme park includes games, rides, "Scary-oke," food and drink, the Mythical Monster Museum, Trail of Terror, and five separate haunted attractions. www.screamspark.com.

**Texas Country Reporter Festival,** Waxahachie. Reporter Bob Philips leads this annual celebration of all things Texas country, which includes live music, crafts and artisans, kids' activities, chefs, and many of the characters featured on Philips's *Texas Country Reporter* show. www.texascountryreporter.com.

**Tyler Rose Festival,** Tyler. Tyler's signature event draws thousands of guests for arts and crafts shows, garden visits, and official festival happenings like Tea with the Queen, the Queen's Coronation, and the famous parade. www.texasrosefestival.com.

# november

**Candlelight Home Tour,** Waxahachie. For three weekends (typically one in November and two in December), check out historically recognized Victorian, Gingerbread, Gothic Revival, and Queen Anne homes decked out in their holiday finery. There's also a Victorian Christmas Festival around the courthouse square. www.waxahachiechamber.com.

# december

**Christmas Capital of Texas,** Grapevine. Parades, caroling, decorating contests, winery tours, family movie events, and North Pole Express trains rides, all in the official Christmas Capital of Texas. www.grapevinetexasusa.com.

**Christmas in the Stockyards,** Fort Worth. Choirs, horseback and wagon rides, kids' activities and games, armadillo races, parades, cattle drives, and lots of food and drink put a Western spin on the holiday. www.fortworthstockyards.org.

**Holiday in Paris,** Paris. For two weekends in December, enjoy dozens of events like historic house tours, vintage car shows, wagon rides, art walks, holiday music performances, extended shopping hours, clog dancing, Christmas pageants, kids' story time, trolley tours, craft fairs, and—of course—Santa. www.holidayinparistexas.com.

**Holiday Lighting Festival,** Denton. Enjoy a traditional small-town holiday with horse-drawn wagon rides, hot cider contests, choirs, dancers, live bands, and more. There's also Victorian Christmas evening at the Bayless-Selby House Museum, and the signature Brave Combo Chicken Dance on the courthouse lawn. www.dentonholidaylighting.com.

**Parade of Lights,** Corsicana. Brightly-lit parade floats toss candy, stuffed animals, and other goodies to the crowds at this annual holiday event. www.corsicana.org.

**Victorian Stroll,** Gainesville. Along with the annual historic home tour, enjoy carriage rides, visits with Santa, wandering carolers and choirs, extended shopping hours, and free edible treats. Takes place the second Thursday–Saturday in December. www.gainesville.tx.us.

# index